To
Chloe Sullivan)

And We Shall Learn through the Dance

Kathleen.S.turner@gmail.com

Great Talking To You,
God's Blessing
& The Read
Enjoy

Kathleen S. Turner

And We Shall Learn through the Dance

Liturgical Dance as Religious Education

Kathleen S. Turner

FOREWORD BY
Reverends Floyd and Elaine Flake

PICKWICK *Publications* · Eugene, Oregon

AND WE SHALL LEARN THROUGH THE DANCE
Liturgical Dance as Religious Education

Pickwick Publications
An Imprint of Wipf and Stock Publishers
199 W. 8th Ave., Suite 3
Eugene, OR 97401

www.wipfandstock.com

PAPERBACK ISBN: 978-1-5326-1949-6
HARDCOVER ISBN: 978-1-4982-4579-1
EBOOK ISBN: 978-1-4982-4578-4

Cataloguing-in-Publication data:

Names: Turner, Kathleen S., author. | Flake, Floyd, foreword. | Flake, Elaine, foreword.

Title: And we shall learn through the dance : liturgical dance as religious education / Kathleen S. Turner ; foreword by Floyd and Elaine Flake

Description: Eugene, OR : Pickwick Publications, 2021 | Includes bibliographical references and index.

Identifiers: ISBN 978-1-5326-1949-6 (paperback) | ISBN 978-1-4982-4579-1 (hardcover) | ISBN 978-1-4982-4578-4 (ebook)

Subjects: LCSH: Dance in religious education. | Christian dance. | Dance—Religious aspects—Christianity.

Classification: GV1783.5 .T87 2021 (print) | GV1783.5 .T87 (ebook)

This book is dedicated to my father, Lawrence Aristead Sumler, and my mother, Emma Melinda Sumler, who inspired me to pursue my God given talents to dance, teach, and choreograph.

Because Your loving kindness is better than life, my lips shall praise You. Thus I will bless You while I live; I will lift up my hands in Your name.

Psalm 63:3–4

Contents

Foreword

For the past forty years, our church worship experiences have been enriched by the movement and passion of liturgical dance. For us, dance was meant to be an integral part of the worship experience; through the years, we have witnessed the combination of this artistic expression and the power of the Holy Spirit draw congregants into the presence of God. To be sure, this phenomenon has penetrated the hearts and souls of believers in ways that sermon and song are unable to. We have seen choreographers and dancers study the biblical text and the words of a myriad of songs with diligence and cultural sensitivity, and then go on to create movements that surely usher in new dimensions of God's glory. We have celebrated our Promised Land experiences with Miriam, danced out of clothes with David, and wept with Jeremiah. We have witnessed the birth of Christ, the miracles that he performed, the Crucifixion, and the Resurrection come alive through dance. The Allen Liturgical Dance Ministry has truly made a profound impact on thousands of worshippers.

For those who have engaged in the liturgical dance experience by actually dancing, I suspect their experience has been even more life-changing. Kathleen Turner was our first director, and she surely laid a foundation that provided young and old alike with an expanded knowledge of biblical principles. Every dance was introduced with Bible Study, and the underlying theological truths of every song were explained so that those who danced truly understood the message of each piece. Because Dr. Turner and other choreographers were trained dancers, they were also able to explain the history of some of the movements incorporated in specific dances. Our dancers were introduced to choreography that reflected their culture, past and present. They danced like David, their African ancestors, their slave foreparents, and their contemporaries. And every dance was a dance unto the Lord.

As you read this book, the world of liturgical dance—and the roles that it plays in Christian Education—will come alive. In Chapter One, you will see historically how dance has been the means by which worshippers have encountered God and been able to express the impact of their encounters. In Chapter Two, the relationship between dance and spiritual growth is explored and demonstrated. Chapter Three reveals how the church can provide the appropriate platform and become the place of personal and corporate learning, as God reveals God's self in ways that will motivate the learner to live a Christian life. Chapter Four uses the biblical text to inform the content and movement of liturgical dance. And finally, Chapter Five gives validity to liturgical dance as the art form that opens the door to biblical worship and establishes its place in various areas of the worship experience.

Hence, we are confident that this book will transform many local congregations and bring them to an understanding of what liturgical dance really is. It is indeed a path that leads to spiritual growth by fostering a deeper relationship with God. We are grateful to Dr. Turner for sharing her life's work with the world. This work will help worshippers discover and experience new levels of God's glory because when dancers have an authentic encounter with God, they are well able to dance down the manifest presence of God.

The Reverend Dr. Floyd and The Reverend Dr. Elaine Flake
Pastor & Co-Pastor of The Greater Allen AME Cathedral

Preface

I believe that liturgical dance is a way to present, reflect, instruct, learn, study, and share religious beliefs with one's self, within one's worship community, and with one's God. Such a belief is confirmed and witnessed within a variety of religious settings, throughout the world, from the beginning of time to this present age. I can attest that, within Christianity, this statement also holds true. This holds true because, as a Christian and a dancer, I have been involved with liturgical dance inside the walls of the church for over a forty-year period. However, I can also attest that there are many within Christianity that do not understand the validity liturgical dance has in the teaching, learning, and understanding of Christian faith. For some Christian denominations, liturgical dance is still not accepted as a valid form of worship, while others have accepted it as a momentary form of worship entertainment. This book will address the power and potential liturgical dance has in nourishing the faith life of congregations.

To give some background, there are a few resources by liturgical theologians and scholars that explore liturgical dance as an effective tool for worship. These investigations have not only validated the role of liturgical dance as a tool for worship, but have extended its role to include the fostering of faith, as a form of prayer, and as an artistic form of sacred expression. French theologian Albert Rouet investigated the indispensability of the arts in the development of faith within the liturgy of the Christian church.[1] Rouet probed the creative forms of music, architecture, the written word, and dance. He explored how each expression brings life to the biblical text found within liturgy and how it brings life to the people who actualize the liturgy. For Rouet, it is this association that fosters faith within the church congregation.

---

1. See Rouet, *Liturgy and the Arts*, 20.

Reverend Robert VerEecke, SJ is the former pastor and director of religious education at St. Ignatius Catholic Church, located on the grounds of Boston College.[2] As post pastor and Jesuit Artist-in-residence at Boston College, his research pursues liturgical dance as a daily life of prayer. VerEecke's writings have not only defined the significance of liturgical dance as prayer but also defended it against criticisms that identified it as pure "entertainment and courtship."[3]

Kimberly Jordan's dissertation explores a black woman's ritual of consecration and offers a historical study of a growing liturgical dance ministry in order to understand contemporary Black sacred settings in which power is materialized through Black women's bodies.[4] Susan Lee Olson's dissertation demonstrates that the language of modern dance, as epitomized in the work of three early modern dance choreographers, has shaped a new tradition—that of liturgical dance—which, in turn, contributes to the realization of the church's ongoing goal of full, conscious, and active participation in the liturgy.[5]

These investigations have energized the research on liturgical dance, continuing to highlight it as a resourceful methodology in defining and deciphering the meaning of faith and faith formation within the Christian tradition. In the field of religious education, there are now explorations in identifying the importance of the aesthetics and specific artistic expressions in teaching the value of faith. This writing will follow the same course of investigation.

Yolanda Smith captured the Negro spirituals as a teaching modality for African American Christian Education. She developed the "triple-heritage model," a model inclusive of the heritages found within the African American Church tradition, which are African, African American, and Christian.[6] Smith proposes that this triple-heritage "is a unit with three vital components that together make up a unique whole . . . They draw upon one another, they flow out of each other, and they build upon each other."[7] Smith has designed a tri-collaborative curriculum model which intersects the spirituals within her triple-heritage model.

2. Gagne et al., *Dance in Christian Worship*.

3. VerEecke, "Shall We Dance," 2.

4. Jordan, "My Flesh," x.

5. Olson, "If Necessary, Use Words," 5.

6. Smith, *Reclaiming the Spirituals*, vii.

7. Smith, "Preserving Faith," 2, 23.

Anne Wimberly's research explains the renewed emphasis by Christian education and church leaders on the pivotal role of education in and through worship.[8] Wimberly contends that every aspect of ministry, including worship, contains educational implications that describe worship as a "distinctive and powerful habitat for integrating the presence of God, the experiences of daily life, and visions of the future."[9] She creates a model that focuses on the "evocative manner in which worship in the black church nurtures the faith and hope of the worshiping congregation."[10]

The work of Gloria Durka and Joanmarie Smith explicitly addresses the aesthetic dimensions of religious education. They sought to establish the claim that unless the process of religious education is aesthetic, it is not education—and it is certainly not religious.[11]

Academic investigations such as the examples mentioned above have paved the way for continued explorations in the field of religious education and the arts. More specifically, as there is a vacuum of resources that connect liturgical dance to the field of religious education, this research has given us an impetus to explore the association between the two. The continual rise of liturgical dance as an artistic form of expression suggests that it offers unique attributes that are conducive for the teaching and learning of faith and faith formation. This book addresses the power and potential that liturgical dance has in nourishing the faith life of congregants through means that are both educative and reflective.

I am grateful to a host of people who have traveled with me throughout this process. I began this investigation as a doctoral student in the Graduate School of Religion and Religious Education at Fordham University in the Bronx, New York. My sincere thanks are extended to Gloria Durka, who advised and encouraged me on so many levels during my investigating and writing on this topic, along with John Ellis, Aileen Giannelli, and Yolanda Smith, who gave sound advice and academic direction during the entire writing process. I wish to thank the ten interviewees: The Reverend Dr. Floyd H. Flake, Bishop Charles Ellis III, Dr. Patrick Evans, The Reverend Eyesha Marable, Mary Jones, Robert Evans, Yvonne Peters, Doreen Holland, and Jay and Lorie Dekie for their genuine honesty and commitment to the use of the arts (especially liturgical

8. Wimberly, *Faith & Hope*, xi.

9. Wimberly, *Faith & Hope*, xii.

10. Wimberly, *Faith & Hope*, xxvi.

11. Durka and Smith, *Aesthetic Dimensions*, xii.

dance) in sharing the Christian message within the life of the church, both inside and out.

I wish to thank faculty member Carolyn Sharp and former faculty members Thomas Troeger and, again, Yolanda Smith of Yale Divinity School, who gave me a platform to begin the writing process, exploring how liturgical dance can be understood through a seminarian perspective. I wish to thank the formal director of Marquand Chapel worship, Siobhan Garrigan, and the formal director of Marquand Chapel music, Patrick Evans, who exhibited a platform where actual teaching within the worship setting can transpire and be meaningful—whether the teaching is of a song, a prayer, or a movement gesture. I am indebted to such an education; a precedent was set for me to explore the teachable moments found within worship.

I acknowledge my home church, The Greater Allen African Methodist Episcopal Church of New York, under the pastoral leadership of The Reverends Floyd H. Flake, DMin, and the Reverend Elaine M. Flake, DMin, where they gave me the space to explore liturgical dance and how it can be incorporated within the worship experience. With the assistance of the Rev. Dr. Renita Weems Espinosa, who first asked me to share my love of dance with Allen's congregation, this exploration would cover a forty-year time frame through The Allen Liturgical Dance Ministry (ALDM), the dance ministry I founded and directed. ALDM presented a platform to determine how liturgical dance can be discovered, experienced, and shared while presenting opportunities for congregations and communities of worship to experience liturgical dance on a personal basis. It also afforded the opportunity to present national and international conferences where many came, shared, and learned the essence and validity of liturgical dance in the Christian context. In addition to the Allen Liturgical Dance Ministry, I am grateful to the many opportunities afforded me to teach, choreograph, and minister liturgical dance throughout the country at churches and Christian worship and arts conferences. I am most grateful that these occasions pushed me to continue retrieving instruction from pastoral leaders, fellow liturgical dance teachers, and attendees who frequented such conferences.

I am thankful to those teachers of dance who pushed, prodded, and dared me to work to find my creative voice within it. These teachers include Mrs. Gloria Jackson, my very first dance teacher, who not only believed that I could be a sound dancer but also a sound teacher and choreographer. I am indebted to my dance teachers at the New York

High School of Performing Arts, SUNY Purchase, and Sarah Lawrence College, who developed my talent for dance and choreography in ways that were invigorating and propelling while challenging me to find my voice in the art form. I wish to thank Fred Benjamin, Dorothy Vislocky, and Dianne McIntyre, who hired me to join their dance companies and helped develop my creativity as a dancer, teacher, and observer of dance. I am grateful to those sacred musicians and composers who engaged me in theological conversations on the theme of praise and worship. Thank you Rev. Gwendolyn Sims Warren, Marshal Carpenter, David Bratton, John Tirro, and Stanley Brown for encouraging and inspiring me to create new and attainable liturgical dance movements through your sacred musical compositions. I am grateful to both colleagues and friends— Carol Hayes, Lucile Hill, Eyesha Marable, Francine Butler, Denese Vera-Wilson, Alisha Jones, Tamara Henry, Jana Feinman, Sarita Guffin, James Abbington, John Witvliet, and Cynthia Wilson—whose conversations on like topics continually propelled me to move forward.

I wish to thank my parents Mr. Lawrence A. Sumler and Mrs. Emma M. Sumler, who both encouraged me to be creative in pursuing my God-given dreams and destiny. My brother Adam and sister Gail, whose patience and support encouraged me when times were lowly and grim. Finally, I wish to thank my husband Curtis Turner, who unselfishly encouraged me to return back to school to further my education in matters that fused both my Christian belief and my love of liturgical dance. He literally made room for me to research, think, and write while proving to be an avid listener to the work that was being designed. Lastly, I am grateful to *Adonai Elohim*, the Great Lord, the all-powerful One who placed within me the need to speak, teach, and create through movement. Thank you, *Adonai*, for equipping me with the unction to push beyond the boundaries of Christian Worship, so that movement can be used to express, declare, inform, and translate the love you have for your creation.

Introduction

The Lifter of My Head

Starting Point

The driving question of this book is: *What are the characteristics embedded in liturgical dance which identify it as religious education within the church as a community place of learning?* I contend that there is a plethora of characteristics within liturgical dance which substantiates it as religious education. These components include liturgical dance as communicator, translator, and teaching tool and they are articulated through gesture, movement, improvisational discovery, and partially or fully choreographed dances. These attributes can translate themes of faith, prayer, love, devotion, sanctification, healing, compassion, missions, and social justice to God's people found both inside and outside the walls of the church. Hence, this writing will aim to define liturgical dance as a manner of expression and as a method for translation and instruction that touches the hearts and minds of God's people in ways that are both sustaining and educative.

From a historical perspective, dance has always been utilized as a tool in the apprehension of and the classification of all things religious. Dance historian Curt Sachs explains the early relationship dance has had with the search for God as follows:

> The dance, inherited from savage [primitive] ancestors as an ordered expression in motion of the exhilaration of the soul, develops and broadens into the search for God, into a conscious effort to become a part of those powers beyond the might of man [humankind] which control our destinies. The dance becomes

a sacrificial rite, a charm, a prayer, and a prophetic vision. It summons and dispels the forces of nature, heals the sick, links the dead to the chain of their descendants; it assures sustenance, luck in the chase, victory in battle; it blesses the fields and the tribe. It is creator, preserver, steward, and guardian.[1]

Sachs explains dance as a medium by which ritual, discovery, and the call for the divine have been expressed since the beginning of time. Dance as full-bodied expression is the only vehicle by which individuals can abide, translate, and exhibit religious belief, rite, and practice physically, mentally, and spiritually.

The Bond between Religious Education and Liturgical Dance

This writing begins with considerations of how dance, from a historical perspective, has been useful in the learning and identification of religious belief. There are two specific examples of the relationship found between dance and faith formation. The first example examines the African slaves and the teaching of Christianity through the "invisible church" during the Antebellum south. The second explores the United Society of Believers in Christ's Second Appearing, also known as the Shakers. Both examples reveal how the element of dance accompanied by song and word were instrumental in the teaching of faith in two religious groups.

This book investigates arts education and its validity to promote learning that is balanced and conducive to the varieties of ways individuals learn. The work of educational theorists Elliot Eisner, Howard Gardner, Maxine Greene, and Jennifer Donohue Zakkai is also reviewed. Zakkai is both a dancer and artist educator for the Galef Institute, which is responsible for developing the school reform initiative, "Different Ways of Knowing," a philosophy of education based on research in child development, cognitive theory, and multiple intelligences. Zakkai's work highlights why and how movement and dance are powerful tools for learning and creativity in classrooms K-6.[2] The work of all four authors is foundational in the creation of a religious education curriculum encompassing liturgical dance as a teaching tool for the church.

1. Sachs, *History of the Dance*, 4.
2. See Zakkai, *Dance as a Way of Knowing*.

The importance of an aesthetic education in nurturing congregations is another topic that is investigated. It shows how John Dewey's ideas on education, aesthetics, and experience can assist faith communities in the teaching, learning, and living experiences that are religious.[3] The work of Dewey provides a firm foundation for the teaching of religious education through experience and the arts within the context of the church as a community of learning.

Three religious educators whose work seems to be influenced by John Dewey will also be considered: Charles Foster, Norma Cook Everist, and Anne Streaty Wimberly. Foster explores congregational learning by developing a format for Christian religious education that is emancipatory and transformational in nature.[4] He sets out to discover how the church can participate in the "formative and transformative events of Christian tradition and witness."[5] Foster's research goes hand in hand with Dewey's understanding of community as communication, where the participation of people within the learning process is assured due to a common understanding. I wish to examine how Foster's meaning making and teaching for meaning help to create an educational, operational, and functioning Christian congregation.

Norma Cook Everist concentrates on the act of re-membering.[6] She promotes the fashioning of a communal encountering curriculum and the elements needed in caring for the learner during an aesthetic learning experience. For Everist, a merging of Dewey's philosophy of education with and through experience can continue to enrich religious education as a way to foster religious experience for the church as a community place of learning.

Anne Streaty Wimberly points to the nurturing experience found in congregational worship as a model for Christian Education within the Black church.[7] A closer look at the nurturing components of faith and hope as found in the worship elements of preaching, music, and prayer are examined. Since a merging of Dewey's philosophy of education with and through experience is presented, it is proposed that it can continue

---

3. See Dewey, *Experience and Education* and Dewey, *Art as Experience.*

4. Foster, *Educating Congregations*, 13.

5. Foster, *Educating Congregations*, 8.

6. See Everist, *Church as Learning Community.*

7. See Wimberly, *Faith & Hope.*

to enrich religious education as a way to teach, foster, and give understanding to religious experience of the church as a community place of learning.

Thus, this writing examines the meaning and value of liturgical dance as a viable tool for religious education and suggests teaching formats that can be implemented within the church through religious education. This is done by first exploring examples extracted from the Old Testament. Dance historian W.O.E. Oesterley believes that starting with the Old Testament is important in establishing the connection between sacred dance and religious belief. He writes:

> The Old Testament offers, either explicitly or implicitly, as we hope to show, evidence of the existence among the ancient Israelites of most of the typical sacred dances of antiquity. By "typical" we do not mean dances in their outward form, but in the intention and object for which they were performed. In dealing with sacred dances, it is only by considering their intention and purpose that a classification of them can be attempted. The Old Testament gives with the compass of its pages certain *points d'appui* which afford convenient staring-points for the consideration of these different types of the sacred dance.[8]

From the perspective of the Old Testament, the resurgence of liturgical dance in a Christian context (from the late twentieth century to the present) has elevated the need to extend its boundaries to include religious education. The work of Margaret Fisk Taylor, Carla DeSola, J. G. Davies—as well as my own—are reviewed. This writing seeks to identify liturgical dance as a tool in the teaching of Christian faith.

Finally, this book is unique in both concept and content as it extends religious education curriculum research to include liturgical dance. Drawing on Maria Harris's working definition of curriculum and its relation to the life of the church allows me to implement liturgical dance as a way to apprehend, share, and exhibit an understanding of how one becomes Christian and how one grows to be more Christ-like.[9] The process of utilizing liturgical dance encompasses the makeup of the whole person—body, mind, and spirit—which contributes to Harris's comprehension of curriculum as one that fashions, molds, and shapes the

---

8. Oesterley, *Sacred Dance in Ancient World*, 8.

9. See Harris, *Fashion Me a People*.

whole person, both learner and instructor.[10] This book promotes liturgical dance as a teaching tool that services the life of the church, creating teaching formats that present a partnership between liturgical dance and religious education.

The Lifting of Voices

This book includes a purposeful sample of interviews with a variety of people who have been affiliated with or affected by the use of liturgical dance as a teaching tool within the life of the church. These interviews involved liturgical dance directors and choreographers, dancers, clergy, parishioners, and a director of music. Each interviewee was presented with a series of questions in advance. The information extracted from these interviews produced present-day feedback on the use of liturgical dance as a tool for learning within a variety of venues that are church related.

Those interviewed cross denominational, gender, age, ethnic, and cultural lines, incorporating a variety of national and international voices. This was essential for including a plethora of experiences that unite the use of liturgical dance within a Christian context regardless of one's denomination, gender, age, ethnic, or cultural associations. The length of time each interviewee had been affiliated with the use of liturgical dance within a church setting established the various ways liturgical dance has serviced the teaching component of church life on a variety of levels, over an extended length of time, and within a variety of circumstances.

The liturgical dance directors and choreographers chosen are established dancers in their own right, having been exposed to professional dance training. The dance training did not have to be within one specific genre of dance (for example, ballet or modern), rather, the director or choreographer was to have had serious exposure to the rudiments of their particular genre. Dancers were selected according to their affiliation with learning and executing liturgical dance movement. They were comprised of both dancers who are professionally trained and those who have had limited professional training. The dancers chosen have a compilation of experiences within the field of doing liturgical dance. The inclusion of both clergy and the director of music ministry was based upon their association with the utilization of liturgical dance in a variety

10. Harris, *Fashion Me a People*, 16.

of venues within the total life of the church. Parishioners were selected from a variety of venues and share what their experiences of liturgical dance have been in developing their personal understanding of faith and religious belief.

The interview was comprised of seven questions which address what liturgical dance is and how it can affect the teaching life of the church:

- From your experience, how would you define the term "liturgical dance?"
- How have you been affected by liturgical dance?
- How has the church or worship community been influenced by its use?
- Explain why you would or would not classify liturgical dance as an instructional tool.
- Should the church incorporate liturgical dance as a learning tool? Why or why not?
- What precautions should be applied in utilizing liturgical dance?
- What suggestions would you offer to religious educators in utilizing liturgical dance as a teaching tool?

The time of each interview was between forty-five minutes to one hour. The interviews were semi-formal since each interviewee was selected by myself. Whether the interview was in person or by phone, these interviews gathered current information from the interviewees to help me determine the criteria for generating settings that highlight the partnership found between liturgical dance and a religious education that promotes liturgical dance as a teaching tool for the church as a community place of learning.

Book Content

The book has five chapters. Each title is extracted or inspired from scriptural texts that speak to the themes covered. These texts are predominately found in the book of Psalms or have been influenced by the verbiage found within Psalms. Each of the chapter titles is accompanied by a simple thematic explanation, clarifying the essence of the chapter.

The Introduction, "The Lifter of my Head (Ps 3:3): The Explanation of the Book" is the introduction, situating the writing within the academic framework of religious education and liturgical dance.

Chapter 1, "My Steps Have Held to Your Paths and Have Not Slipped (See Ps 17:5): A History of Two Communities," reviews the historical use of dance. Marianne Sawicki's work on historical methods and religious education supplies the blueprint to discover the history of dance and religious teaching found among two historic religious communities.[11] The first is the enslaved African community and "invisible church" during the Antebellum period and the second community is the Shakers.

Chapter 2, "I Will Mediate on Your Wonders (See Ps 119:27): The Significance of Arts Education," examines the validity of arts education as a source of learning. The chapter investigates the relationship between arts education and religious education and the use of dance as a way of knowing, utilizing the work of Howard Gardner, Elliot Eisner, Maxine Greene, and Jennifer Donohue Zakkai. This writing gives foundation to creative and imaginative ways of teaching inside the walls of the church through the writings of Maria Harris while Carla DeSola and Arthur Easton explore the connection between dance, religious education, and worship.

Chapter 3, "Teach Me and Give Me Understanding (See Ps 119:33–4): Experiential Learning and the Church Community," draws on John Dewey's theories of education and aesthetic education through experience. This chapter describes what it means for the church to be a community place of learning. Through the works of C. Ellis Nelson, Charles Foster, Norma Cook Everist, and Anne Streaty Wimberly, it also examines Dewey's influence on the church as a community place of learning and the use of the arts within such a setting.

Chapter 4, "Praise God with Dancing (See Ps 149:3): An Investigation into the Meaning and Application of Liturgical Dance," defines and describes liturgical dance, drawing from information supplied by written texts ranging from the Old Testament and doctrines of the early Church Fathers to liturgical dance artists and interviews. It identifies its educational attributes through the use of description, interpretation, and evaluation of movement, gesture, and language in the context of the use of dance within specific church teaching and learning events.

11. Sawicki, "Historical Methods," 375–389.

Chapter 5, "And We Shall Learn through the Dance: Exploring the Instructional Relationship between Liturgical Dance and Religious Education," is the final chapter and proposes the principle of listening as explained by Margaret Crain.[12] This notion assists in formalizing the four formats that establish the partnering relationship found between liturgical dance and religious education. These four formats merge liturgical dance and religious education in the areas of worship, classroom teaching, prayer, and evangelism.

In summary, this book seeks to help fill the vacuum of resources that connect religious education and liturgical dance. Since liturgical dance continues to rise as a form of worship expression, it is also fitting to associate it with the teaching of faith and faith formation because of its unique qualities and attributes. It is my hope that this book will inspire many seminarians, professors, pastors, dancers, musicians, religious education teachers, youth directors, and congregational members to seek the power and potential that liturgical dance has in the nourishing of one's faith life and to accept the invitation to *learn through the dance*.

12. Crain, "Listening to Churches," 93–109.

Chapter 1

My Steps Have Held to Your Paths and Have Not Slipped

A History of Two Communities

Introduction

The history of religious education shows that various tools were utilized in teaching about faith and religion. The arts were one such tool. History records that the arts have been effective in the teaching of Christianity and religious education. Their usage reveals much about the faith communities who found their inclusion helpful in fostering the life of faith. The artistic forms of song, word, and dance are expressions utilized by many faith communities whose religious walk appears to neither falter nor slip. For reasons that will be explored in the chapter below, these artistic tools remain helpful in recalling memories and historical events while fostering Christian and religious identity. The aim of this chapter is to describe and analyze the way two historical faith communities have used the arts in the life of faith.

Marianne Sawicki describes religious education as a "traditioning," a handing on of what has been handed down.[1] It contains stories of rituals, belief systems, and the interplay of activities that give expression to one's religious beliefs. For Sawicki, the historical is where one finds the correlation between what the religious traditions are and how they are

1. Sawicki, "Historical Methods," 377–378.

taught. She identifies the religious tradition found within the biblical narrative and then names the teaching and policy methods that were utilized in teaching the religious tradition. She creates a comprehensive historical method through which religious educators can teach by not just retelling the story but also finding and expressing the religious experience behind it. According to Sawicki, the religious experience and its comprehension should be a primary focus of religious educators.

It is within such a methodology that the use of the arts as a teaching tool is at its best. This chapter explores the power of recalling memory and historical events as well as how a community of faith is formulated in order to teach and shape Christian identity. Sawicki observes the overall creation of a religious community through the successive sharing of the gospel message from one person to another and how such an act transforms the faith identity of that community.[2] This analysis provides background to Sawicki's notion of traditioning, the handing on of what has been handed down in religious education. It is followed by an examination of the historical use of the arts—more specifically, song, word, and dance—in religious education and faith formation in two specific faith communities: the African slaves and the teaching of Christianity through the "invisible church" during the Antebellum South and the United Society of Believers in Christ's Second Appearing, also known as the Shakers. The theological underpinnings of the Shaker belief system will not be presented, however, since their controversial views of Christianity (particularly the acceptance of the male and female duality of Christ as witnessed through Jesus and Mother Ann) are not germane to this study. The tensions and conflicts between their theological beliefs and those of other Christian denominations will not be addressed. Similarly, considering that the period of slavery in the Antebellum South was more readily exposed to Protestantism than Catholicism, here, only the use of song, word, and dance in the birth of the Black church under Protestantism will be examined. Hence, references to the influence of Catholicism upon slaves in Louisiana (where African pantheons and rituals were mixed inside their comprehension of Catholicism) will not be addressed.[3]

2. See Sawicki, *Gospel in History.*
3. Raboteau, *Slave Religion*, 88.

The Steps that Form a Community of Faith

This section describes how the church and Christian communities were formed. Marianne Sawicki submits that the telling of the Christian gospel message began with the simple telling of the story—the sharing of the gospel from one person to another. Sawicki's thesis, however, is based on the questions, "How did the gospel get itself told and retold in successive generations," and, "How did that telling transform the quality of human living for the ordinary people?"[4] Her text seeks: "To follow the 'low road' of the gospel's travel from mouth to mouth, heart to heart, among ordinary Christians. The writings of learned scholars and the achievements of ecclesiastical administrators are regarded as secondary to this grass-roots communications process."[5] Sawicki hopes that her inquiry will touch the ordinary, present-day Christian so that they will benefit from the recovery of such a heritage.

Sawicki locates her investigational tactic under the field of phenomenology, which focuses on the impact particular realities have upon human consciousness. This method is subjective, taking the human subject as its starting point, since subjectivity is the quality which distinguishes human beings from things. Subjectivity, Sawicki contends, promotes not only the knowing of human beings but also, and more importantly, that human beings know that they know. Within that knowing, all humans come into possession of who they are as informed knowers. For Sawicki, this subjectivity takes place among people as well as between individual persons and things. She writes: "Intersubjectivity is the quality of being human together in some sort of group, and knowing that the group itself also has being—a being different from the being of things, and also different from the individual subjectivities who enact the group."[6] Communication—and, in particular, the telling of stories—is what sustains both subjectivity and intersubjectivity. It is what creates and maintains both the personal being of persons and the social being of groups. Sawicki points out that the phenomena in which this creation and maintenance occur are the events which make up the field that phenomenology studies.

According to Sawicki, the Christian regards the gospel as God's word, God's way of communicating with God's people. This gospel is a powerful revelation of God's loving intention toward humanity. She

4. Sawicki, *Gospel in History*, 6.

5. Sawicki, *Gospel in History*, 6.

6. Sawicki, *Gospel in History*, 6–7.

surmises, however, that the power of God's word is also its weakness because it needs help to get from person to person—it needs ministers. She suggests that when the gospel is referred to as the "word of God" or "revelation," this usually refers to three different realities: a book, a person, and a process. The book refers to the Bible, comprised of those many books that record God's historical contact with God's people through reflections upon events that discern a pattern of God's love and care for the people of God. Sawicki describes the recording this way:

> This contact—which we call "revelation"—seems to have been conveyed in an experience of outrage at the dissonance between evil encountered in the world and the inherent goodness of the creator. Sometimes God's presence and action seemed localized in a place, like a mountain or the Temple, or in the Law, or in a whole people of Israel, or in the person of Jesus, or in the evangelizing activities of Christian missionaries. Each of these was a window onto the provident goodness of God, which was without limit.[7]

The Bible, Sawicki indicates, became regarded as the word of God, which signified a special communication from God.

For Sawicki, Jesus is the human word of acceptance of everything that God is and wants. To pray "in the name of Jesus" means to enter into this back-and-forth exchange, the rhythm of relationship with God that made up the inner core of the human being of Jesus.[8] The concept, "God's word," then, points both to the Bible and to Jesus Christ. Sawicki also points to a third meaning to the term "God's word." She asserts that the book and the historical individual, Jesus, who died twenty centuries ago, do indeed present communication from God to human beings, but such communication is not confined to them alone. God's word is also that process which continues every day, in every human life. For communication to be successful, it must be received. God said everything there was to say in Jesus, but God's communication cannot be completed until the last human being in history has responded to God's invitation. Therefore, the Bible is still becoming the word of God for each and every person who picks it up and receives its message:

> The strength of God's word—book, person, process—is that it is gentle, persuasive, and respectful of the characteristics of human

7. Sawicki, *Gospel in History*, 8.
8. Sawicki, *Gospel in History*, 8.

nature. God's word, then, is needful of help, that is, of helpers.
The ministry of the word ministers *to God's word*, by helping
it take flesh, happen, live, and become effective. The ministry
of the word ministers *to people* when it administers or applies
God's good news to their circumstances and particular needs.[9]

When God's word is effective, Sawicki claims, it becomes a part of the
ongoing flow of communications through which people participate in
human society and find their place in it. The process by which individuals become members of a society is called socialization and the reality
of society itself is sustained through the continuous traffic of communication—the sending and receiving of messages. This is also true of the
church, which is a society of individuals linked by means of the gospel
message. The church is the result or outcome of the telling of the gospel
story in the history of humanity. For Sawicki, the church is a particular
way of being human; a way that is made possible by the recognition that
the deepest meaning of human existence is to love and be loved by God.
She writes, "The church *is* a particular way of being together *because* its
members are those who have accepted the gospel."[10] The quality of being
together is contingent upon the quality of the meanings those within the
church share. Therefore, Sawicki suggests that those who have received
their personal identities from the gospel story have the assurance that
God intends to provide all the goods and all the meaning that are necessary for human life. Christians often think of the church, then, as the
hearer of God's word.

As Sawicki states, the church is the agent of the gospel, since it pro-
claims the gospel story to the world:

The activities which are identified as ministries of the word
are activities of the church itself, done by church members on
behalf of the church rather than in their own name. These activities include evangelization, catechesis, preaching, liturgical
and paraliturgical celebrations of the word, theological writing
and teaching, religious journalism in both broadcast and print
media, Bible study, and other forms of religious education.[11]

Christians who participate in these activities are called ministers of God's
word. Therefore, they see themselves working for the church, not only in

9. Sawicki, *Gospel in History*, 9.

10. Sawicki, *Gospel in History*, 10.

11. Sawicki, *Gospel in History*, 10.

the service of the gospel but also in the service of all humanity. Sawicki stipulates that the church itself is not an individual, personal subject, so it cannot literally act. Rather, it is enacted, as a mode of being human, in the actions of Christians who act on its behalf. The church is thought of as both the announcer as well as the hearer of God's word. It is the medium through which the gospel message travels to people in lands and times that are far distant from those in which Jesus and the biblical books first appeared. Using metaphorical language, she explains that the medium through which God's overwhelming love and longing for all humanity was of common form and language. It traveled through the sound and air waves of simple conversations and the simple writing of early texts. The church renewed and continues to renew the materials which have physically carried the gospel to our present day via new biblical translations, the bible encoded on microfilm, and stored in computer files as well as in the memories of people who have learned parts of the scriptures by heart. The church itself is the body of Jesus Christ—in which God's reconciling word continues to address the world—and the church renews Christ's sacramental presence in the communion celebration. Whether it is materially, mystically, or sacramentally, the church, according to Sawicki, is the channel or carrier of God's word.[12]

The church itself embodies the message of the gospel and what the gospel promises. Sawicki points out that the church is a universal community, making no distinction by race, sex, or class. The gospel's offer of salvation, conveyed through the church, is for everyone, open to all. The gospel asserts the providence of the Father and the ecclesial community provides for the material welfare of its needy members. According to Sawicki, before it even speaks a single word of sermon, the church community has already delivered its version of the gospel message by simply being what it is.

It is at this juncture that the gospel—identified both as God's word and the community known as the church—must be extended to explore how such a gospel was translated and handed from person to person. Sawicki's understanding of religious education as a "traditioning," involves tradition, what one hands down; the stories which describe the origins of the community; values and rules of behaving that delimit what is appropriate for the community; and rituals and customs that express

---

12. Sawicki, *Gospel in History*, 10.

and enshrine those meanings.[13] It is necessary to find individual identities and our identity as a people through the symbols, myth, values, and meanings received from the past in its story form—that is, to find ways to continue to tell this story, truthfully and faithfully.

It is here that the symbols, myth, values, and meanings of how the gospel was communicated amongst the African slaves during the antebellum period will be analyzed. Specifically, the artistic tools of song, dance, and word were effective in shaping and sharing the gospel message among the enslaved African community. As a result, religious traditions were created and, though invisible to many, a newly formed religious community was birthed.

The Invisible Institution in the Antebellum South

The Early Steps of the Invisible Church

From the abundant testimonies of fugitive and freed African slaves, much can be learned about the religious experience of the enslaved community. The slave community had an extensive religious life of its own, hidden from the eyes of the master. Albert Raboteau reported these words of explanation from a former slave:

> The old meeting house caught on fire. The spirit was there. Every heart was beating in unison as we turned our minds to God to tell Him of our sorrows here below. God saw our need and came to us. I used to wonder what the people shout but now I don't. There is a joy on the inside and it wells up so strong that we can't keep still. It is fire in the bones. Any time that fire touches a man, he will jump.[14]

It must be noted, however, that the religious experience of the African slaves was by no means fully contained in the visible structures of the institutional church found on or near the plantations. In most cases, all of these institutions were still governed under the tyranny of slavery, as the suspicious slave owners kept watchful eyes to make sure unlawful insurrections did not occur due to a growing belief in a delivering God.

13. See Sawicki, "Historical Methods."
14. Raboteau, *Slave Religion*, 64.

The Praise House and The Ring Shout

The "Praise House" or "Pray's House," was the name of the accepted establishment—acceptable by some white slave owners—where the slaves
held their religious meetings and services. Praise Houses developed during the 1860s on seacoasts of South Carolina and Georgia, but were not
limited to those areas. Others were known in Florida, specifically within
the population of the Baptist slaves.[15] The slave owners permitted such
activities as they realized it kept the slaves both confined and occupied.
Costen states, "For this reason, Praise Houses could technically be called
the first 'visible' institutions or creative worship spaces in which African
American worship traditions were developed."[16]

There were several principle traditions—extracted from various
African cultures—represented amongst the slave populations that were
implemented during worship in the Praise House. One such principle
was the connectedness and sacredness of all things that led to an affirmation of life, where the Africans were compelled to participate fully in
the whole of life. Yolanda Smith proposes that this aspect of the African
worldview can be seen in African music, dance, folklore, storytelling, and
proverbs.[17] Through these modes of expression, Smith indicates that Africans share their beliefs and feelings; rehearse their history; critique the
establishment; set forth their worldview; observe rituals and ceremonies;
communicate with others within the community; govern their moral behavior in relationship to God, humanity, and creation; impart wisdom for
full participation in life; and provide guidelines for instruction. Such an
African worldview, Smith points out, embodies a sense of connectedness,
unity, sacredness, and life.

The use of African song and movement within the Praise Houses
of the 1860s laid a firm ground for the establishment of the call and response song pattern and the "Ring Shout" movement that followed. This
was a unique worship order which flourished in the late nineteenth century. For example, the shout is not, as the name might suggest, merely a
loud vocalization of religious experience but rather a religious or semi-
religious activity combining music, devotion, and movement.[18] The use
of the call and response is a characteristic commonly seen in African

15. See Alho, *Religion of the Slaves.*

16. Costen, *African American Christian Worship,* 50.

17. See Smith, *Reclaiming the Spirituals.*

18. See Courlander, *Negro Folk Music.*

music and its presence in the spirituals was "strong evidence of an African survival in the New World."[19]

Costen highlights the importance of the story teller—the *griot*, in African culture—who was responsible for holding the history of the community in story, song, and even dance. The songs that grew out of this tradition were antiphonal in shape, with varying call and response musical patterns that "lead themselves to interlocking in overlapping phrases."[20] Melva Costen explains that the "syncopation and highly rhythmic patterns evoked intricate, physical, and instrumental accompaniment or hymnic musical patterns with slow harmonic progressions."[21] The use of this call and response pattern allowed the entire community to participate in remembering the facts of their family, religious and tribal traditions, and histories in a form that used recitation, choreography, and music. The *griot* would begin the story, song, or dance and the community was invited to listen or join in by responding to the story using one of three forms—either by word, song, or dance. The strength of this pattern of remembrance kept the history of the community alive and vibrant while the stories, songs, and dances were used to help evaluate where the members of the community were in relation to that history.

This particular pattern of call and response framed the worship event within the Praise House. The bodily movement of the Ring Shout was considered anything but exalted by white Christians, who associated it with sexual activity and barbarism at a time when sacred dance was no longer a force in Western religious ceremonies. Sterling Stuckey states that the opposition to the Shout was perhaps the principal means by which slaveholders attempted to break the mold of African culture in America.[22] Therefore, the push to teach the enslaved community more acceptable psalms and hymns was of crucial importance to the slave masters.

Within the Praise House, there was always a designated song leader—who led all of the songs—while the congregation either sang the songs collectively, followed the songs by having them lined out, or sang in the call and response framework.[23] Apparently, within the early start

19. Smith, *Reclaiming the Spirituals*, 60.

20. Costen, *Spirit and Truth*, 10.

21. Costen, *Spirit and Truth*, 10.

22. Stuckey, "Christian Conversion," 47.

23. The method of lining out a song followed a particular pattern of instruction. The leader would sing one line of the song and the congregation would immediately

of the service, there was already an inclusion of physical movement that accompanied the continuous singing which brought everyone into unison. The use of polyrhythmic clapping and rhythmic tapping of the feet throughout the singing of songs established the unification of the entire body of all persons in attendance.[24]

Recognizing the association between the African roots of the slaves with the development of the Negro spiritual brings into focus the relationship between rhythm, song, and movement. In *Black Song: The Forge and the Flame*, John Lovell Jr. explores the connection between all three elements. Handclapping took the place of the drum and shouting and other highly rhythmic body movements were substituted for the dance. The rhythm of many spirituals indicates the necessity of handclapping and body movement to support the singing of the songs. Lovell states:

> Behind the instrumental music . . . lived and prospered a singing Negro music, in solo and in choir. That the spiritual is an African song associated with dances and instruments helps to account for its remarkable gift of rhythm. The fact that, in the heart of the African, music is ever-present gave these rhythms depth and unerringness. Whoever sings spirituals today without a sense of varying dance rhythms is probably not getting as much from them as [they] might.[25]

The various texts that capture the actualization of the Ring Shout are quite similar. It is a ritualized dance, done collectively by women, men, boys, and girls. Usually performed at the end of the service, it could last up to five hours. As everyone is invited to participate, the Ring Shout is considered a folk dance. Even as it underwent transformation in the face of the pressing challenge of slavery, the Ring Shout emerged as an ideology embedded in the artistic experience and a form of dance ceremony in which a religious vision of profound significance was projected.[26]

The Ring Shout was distinguished from "dancing" by the shuffling of the feet against the floor. Its circular formations and foot movements include the use of shuffling rather than the lifting up of the feet. In dancing, which was considered wrong and sinful, the crossing of the legs

---

follow, singing the exact same line. This method of song singing was not limited to the African American slave. Many cultures that experienced illiteracy among the community utilized this same technique. See Costen, *Spirit and Truth*, 47–50.

24. Costen, *Spirit and Truth*, 51.

25. Lovell, *Black Song*, 219.

26. See Stuckey, "Christian Conversion."

and the lifting of the feet up off the floor were essentially physical signs that dancing was being performed. The Ring Shout provided a scheme through which to reconcile the use of dance within African religious behavior and the prohibiting of dance within the Euro-Christian tradition. Harold Courlander declares that the circular movement, shuffling steps, and stamping conform to African traditions of supplication, although, by definition, this activity was not recognized as a "dance." If one violated this compromise, however, going too far, they would have committed an irreverent act. This was not allowed during the Ring Shout. A person who violated this commonly understood proscription by crossing the feet—that is to say, by "dancing"—would be admonished or evicted from the service. Courlander captures one man's testimony of being removed from service because of such a violation:

> Well, don't you know, them folks all shouting, rockin', and reelin', and me in the middle; and I ask you if it wasn't the Holy Ghost that come into me, who was it? Those feet of mine wouldn't stay on the ground in no manner, they jumped around and crossed over, back and forth, and the next thing I know they turned me out of the church.[27]

Melva Costen shares a description of the Ring Shout:

> The true "shout" takes place on Sundays or on "praise nights" through the week, and either in the praise-house or in some cabin in which a regular religious meeting has been held. . . . The benches are pushed back to the wall when the formal meeting is over, and old and young, women and men, . . . boys, . . . [and] young girls, . . . all stand up in the middle of the floor, and when the "sperichl" (spiritual) is struck up, begin first walking and by-and-by shuffling round, one after the other, in a ring. The foot is hardly taken from the floor, and the progression is mainly due to a jerking, hitching motion, which agitates the entire shouter; and soon brings out steams of perspiration. Sometimes they dance silently, sometimes as they shuffle they sing the chorus of the spiritual, and sometimes the song itself is also sung by the dancers. But more frequently, a band, composed of some of the best singers and of tired shouters, stand at the side of the room to "base" the others, singing the body of the song and clapping their hands together or on the knees. Song and dance alike are extremely energetic, and often, when the shout lasts into the

---

27. Courlander, *Negro Folk Music*, 195.

middle of the night, the monotonous thud of the feet prevents sleep within a half mile of the praise-house.[28]

Several accounts highlight the Ring Shout done by the elders of the community. Their motional patterns, postures, and gestures allowed for both excitement and grace to activate the worship atmosphere. Their standing manner—the use of bent knees, their feet flat against the floor, and their arms opened wide for balancing purposes—were not only elegant to watch but also confirmed, once again, its African influence and derivation.

During the dance, the shoulders remained very close together while the shouters swayed their bodies from side to side, in a circle, forming "the ring." Its use of the circle suggests a certain wholeness that encouraged the spirit of community, where the dancers moved counterclockwise in the ring.[29] The dance started off slowly and would gradually increase in tempo as the song progressed. For example, in using the song, "I Can't Stay Behind," the words of the chorus/response are, "I can't stay be-hind, my Lord, I can't stay be-hind," while the words in the verse text varied. However, within the song, the response words seem to change depending upon the verse. Using the first verse, the call verse begins with "dere's room e-nough" (three times), "in de Heaven, my Lord," while the choral response is "room e-nough" (three times), "I can't stay behind."[30]

In the Ring Shout, the congregation circles around in a ring, shuffling their feet against the wooden floor, moving their torsos from side to side while the verse is sung by the leader (or leaders). The congregation responds by either singing the chorus or, if they get the spirit, they begin singing the entire song—but the Ring Shout continues all the same. In this particular example, the real response to the song done by the congregation is the Ring Shout. It continues as the standard and full bodied response to the shout song being sung.

Although the Ring Shout was most commonly done in a group setting, it must be noted that there were instances where individuals would do movements that were separate and apart from the community of dancers. It was at these times that such individuality enhanced the Ring Shout to be more than simply a group endeavor within African religious worship. Stuckey describes this as follows:

28. Costen, *African American Christian Worship*, 53.
29. See Stuckey, "Christian Conversion."
30. Allen et al., *Slave Songs*, 6. For the complete text of the song, see Appendix A.

The more powerful yet more subtle Shout in which the dancer leaps into the air, turning in a counter-clockwise direction, merits mention as a means by which *individual* Ring Shouts were similar to, yet different from, the more standard Ring Shout. Fredrik Bremer provides a fine description of this subtle form of inscribing in space, through dance, one's religious values. She describes solo performances of groups of Africans leaping and spinning in the air in New Orleans in the 1850s and calls the effect of the whole an "African Tornado," which is richly suggestive since tornadoes, in this hemisphere, move in a counterclockwise direction. Variants of this type of Shout were found elsewhere in the South and even in the North.[31]

The Ring Shout, in both song and dance, served as a sense of knowing where God is in the midst of the life of the slave. The Ring Shout was a type of monitoring system where the slaves were able to be absolutely present when the spirit of God filled the room. When the congregation engaged in the Ring Shout, it was the use of singing, rhythmic clapping and accompaniment, patterned movement, and intense emotional expression that produced devotional activity.[32] For the African slave, all such elements were associated with worship.

The worship events in the Praise House gave African slaves a sense of empowerment and reality that sustained them. The entire community joined in and the effect was a communal awareness of the ever-sustaining presence of God as deliverer in their midst. The community of worshipers all became the central *griot* and this afforded them opportunities to reflect, build, and strengthen one another's faith, to press forward in their present state of slavery. The call and response moment enabled the slaves to see themselves more in their future liberated state as opposed to their present state of servitude.

Religious Education Traditioning through Song, Word, and Dance

In "A Legacy of Hope," Anne Wimberly points out that, during slavery, the Bible became the primary text for African American Christian educational initiatives. It served as a sense-making document, providing the lens through which African slaves looked at the world and their situation

31. Stuckey, "Christian Conversion," 48–9.
32. Courlander, *Negro Folk Music*, 196.

within it. The Bible provided stories which they could identify with and from which they could find direction and hope. These stories became their own. Wimberly explains this further:

> They were attracted primarily to the narratives of the Hebrew Bible dealing with the adventures of the Hebrews in bondage and escaping from bondage, to the oracles of the eighth century prophets and their denunciations of social injustice and visions of social justice, and to the New Testament texts concerning the compassion, passion, and resurrection of Jesus. With these and other texts, the African American Christians laid the foundations for what can be seen as an emerging 'canon.' In their spirituals and in their sermons and testimonies, African Americans interpreted the Bible in the light of their experience.[33]

As Albert Raboteau points out, within the use of the spiritual, there was a sense of the sacred at work. The present state of the slaves was extended or "traditioned" so that the biblical characters, teachings, and events of Old and New Testaments became dramatically alive and present to the African slave. Raboteau adequately describes an example of Sawicki's traditioning by explaining how the faith concepts of Christianity are handed down from generation to generation. He portrays this process as follows:

> The slaves' religious community reached out through space and time to include Jacob, Moses, Joshua, Noah, Daniel, the heroes whose faith had been tested of old. From the New Testament they remembered "weeping Mary," "sinking Peter," and "doubting Thomas," again noting the trails of faith through which these "true believers" had passed: Mary weeping in the garden because she did not know where Jesus's body had been taken, until he appeared to her in his risen glory; Thomas doubting that Jesus had risen until Jesus appeared to him and said, "Blessed are those who have not seen, yet believed"; Peter sinking beneath the waves of the Sea of Galilee because he was weak in faith, until Jesus, walking upon the water, reached out to save him.[34]

These were the models or analogues that reminded the slaves to hold on to their faith despite grief, doubt, and fear. These biblical figures also gave life and vision to new songs that taught and formulated faith through word and movement. The newly formed spirituals gave life and

33. Wimberly, "A Legacy of Hope," 8.

34. Raboteau, *Slave Religion*, 250.

direction in learning and comprehending faith. Wimberly explains that the slaves saw God as the "Spirit that incorporated an understanding of God's goodness and liberating activity" within their lives on a continuous basis.[35] This image of God contradicted the image presented by the missionaries of God being an oppressive Being. Jesus was the spirit of God in human form, the suffering servant who knew all about their troubles. Even though the enslaved Africans suffered, they were assured that Jesus would be with them and never leave them.

Sharing the Bible through storytelling gave credence to the reality that God, Jesus, and the Holy Spirit existed and worked righteously on behalf of the slaves. Such stories also validated the life experiences and turmoil faced by the slaves. Wimberly submits that the story-telling of the Bible and their attentive listening to these stories became a means of expressing and teaching values of perseverance, endurance, and patience. Until the enslaved community was able to learn to read the Bible for themselves, storytelling was the means by which they learned not only the theology of Christianity but also learned to formulate their own comprehension of a theology that worked on their behalf. The use of storytelling within the Praise House shaped the church for the African slave community because it was the outcome of the telling of the gospel story. Just as Sawicki suggests, the church, and in this case the Praise House, was the way through which slaves found and felt human recognition. For the enslaved community, the deepest meaning of human existence was to love and be loved by God. As Sawicki explains, the church *is* a particular way of being together *because* its members are those who have accepted the gospel. For the slaves, the Praise House was their own church environment.

The use of spirituals was another form of Christian education through oral expression. Wimberly claims that these songs "were declarations and testimonies of an enslaved people's journey of slavery and their understanding of Christianity at work in that journey."[36] For Wimberly, the spirituals both mirrored and sustained their faith in the God of history. She highlights that, in the process of the African slave's communication through song, they taught the biblical message and the meaning of continuing in faith and hope in spite of trials and tribulation. Both the music and dance mirrored and sustained their faith not only in the God

---

35. Wimberly, "A Legacy of Hope," 5.
36. Wimberly, "A Legacy of Hope," 10.

of history but also the God of the "now" moment. Through songs, the biblical message of hope encouraged faith and perseverance, becoming a force to withstand the trials and tribulations the enslaved Africans were presently facing. Such messages were hidden away in the deepest recesses of their hearts, minds, and souls. They inspired the slaves to push forward and to continue living, day in and day out.

Drawing upon the work of Wyatt T. Walker, Yolanda Smith explores the fundamental educational characteristics of the Negro spirituals. One educational characteristic of the Negro spiritual is the *deep biblicism* of the Bible, specifically Old Testament imagery.[37] Such imagery can be found in the song, "Ezek'el Saw de Wheel," which is based on Ezekiel's vision found in Ezekiel 1:4–28.[38] Smith explains that if there was not a direct biblical reference, there were always biblical overtones and implications found within the spiritual. Courlander shows how the image of a train, used frequently in Negro spirituals, "represents more modern transportation to the same ultimate destination for those who have found salvation."[39] The use of the Ring Shout in songs such as "King David" represents, for Courlander, "the driving character of a moving train, and it ties the train image to that of the chariot, for which it is only a modern substitute."[40] In some spirituals, there were specific biblical stories such as found in the song, "Joshua Fit de Battle of Jericho," which deals with Joshua's battle for the city of Jericho as found in Joshua 6:1–27.[41]

There are other fundamental educational characteristics of the spirituals. Smith suggests that the *eternality of the message* is one such characteristic.[42] The message of many of the spirituals is both universal and contemporary, allowing for numerous spirituals to transcend time and continue to speak to the human condition today. Another characteristic Smith suggests is their *double* and *coded meanings* found within the spirituals. Smith points out that this allowed for the slaves to communicate secret messages with one another without being detected by their masters. An example of this is in the spiritual "Go Down, Moses," which reflects the slaves' strong identification with the oppression of the

---

37. Smith, *Reclaiming the Spirituals*, 58.
38. Smith, *Reclaiming the Spirituals*, 57.
39. Courlander, *Negro Folk Music*, 41.
40. For the complete text of the song, "King David," see Appendix B.
41. Smith, *Reclaiming the Spirituals*, 59.
42. Smith, *Reclaiming the Spirituals*, 59.

children of Israel who communicated their belief in a God that identified with their suffering and would one day liberate them. Smith cites the
words of the spiritual:

> When Israel was in Egypt's land: Let my people go;
> Oppressed so hard they could not stand, Let my people go.
> Go down, Moses, Way down in Egypt land,
> Tell ole Pharaoh, Let my people go.[43]

Another characteristic of spirituals is *repetition*—in melody, lyrics,
or both—with minimal changes throughout the song. Repetition, also of
African influence, helped facilitate a corporate memory and contemporary significance.

Their *unique imagery* is another fundamental characteristic. According to Smith, the images described by the spirituals were often so
vivid and dynamic that a person could visualize or even feel the images
being portrayed. Smith concludes by explaining how spirituals could be
defined as the form of music that arose from the unique convergence of
African culture, the slave experience, and the Christian religion.[44]

The songs were adapted to their situations at the very moment that
the leader changed the first line of the spiritual, and the rest of the church
followed that lead. While the essence of the songs was spiritual, they
were also educational, as the slaves learned that God moved in such an
instance on their behalf. Their religious knowledge was increasing about
the God of the Bible as well as their understanding of the God who called
them his very own. The dances helped them to realize this in the physical form. As they moved and gathered together, their very beings were
engaging in a war that was struggling to go on without end. This war had
ebbs and flows, carrying them through moments of deep depression and
stillness. One can only imagine what type of life the slaves led and the
visible and invisible chains that enclosed them. But it was the song and
dance which taught that God was near to them and to their situation.
Raboteau describes their religious life as follows:

> Spanning almost two hundred and fifty years, [the] slaves
> came to accept the Gospel of Christianity and at the same time
> made it their own. It is important to remember that it was a
> dual process. The slaves did not simply become Christians; they

43. Smith, *Reclaiming the Spirituals*, 60.
44. Smith, *Reclaiming the Spirituals*, 61.

creatively fashioned a Christian tradition to fit their own peculiar experience of enslavement in America.[45]

The actualization of God's presence was witnessed by the slaves through their testimonies, songs, and dances from which many generations thereafter have been able to glean their strength. Smith contends that the messages undergirding the spirituals are both universal and contemporary and should not be considered as historical works alone. She writes, "The messages of numerous spirituals have transcended time and continue to speak to the human condition even today."[46] So much is to be learned from them, their worth is priceless for humanity. Such stories, songs, and movements laid the foundations for "what can be seen as an emerging canon."[47] As Wimberly demonstrates, in times of deep doubt and fear, African Americans interpreted the Bible in light of their own experience through movement, spirituals, sermons, and testimonies.[48] People today are *still* learning about faith by their example.

The Shaker Movement

History, Belief, and Doctrine

Ann Lee was a twenty-two-year-old woman who was attracted to the "shaking Quakers," led by James and Jane Wardley. By virtue of her gift of leadership—as well as strange visions and revelations—Ann Lee assumed a dominant role in the movement in 1758, transporting nine of its members to America in 1774. Known as Mother Ann, Lee was accepted as the female reincarnation of the Christ spirit, proclaiming herself to be "Ann the Word," and the Bride of the Lamb. Scholar Edward Deming Andrews explains that, within the sacred ecclesia of the Shaker movement—later to be known as the millennial or resurrection church—salvation was only possible by confessing and forsaking all fleshly practices. The Shakers assembled in the wilderness of Niskeyuna, New York (later Watervliet, New York) and held secret meetings in which members danced with the ecstasy of a chosen and exalted people.

45. Raboteau, *Slave Religion*, 209.
46. Smith, *Reclaiming the Spirituals*, 59.
47. Raboteau, *Slave Religion*, 8.
48. See Wimberly, "A Legacy of Hope."

Andrews describes both the notion of salvation and lifestyle exemplified by the Shaker colony as follows:

> They found a fellowship literally following the example of the primitive apostolic church: men and women living together in celibate purity, holding all goods in common, working industriously with their hands, speaking and singing in unknown tongues, worshipping joyfully, preaching that Christ had actually come to lead believers to a perfect, sinless, everlasting life—the life of the spirit.[49]

The Shakers developed several colonies throughout the northeast, including Massachusetts. It was here that Father Joseph Meacham developed a more consistent and elaborate belief based upon Lee's mystic faith after she passed away in Hancock, Massachusetts in 1784. His understanding of the Shaker belief system was based upon the doctrine of the four "dispensations," namely, "those periods in the history of [humanity] from Adam to Abraham to Moses to Jesus to Ann, during which God had gradually unfolded his plan of salvation."[50] The equality of the sexes had been established by Mother Ann, known as the prophetess, who compared her position as head of the true church to that of a wife after the husband (Jesus) was gone. However, it was Father Meacham who put this principle into communal practice, elevating Lucy Wright to leadership over the sisterhood and, thereafter, appointing women to positions of equal privilege and responsibility.[51]

The seven principles of Shaker theology are: "Duty to God, duty to [humanity], separation from the world, practical peace, simplicity of language, right use of property, and the virgin life."[52] These seven principles formed the practical and external law of the Shaker life based on the twelve Christian virtues of faith, hope, honesty, continence, innocence, simplicity, meekness, humility, prudence, patience, thankfulness,

---

49. Andrews, *Gift to be Simple*, 3–4

50. Andrews, *Gift to be Simple*, 5.

51. The doctrine of a dual Deity or masculine-feminine Godhead—though a logical extension of the concepts of a dual messiah and a coordinate sexual order—seems not to have been expressly formulated until Benjamin Youngs wrote the standard work on Shaker theology, "The Testimony of Christ's Second Appearing," (1808). Within "A Summary View of the Millennial Church" (1823), the doctrines of the manifestation of the Christ spirit in Mother Ann, "spiritual regeneration" and the "new birth" are further clarified.

52. Andrews, *Gift to be Simple*, 5.

and charity. The twelve Christian virtues come from a variety of New Testament teachings. Faith, hope, and love can be found in 1 Corinthians 13: 1–7 and 13:13 while the other ten principles are associated with the fruit of the Spirit, found in Galatians 5:22–26.

Shaker Worship through Song and Dance

A typical Shaker worship service was comprised of a variety of religious happenings. Andrews describes it this way:

> In a Shaker worship, there were inseparable forms of expressing praise, joy, yearning, or union. The first Believers were seized by such ecstasy of spirit that, like leaves in the wind, they were moved into the most disordered exercises: running about the room, jumping, shaking, whirling, reeling, and, at the same time, shouting, laughing, or singing snatches of song. No form existed: someone would impulsively cry out a line from the psalms, part of a hymn, or a phrase—perhaps in an unknown tongue—bespeaking wild emotion; someone might prophesy; another would exhort his listeners to repentance; another might suddenly start whirling like a dervish; then, as in a Quaker meeting, all for a time would be silent. After an order of worship was instituted, songs were sung without movement and dances paced without songs, but usually the procedure deliberately duplicated what had originally been involuntary: songs were danced, and the measures of the dance accentuated by the rhythm of the song.[53]

The above description reveals the earlier atmosphere of Shaker worship. Andrews supplies another example of dancing in the earlier stages of Shaker worship during their first meetings at Niskeyuna. Andrews writes:

> Everyone acts for himself, and almost every one different from the other; one will stand with his arms extended, acting over odd postures, which they call signs; another will be dancing, and sometimes hopping on one leg about the floor; another will fall to turning around, so swift, that, if it be a woman, her clothes will be so filled with the wind, as though they were kept out by a hoop; another will be prostrate on the floor; another will be talking with somebody; and some sitting by, [smoking] their pipes; some groaning most dismally; some trembling extremely;

53. Andrews, *Gift to be Simple*, 7.

others acting as though all their nerves were convulsed; others swinging their arms, with all vigor, as though they were turning a wheel, etc. Then all break off, have a spell of [smoking], and sometimes great fits of laughter . . . They have several such exercises in a day, especially on the Sabbath.[54]

Shaker worship was also shaped by the church structure they occupied. Shaker churches were first raised in New York and New England in 1785 and grew to include a barrel roof top church in 1822. This is when the pattern and consistency of Sabbath worship began to take shape. Andrews points out that as the assembly met for worship in the meeting house they would follow the "Church order," which had a pattern of filing into two lines, with the elders or men in the lead, while the sisters followed. The brethren would enter the church by the right door and the sisters entered by the left. Both groups took their places silently, according to position and age, on long wooden benches that were removed once the service began.

Robert and Viola Opdahl explain that Shaker worship initially followed the same course of revelation as that of Mother Ann.[55] The men and women received gifts of songs—melodies without words that were hummed or sung without nonsense syllable. They state that the performance of songs often led to dancing. As explained above, during the early years of the Shakers, the dancing was unstructured, without any concern for or attention to what others in the room were doing. This type of worship continued for nearly two decades, which is why they acquired the name, "Shaking Quakers."[56] The first formal group called into "gospel order" under Mother Ann was formed in 1787 and, as the Opdahls share, they settled into a united community in New Lebanon, New York. As the Shaker communities expanded through missionary efforts throughout New England and the United States, there arose the need to address such issues as worship order, property, and the defining of relationships between the sexes.[57] After Mother Ann's death, the leadership was given to Father Joseph Meacham and Lucy Wright, his female counterpart. An order was established and all other Shaker communities were expected to follow the model of order established in New Lebanon. The individual

54. Andrews, *Gift to be Simple*, 144.
55. See Opdahl and Opdahl, *Shaker Musical Legacy*.
56. See Opdahl and Opdahl, *Shaker Musical Legacy*.
57. Opdahl and Opdahl, *Shaker Musical Legacy*, xxiv.

ecstatic shaking and twirling was channeled into choreographed dances that accompanied songs that fit them. Opdahl and Opdahl report that the newly gathered communities were given instruction in the dance and songs through visits from Father Meacham and Lucy Wright and others from the New Lebanon order.

The organization of the millennial church into communities holding a "joint interest" of common property was the work of Father Joseph Meacham. The original eleven societies were divided into five bishoprics, each with its own ministry, responsible to the "lead" society at New Lebanon.[58] As Andrews explains, each society patterned its government on the example of the central society, which was subdivided into several family groups, controlled by subordinate officers, and named according to their location from the central Church (e.g., East family, South family, etc.). Andrews describes the millennial society further:

> Each family was an independent economic unit, consisting of from thirty to perhaps a hundred members, governed by an order of two elders and two eldresses who had the spiritual care of the group and oversight of all the family's affairs. An order of deacons and deaconesses was directly responsible for temporal concerns, while one or more trustees held the consecrated property of the unit. Family leaders were appointed and supervised at New Lebanon by an all-powerful, self-perpetuating central ministry composed of two elders and two eldresses, and in the other societies by the branch ministries.[59]

In 1812 and 1813, the Shakers printed their first hymnal, *Millennial Praises*, so that copies could be distributed amongst the Shaker societies that had been established. The Opdahls explain that since the *Millennial Praises* offered the hymn words without music, the Shakers began to record song melodies in manuscript hymnals, using a variety of systems to represent the different notes of the scale. They describe the varied note systems the Shakers used as follows:

> They used traditional round notes and the shape notes of the New England singing schools, but they also devised a unique system of notation created by placing letters that represented notes in a straight line or on a four—or five—line staff. There was great variety in these systems of "letteral notation" and a

58. Andrews, *Gift to be Simple*, 5.
59. Andrews, *Gift to be Simple*, 5.

greater debate among shakers on which system was best for adoption by all Shaker communities.[60]

Keeping in union with all other Shaker communities was essential to both the doctrine and lifestyle of the Shakers. Opdahl and Opdahl point out that the Shakers tried to secure uniformity and fairness among all its members, striving for consistency in rules and regulations, costume, architecture, diet, household furnishings, and worship. In attempting to ensure that Shakers in Maine would sing not only the same words but the same tune, tempo, and pitch as Shakers in Kentucky, a "tone-ometer" was developed to set the pitch of songs and a "mode-ometer" to set the tempo at which they were sung. This led to the printing of two different musical instruction manuals, *A Short Abridgment of the Rules of Music*, written by Isaac N. Youngs in 1843 and *The Musical Expositor*, written by Russell Haskell in 1847.

Shaker ritualism was composed of tunes, songs, marches, ring dances, and other forms of devotional exercises that were composed and intended for communal use. As Andrews suggests, their form and character were particularly social: the songs reflected in content the thought and aspiration of the whole group and their tempo was adapted to prescribed parts of the service and dance techniques which the eighteen societies had all adopted in common. They were perfected in the week-day singing meetings of the families and, according to Andrews, they were passed on to the community in the united Sabbath worship. As hundreds of songs were composed, they were exchanged among different families and given as gifts to particular elders and eldresses, or beloved brothers and sisters. "Popular pieces such as 'Come life Shaker life,' 'Tis the Gift to be Simple,' and 'My Carnal Life I will Lay Down' became authentic symbols of a distinct folk culture."[61]

The Shakers rationalized the use of dance because it was performed as "a worship among the ancient people of God."[62] The use of dancing was strongly affiliated with biblical references; therefore, they justified dance as "a gift of God to the church."[63] Andrews cites numerous scriptural references used by the Shakers to justify the use of dance within their life of worship, such as: the dance of Miriam, the prophetess, who

60. Opdahl and Opdahl, *Shaker Musical Legacy*, xxiv.

61. Andrews, *Gift to be Simple*, 7.

62. Andrews, *Gift to be Simple*, 146.

63. Andrews, *Gift to be Simple*, 146.

celebrated the children of Israel's deliverance from Egypt's bondage
(Exod 15:20–21); the daughter of Jephthah, who welcomed her father
with dancing after his victory over the children of Ammon (Judg 11:34);
David's dancing before the Lord when the ark was returned to the City of
David (2 Sam 6:16); and the exhortations of Psalm 149 and Psalm 150,
encouraging people to praise the Lord through dancing. This assurance
gave the Shakers enough grounding to establish the use of dance as a tool
for worshiping God.

As Andrews describes it, the service began with a devotional hymn,
followed by a discourse directed to the public as followers of the faith.[64]
Dance songs—called "labored" songs—took place once the meeting was
well under way. They were called labor songs because, within the dance,
their laboring or physical exercises expressed the inner workings of the
spirit.[65] This was understood by every believer because of their own life of
labor in working either in the field or workshop for the temporal welfare
of the Society. They labored in worship to awaken their feelings to the
spiritual gifts that would be bestowed on them during the course of the
service. Andrews and Andrews explains that: "The peculiar 'laboring' of
the Believers in their religious dances and rituals was patterned on the
dances of angels seen in a vision by Father Joseph Meacham."[66]

Early labor songs had a medley or short song text to accompany
the dance, and each song was numbered according to the type of dance
being performed.[67] The joy of salvation experienced by the worshiper was
expressed through leaping, shuffling, and whirling, all done as the spirit
moved them. Mother Ann "wisely refrained" from instructing how the
Shaker worshiper was to dance.[68] It was Father Joseph Meacham who
was led to develop a protocol for all Shakers dancing within the worship
services. As Patterson explains:

> It was Father Joseph Meacham who, by the revelation of God,
> transformed this "promiscuous dance" into the ordered cer-
> emony called "laboring." In one or another variation of its two

64. Andrews, *Gift to be Simple*, 21.

65. Patterson, *Shaker Spiritual*, 99.

66. Andrews and Andrews, *Visions of the Heavenly Sphere*, 9.

67. Patterson, *Shaker Spiritual*, 99–130. The forms included the Back Manner
form, the Holy Order form, the Turning Shuffle, the Skipping Manner form, the Regular Step form, the Drumming Manner form, and the Walking Manner form.

68. Patterson, *Shaker Spiritual*, 99.

forms—the dance and the march—laboring was practiced in Shaker worship from 1788 until nearly 1930.[69]

Various photos of the Shakers dancing show that there were particular spatial patterns which were utilized. One form had the men and women directly facing one another, while others had each group create rectangular formations opposite each other. There were also circular formations—the women encircled in an inner circle while the men created an outer circle. The most common understanding of the "typical" Shaker movement had to do with the shaking of the hands, representing the shaking off and the shaking away of one's sins. There was never to be any formalized contact between the men and the women when dancing. Therefore, all the established choreography had both genders dancing apart from one another.

One prominent dance of Father Meacham was named the Holy Order dance.[70] Patterson captures the essence of this dance through the words of Father Meacham:

> "I received this manner of worship by the Revelation of God and it must be handed down through you, from generation to generation." Holy Order was, in fact, one of only two early laboring manners to be long used in worship. . . . For years, it opened the Sunday afternoon services. . . . As late as 1868, a writer at Union Village called it the Church's "most solemn & beautiful order of worship."
>
> To execute the dance, the worshipers formed into ranks on one side of the meeting room, the brethren and sisters in separate bodies. The two groups faced the band of singers standing in a line along the opposite wall. During the first half of the tune, which was sung twice, the laborers alternately advanced and retreated three steps, turning (brethren to the right and sisters to the left) and shuffling after the third and sixth steps and shuffling, without turning, after the ninth and twelfth steps. During the second half of the tune, which was sung only once, the dancers shuffled in their places facing the singers.[71]

69. Patterson, *Shaker Spiritual*, 99.

70. Patterson, *Shaker Spiritual*, 107.

71. Patterson, *Shaker Spiritual*, 108. One song text sung while doing the Holy Order dance was labeled the "Holy Order Tune No. 8." The words are as follows: "With him in praises we'll advance, And join the Virgins in the dance" (Patterson, *Shaker Spiritual*, 111).

Another dance Father Meacham taught was the "square order shuffle," which, Andrews writes, was also attained in a vision. He describes the dance this way:

> The "shuffling manner," as described by Youngs, "consisted in taking three whole steps forward, turning, and taking three back, setting the foot straight forward at each end, and then going forward again three steps, and taking a double step, or 'tip tap,' as it is called, then receding three steps, with a 'tip tap'; this takes the turn part of the tune once; then it is repeated, in the same manner, then shuffle the set part once over."[72]

Another category of dances was the true "ring" dances, which were developed in 1822, soon after the death of Mother Lucy. In its earliest form, the singers stood in the middle of the room. The brethren and the sisters, in separate files, placed themselves in a circle, advancing at the turn part of the tune. At the set part, they would turn inward, dancing a single shuffle.[73] According to Andrews, "Sometimes the round dances— the so-called 'ring shuffle,' for instance—were slow, but often they were 'merry measures,' done to a bounding elastic steps, with hands 'motioning the time,' to quicken the spiritual elements and stir up zeal."[74] He explains:

> A circle of singers might face inward, in the center of the room, while around them moved two groups of dancers, two or three abreast, dancing opposite directions to form "a wheel within a wheel." In its most elaborate pattern, developed later, four concentric circles of dancers were employed to symbolize the four dispensations or spiritual cycles of shaker theology: the lion epoch, from Adam to Abraham; the calf epoch, from Abraham to Jesus; the face-of-a-man epoch, from Jesus to Mother Ann; and the flying-eagle epoch (the outer, greatest, all-inclusive circle), the period of the millennial church-Shakerism, "rising above the earthly order . . . into the pure and holy sphere of abstract Christianity." Walt Whitman, witnessing a "wheel" dance in about 1853, was told that the singing in the center represented "the harmony and perfection to which all tend and there is God."[75]

72. Andrews, *Gift to be Simple*, 147.

73. Andrews, *Gift to be Simple*, 149.

74. Andrews, *Gift to be Simple*, 149.

75. Andrews, *Gift to be Simple*, 152.

The music of the Shakers expressed the doctrine of the Shakers. The hymns and anthems voiced the doctrines of the sect while the exercise songs expressed the inner spirit. One of the favorite images used by the believers was the image of the vine. The song "Living Vine" was composed in the year 1808, and its strong doctrinal message, biblical allusions, and polemical tone make it a typical Shaker hymn:

> Christ is the true & living vine, Vine in ancient days this was made known
> And now he's come the second time descending from the Fathers throne.
> He first appeared in the male, there did Imman'els Glory shine
> His second coming in Female is still the true and living Vine.[76]

The Shakers' life was a continual reminder of the doctrines that they upheld. They lived their life of faith through their work and worship which included word, song, dance, and art. One example of artwork that was key to the Shakers was the "Tree of Life," created by Hannah Cohoon.[77] In 1854, Sister Hannah Cohoon reportedly received an image of this tree in a vision. She describes it as follows:

> City of Peace Monday, July, 3rd 1854. I received a draft of a beautiful Tree pencil'd on a large sheet of white paper bearing ripe fruit. I saw it plainly; it looked very singular and curious to me. I have since learned that this tree grows in the Spirit Land. Afterwards the spirit shew'd me plainly the branches, leaves and fruit, painted or drawn upon paper. The leaves were check'd or cross'd and the same colors you see here. I entreated Mother Ann to tell me the name of this tree: which she did Oct. 1st 4th hour PM by moving the hand of a medium to write twice over Your Tree is the Tree of Life.[78]

Andrews and Andrews point to the tree of life, the fruit-bearing trees, and the "beautiful and pleasant smelling flower," as representing the unspoiled loveliness of a Garden of Eden, a type of heavenly setting Cohoon's art promotes.[79]

---

76. Andrews, *Gift to be Simple*, 159. For the complete text of the song, "The Living Vine," see Appendix C.

77. For an example of Shaker art, "The Tree of Life," see Appendix D.

78. Andrews and Andrews, *Visions*, 70.

79. Andrews and Andrews, *Visions*, 70.

The Shakers and Frobel's Educational Philosophy

The teaching and educational principles found within the Shaker religion stemmed from the central belief that all the gifts were employed by the spirits of Mother Ann, the first witnesses, and other religious teachers for educational purposes. The "Era of the Manifestations," was a ten year revival period of the Shakers which began in 1837 in the Watervliet, New York colony. According to Andrews and Andrews, this era:

> Was marked by a profusion of what the Shakers called "gifts"—the giving and receiving of diverse spiritual presents—which were the product of an afflatus so absorbing that no one at the time questioned the propriety of translating inspiration, or revelation, into terms of graphic imagery and colored symbols.[80]

The Shaker gifts were many. Gifts were attained through laboring, which, as explained earlier, meant that one had to strive to become properly receptive to spiritual influence. Andrews and Andrews explain that to have spiritual experiences or to be receptive to spiritual influence, one had to attain the gifts of clairvoyance, clairaudience, prophecy, and tongues. Such gifts were precious to the Shaker believer. Visions were seen "in which the sun, moon, stars, mountains, rivers, plains, vegetables, fruits, animals, and a thousand particular things and circumstances in nature were used as emblems of things in the spiritual world, or Kingdom of Christ."[81] The Shakers believed that such manifestations, no less than the visions of the ancient Hebrew prophets, the miracles at Pentecost, and the mystical experiences of the spiritual reformers of the sixteenth century, were signs of a new dispensation, a new heaven on earth. The receiving of such gifts was often accompanied by physical manifestations such as jerking the head, whirling the body, bowing, and shaking.[82]

There were also other gifts, such as the gift of song, the dancing gift, the whirling gift, the laughing gift, the gift of love, the warring gift—in which "the worshipers stamped, hissed, and drove the Devil out of the room"—and the healing gift.[83] Educational training stemmed from how the spirits utilized these gifts in teaching Shaker doctrine within the community, as elaborated in the following passage:

80. Andrews and Andrews, *Visions*, 4.
81. Andrews and Andrews, *Visions*, 9.
82. Andrews and Andrews, *Visions*, 12.
83. Andrews and Andrews, *Visions*, 12.

These spirits made use of the object-lesson methods of the Froe-
belians, then in vogue, to illustrate ideas, at first with simple,
and then with more complex, materials. "Simple deductive
reasoning first," the eldresses explained, "abstract thought and
broader, advanced deductions later, with simplicity, receptivity,
obedience, humility and teachableness as the necessary foundation for true spiritual education, seems to have been the plan of
development of the unseen teachers."[84]

Frederick Froebel's educational philosophy greatly enabled people
to realize their true essence by living in tune with the Creator's purposes.
Froebel believed that if education was to be transmitted successfully, it
was extremely important to adapt the content and methods of the teaching to the natural development of the person.[85] Froebel's research centered on the child, and how the child was to see God clearly revealed in
all of God's manifested works. Founder of the kindergarten movement,
Froebel compared the child to a plant in a garden whose nature cannot
change but who can grow healthily with the aid of a good teacher.[86]

It does not seem unusual for the Shakers to adapt a Froebelian
approach to education since their society's religious beliefs were based
upon the theological principles of rendering their lives to serve God
and humanity, to be separate from the world, to practice peace, and to
live a virgin, pure, and simplistic life. Therefore, the teaching doctrine
of starting from the simple and advancing to the abstract would render
the use of the arts—specifically dance, word, and music—at full capacity,
to model not only what is taught but also how it is transferred. Andrews
cites Therese Blanc, a Catholic writer, who observed the Shakers' dance
as a thing of beauty.[87] In Blanc's observations, she addresses the use of
the Shakers hands and feet as demonstrations of movement that express,
define, and clarify not only beauty but also the understanding of how
one receives blessings and renders prayer through the act of grace. For
Blanc, this demonstration appeared to exemplify the simple yet profound
meanings of grace and prayer. From the simple to the abstract, the two
terms were clearly defined through the use of both dance and song. Blanc
explains the movement in the following way:

84. Andrews and Andrews, *Visions*, 51.

85. Elias, *History of Christian Education*, 144.

86. Elias, *History of Christian Education*, 144.

87. Andrews, *Gift to be Simple*.

The movement of their hands—stretched forth to receive blessings or to offer to one's neighbor in prayer the grace he seeks—
seems of very noble symbolism. And their feet barely touch
earth in the rapid processional, accompanied by hymns to tunes
sometimes very lively, at others remarkable for the repeated return (of) the same note, as in oriental music.[88]

Doris Humphrey's Shakers

As a dance major at the New York High School of Performing Arts[89],
the author participated in the modern department's performance of
"Shakers"—first choreographed by Doris Humphrey in 1931—at the
Senior Dance Concert.[90] Some of the movements were direct replicas of
the original Shaker gestures while others were choreographed according
to Humphrey's creative license. Even so, the dance was choreographed
based upon the life of the Shakers and their religious beliefs. Dance critic
and historian Marcia B. Siegel explains Humphrey's choreographic approach as follows:

> What [Humphrey] did in "Shakers" was to extract the essence
> of Shaker belief, practice, and psychology, to clothe all this in a
> form apparently so simple and direct that the audience is over-
> come before it realizes how much meaning has accumulated.[91]

Siegel believes that Humphrey's motivation for choreographing the work
arose from her preoccupation with form and because she liked the idea
that they expressed their faith through dancing.[92]

Humphrey utilized floor patterns within the dance "to define the
character of the society she was presenting."[93] The movements were rigid,
sharp, and quite static, with much emphasis placed on both the body
bowed and on the body tall and erect. Movement gestures consisted of

88. Andrews, *Gift to be Simple*, 157.

89. The New York High School of Performing Arts is now formally called LaGuar-
dia School of the Arts at Lincoln Center in New York City.

90. Doris Humphrey (1895 to 1958) was one of the pioneers of modern dance and
a major contributor to the field as both a teacher and a choreographer. The dance was
reconstructed by Jo Ann Bruggermann, a dancer and certified Laban notator, through
a dance language called Labanotation, created by Rudolf Laban.

91. Siegel, *Shapes of Change*, 58.

92. Siegel, *Shapes of Change*, 59.

93. Siegel, *Shapes of Change*, 59.

the shaking of hands, the elevation of the body with jumps and turns, shuffles, and the stamping of the feet, while keeping linear and circular spatial formations going. Siegel believes that the circle of religious ecstasy—and its further development, the spiral—represents freedom and release from earthly temptation and the necessity for self-imposed control.[94] Throughout the entire dance, the women and men were separated by the center figure, the Eldress, who represented Mother Ann. The Eldress is the only one who spins, as she is in direct contact with God. In Humphrey's dance, however, those who served as the other communicants partook in the circle where dancers knelt around the Eldress, their scooped arms and upper bodies moving around in the process of getting free from sin.

During the dance, there were moments of complete movement arrests; at such times, the choreographed movement of the Eldress appeared to prophesy to the entire group. Spoken word and movements were used by the Eldress to project prophetic utterances. Siegel vividly describes the words of the Eldress during this moment of highly energized motion:

> The jumping begins again, growing faster, only to be halted by the Eldress. She stands on her box and claps her hands several times, then shouts: "It hath been revealed. Ye shall be saved. When ye are shaken free—of sin!"[95]

Although many Christians question Shaker theology, their lifestyle exemplified faith nurturing, faith building, and religious education. Shaker life influenced many generations in how they lived out their faith in an ever-changing world. Thomas Merton, for example, was influenced by their life and walk. He reflects upon the Shakers in this way:

> I will not rush at it and I will try to profit by their example and put into practice some of their careful and honest principles. It would be a crime to treat them superficially and without the

---

94. Siegel, *Shapes of Change*, 66.

95. Siegel, *Shapes of Change*, 66. Whether it was during rehearsal or performance, these words rang vividly. It was at such times that every dancer imagined the powerful and effective impact the Shaker theology and lifestyle had upon the entire Shaker community, especially its youth. Such moments allowed both the dancers and audience to reflect upon the Shakers; who they were and the relationships they modeled amongst themselves. The dancers witnessed their relationship to their God and belief system, but also their relationship to the viewers and observers. Whether as dancers or as the audience, it always appeared during the execution of the dance that all were being educated at a deeper level about the life and faith of the Shakers.

deepest love, reverence, and understanding. There can be so much meaning to a study of this kind: meaning for twentieth century America which has lost so much in the last hundred years—lost while seeming to gain. I think the extinction of the Shakers and of their particular kind of spirit is an awful portent. I feel all the more akin to them because our own Order, the Cistercians, originally had the same kind of idea of honesty, simplicity, and good work for a spiritual motive.[96]

Like Thomas Merton, there are others who were also influenced by the life and theology of the Shakers. The gospel of Ann Lee and its development through Father Joseph Meacham filled the hearts of their believers, and the use of both song and dance appeared to leave them with overflowing joy. Andrews and Andrews contend that the Shaker doctrine found its own ways of expression in biblical-like messages and finally in its imaginative graphic forms. Just as Sawicki refers to the church as a society of individuals linked by the message of the gospel, so was the Shaker Society. It was a church that resulted from the telling of the Shaker gospel and its relationship to humanity. Sawicki proposes that the church is a particular way of being human—a way that is made possible through the recognition that the deepest meaning of human existence is to love and be loved by God.[97] So was the Shaker society one that presented resurrected life for all who believed. As the doctrine was handed down and communicated through word, song, dance, and art, so did the entire Shaker society respond in a particular way of being together. Its members were those who wholeheartedly accepted the Shaker message.

Conclusion

Sawicki explains that the collective experience of past myths, symbols, and meanings paves the way for the ongoing religious experience of those who belong to the same religious community. As she puts it:

> The past, then, is accessible as a dimension or component of the present. The classic myths, symbols, and meanings which are expressed in historical religious narratives also are given as background for ongoing experiences and lifestyle of the people who belong to the religious community whose narrative it is. The pastness of these meanings is also their "suchness"

96. Merton, *Seeking Paradise*, 22.
97. Sawicki, *Gospel in History*, 10.

in the continuing flux of experience, they are the constant component.[98]

For the enslaved African community, their history of worship styles paved the way for a plethora of religious experiences found in many Protestant denominations of both African and non-African descent. From the Ring Shout, the Negro Spiritual, and the preached word arose various Christian denominations that utilize the art forms of music, dance, and spoken word in new and refreshing ways within their worship practices. For example, in contemporary times, members of Pentecostal denominations are known to exhibit their devotion and spiritual experiences with God using all three artistic expressions. The Church of God in Christ (COGIC) and the Holiness Church are branches within the Pentecostal denomination that are predominately Black. They, too, regularly utilize all three artistic forms to exhibit their love and communion with the Godhead. Outside of these examples, however, it is more common to see the use of the arts today by individual churches within a denomination where their expressions are unique to their own religious experiences. This holds true for congregations of both African and non-African descent.

Unfortunately, this was not the case with the Shakers. Their order declined in numbers after the Civil War and therefore lost "that inner vitality of spirit which was the well-spring of its exuberant worship."[99] More than half a century ago, Andrews describes the disappearance of the Shakers in this way:

> The voice of the world grew more and more insistent, to the brethren especially, and Mother Ann's voice more distant. As the century advanced, the Shakers still sang of union, of holiness, of the joy of the virgin life. They still marched solemnly on their way to the heavenly Jerusalem. The preachers continued to argue the virtues of purity and a consecrate communal fellowship apart from the world. But worship was in the main a mechanical repetition of the old forms, revealing indeed the same saintly devotion to cause, but lacking the freshness of a movement renewed from within . . . The dance became more sedate; the whirling and reeling ceased; the hymns, sung to the accompaniment of a harmonium or organ, failed to express that elusive quality which gave them Shaker significance. Though it may be many years yet before the last Believer leaves the last

98. Sawicki, "Historical Methods," 379–380.
99. Andrews, *Gift to be Simple*, 157.

surviving community, the contributions of "the children of the free woman" to the religious folk art of America long ago came to a close.[100]

There were several factors, then, which contributed to the demise of the Shakers, including living a virgin life (where procreation among the Shakers was impossible) and the country's upward sprint in the areas of science and politics (which promoted a more individualistic way of being). According to Sawicki's interpretation, there were no more members who relied on the community's heritage of narratives and their meanings. Such an absence ceased to promote ongoing experiences for individuals that were renewed from within the soul.

Both examples investigated in this chapter can enrich our understanding and appreciation of the union found between religious education and the arts. Even though this union has not flourished consistently, it can be greatly recovered and enhanced at the present time. W. O. E. Oesterley wrote of the "extraordinary uniformity" that exists in human culture, giving rise to a state of standards that are neither borrowed nor stolen but, rather, inhabit the soul of the human being.[101] His views are supported by the examples of the two communities cited in this chapter. The "steps" of both communities could be described as those that were directed and connected to strong and firm religious beliefs. In both cases, each religious community explored in this chapter possessed an unwavering faith so sturdy that they neither stumbled nor slipped.

The next chapter investigates the validity of arts education as a source of learning or, more specifically, the relationship between arts education and religious education and the use of dance as both a teaching and learning tool. It is through this exploration and with the help of the Holy Spirit that the church can move forward to sing, dance, and believe in a Godhead whose love for the church warrants such a physical response from its members.

100. Andrews, *Gift to be Simple*, 157.
101. Oesterley, *Sacred Dance*, 2.

Chapter 2

I Will Meditate on Your Wonders

The Significance of Arts Education

Introduction

This chapter investigates the validity of arts education and aesthetic education as a source of learning. While also acknowledging the import of music, visual art, and drama, this chapter especially highlights the importance of dance. Although there are a variety of dance forms, it is dance as a way of knowing, its aid to the field of education, and how dance affects the development of sound and imaginative curriculum that is to be investigated. From this position, the chapter then examines the use of art and aesthetic education within the field of religious education. The wonders of dance as both a teaching and learning tool are to be analyzed by bridging the two forms of arts education and religious education together.

This chapter begins by considering Howard Gardner's theory of Multiple Intelligences in relationship with an arts education, emphasizing how the use of these intelligences are framed within the domain of the discipline or craft in which they operate.[1] From here, the use of the imagination in the context of education and the arts is identified through the writings of Maxine Greene, Elliot Eisner, and Howard Gardner. Eisner's work in designing curriculum artistically is also analyzed. This section concludes with a study of dance education through

1. See Gardner, *Multiple Intelligences*.

the lens of Jennifer Donohue Zakkai. It is from here that the wonders of the imagination, dance, and aesthetic education in relationship to both the church as a learning community and to religious education as a field of study are explored. The writings of Carla DeSola, Arthur Easton, and Maria Harris are also considered in order to probe the wonders of dance and its usefulness as a teaching and learning tool for religious education.

An Exploration of Howard Gardner's Multiple Intelligence Theory

Howard Gardner's theory of Multiple Intelligences defines a set of various intelligences as procedures for doing things that include analytical, methodological, and artistic forms of knowing. Gardner proposes that these intelligences can function both as subject matter and as the preferred means for instilling diverse subject matter, thus creating options between student and educational material as well as between religious learner and faith formation. In the book *Multiple Intelligences*, Gardner summarizes his Multiple Intelligence theory as follows:

> I introduced the theory of multiple intelligences (MI) in the early 1980s. As the name indicates, I believe that human cognitive competence is better described in terms of a set of abilities, talents, or mental skills, which I call *intelligences*. All normal individuals possess each of these skills to some extent; individuals differ in the degree of skill and in the nature of their combination. I believe this theory of intelligence may be more humane and more veridical than alternative views of intelligence and that it more adequately reflects the data of human "intelligent" behavior. Such a theory has important educational implications.[2]

As an avid believer and promoter of the Multiple Intelligence theory, Thomas Armstrong suggests that Gardner's theory of intelligence has more to do with the capacity for solving problems and fashioning products in a context rich and naturalistic setting.[3] These intelligences include the following eight: musical, linguistic, bodily-kinesthetic, logical-mathematical, spatial, interpersonal, intrapersonal, and naturalist.

---

2. Gardner, *Multiple Intelligences*, 6.
3. See Armstrong, *Multiple Intelligences in the Classroom*.

In his expedition of Gardner's theory, Armstrong defines *linguistic intelligence* as the ability to use words effectively, whether orally (as a storyteller or politician) or in writing (as a poet, playwright, or journalist). This intelligence includes the capability to manipulate the structure of language, the phonology of language, the semantics of language, and the pragmatic dimensions of language. He defines *musical intelligence* as the capacity to perceive as a music aficionado, discriminate as a music critic, transform as a composer, and express musical forms as a performer by being sensitive to the rhythm, pitch, melody, timbre, or tone color of a musical arrangement. One can have a figural understanding of music (which includes a global intuitive ability), a formal understanding (which has more of an analytical or technical comprehension), or both. The *bodily-kinesthetic intelligence* expresses the bodily vessel of the individual's sense of self, their most personal feelings and aspirations, as well as the physical self to which others respond in a particular way because of their unique human qualities. This intelligence allows the individual to use the whole body to express ideas and feelings while facilitating the hands in producing or transforming materials such as a craftsperson, sculptor, mechanic, or surgeon. The *logical-mathematical intelligence* has the capacity to use numbers as a mathematician or tax accountant and to reason well as a scientist or computer programmer. Armstrong surmises that this intelligence includes sensitivity to logical patterns, relationships, statements, propositions, functions, and other related abstractions. The *spatial intelligence* has the ability to perceive the visual-spatial world accurately as one who hunts, guides, or scouts and to perform transformations on those perceptions as an interior decorator, architect, inventor, or artist. Armstrong suggests that this intelligence involves sensitivity to color, line, shape, form, space, and the relationships that exist between these elements. It includes the capacity to visualize, to graphically represent visual or spatial ideas, and orient oneself appropriately in a spatial matrix. The *interpersonal intelligence* has the ability to perceive and make distinctions in the moods, intentions, motivations, and feelings of other people. This intelligence includes sensitivity to facial expressions, voice, and gestures, the capacity for discriminating among many different kinds of interpersonal cues, and the ability to respond effectively to those cues in some pragmatic way. The *intrapersonal intelligence* involves self-knowledge and the ability to act adaptively on the basis of that knowledge. According to Armstrong, this intelligence includes possessing an accurate and honest picture of oneself, an awareness of one's inner moods, intentions, motivations, temperaments, and desires, and the capacity for self-discipline, self-understanding, and self-esteem. The *naturalist intelligence* has an expertise in the recognition and classification of the numerous species—the flora and fauna—of an individual's environment. This includes sensitivity to other natural phenomena such as cloud formations and mountains, and, for those living in an urban environment, the capacity to discriminate among non-living forms, such as cars, sneakers, and album covers.

Gardner cautions educators not to mistakenly make the Multiple Intelligence theory an educational goal to be achieved within an academic environment. He believes that educational goals should reflect "one's own values" because they "can never come simply or directly from a scientific theory."[4] For Gardner, once one reflects on one's own educational values and states one's own educational goals, then the alleged existence of multiple intelligences can prove to be very helpful. In particular, if one's educational goals encompass disciplinary understanding, then it is possible to mobilize several intelligences to help achieve that lofty goal.

Gardner proposes that, regardless of cultural influence, it becomes important to consider individuals as a collection of aptitudes rather than as having a singular problem-solving faculty that can be measured directly through school or occupational examinations. He contends that the diversity of human abilities is created through the differences in these profiles. For him, an individual may not be particularly gifted in any one intelligence, and yet, because of a particular combination or blend of skills, he or she may be able to fill some position uniquely well.[5] Therefore, it is imperative that the assessment of a particular combination of skills be earmarked as it pertains to an individual's vocation or hobby. Gardner's Multiple Intelligence theory leads to three conclusions:

1. All of us have a full range of intelligences; that is what makes us human beings, cognitively speaking.

2. No two individuals—not even identical twins—have exactly the same intellectual profile because, even when the genetic material is identical, individuals have different experiences (and identical twins are often highly motivated to distinguish themselves from one another).

4. Gardner, *Frames of Mind*, xvii.
5. Gardner, *Multiple Intelligences*, 22.

3. Having a strong intelligence does not mean that one necessarily acts intelligently. A person with high mathematical intelligence could use her abilities to carry out important experiments in physics or create powerful new geometric proofs—but she might also waste them by playing the lottery all day or by multiplying ten-digit numbers in her head.

It is from this perspective that Gardner distinguishes between intelligence, which is a biopsychological construct, and a domain, which is the discipline or craft that serves as the sociological setting in which the intelligence(s) operate in. Gardner cautions that there is a danger of mixing or confusing the two: "No doubt there are interesting connections between the kinds of intelligences human beings possess, the kinds of domains that we develop, and how those intelligences and domains map onto one another, but it is analytically confusing to mix these two kinds of entities."[6] The mixing of these two entities can lead to assumptions by an instructor concerning the learning capabilities of a student concerning particular subject matter. Gardner warns that those in the field of education are well advised to assess intelligences by watching people who are already familiar with and have some skills in these pursuits or by introducing individuals to such domains and observing how well they can move beyond the apprentice stage, with or without specific supports or scaffolding.

Further, Gardner suggests it is more appropriate to speak about one or more human intelligences—or human intellectual proclivities—that are part of an individual's birthright. This is why Gardner classifies these intelligences in neurobiological terms. To further clarify the concept of *domains*, those disciplines through which the intelligences are expressed, Gardner writes the following:

> Human beings are born into cultures that house a large number of *domains*—disciplines, crafts, and other pursuits in which one can become enculturated and then be assessed in terms of the level of competence one has attained. While domains, of course, involve human beings, they can be thought of in an impersonal way—because the expertise in a domain can in principle be captured in a book, a computer program, or some other kind of artifact.[7]

6. Gardner, *Multiple Intelligences*, 32.
7. Gardner, *Frames of Mind*, xxx.

Once one achieves a certain competence, the *field* becomes very important. As Gardner suggests, the field is the sociological construct that includes the people, institutions, award mechanisms, etc. that render judgments about the qualities of individual performances. On the one hand, the field has the capacity to judge one as competent, thereby leading one to become a successful practitioner. On the other hand, however, according to Gardner, the field can also prove incapable of judging work or can judge the work as being deficient, leading one's opportunity to achieve to be radically curtailed.

Gardner contends that the trio of *intelligence, domain,* and *field* has proved not only useful for unraveling a host of issues raised by Multiple Intelligence theory but is also particularly fruitful for studies of creativity. The question becomes: where is creativity located within the human construct? Gardner declares that creativity should not be thought of as existing principally in the brain, the mind, or the personality of a single individual. Gardner explains this further:

> Creativity should be thought of as emerging from the interactions of three nodes: the individual with his or her own profile of competences and values; the domains available for study and mastery within a culture; and the judgments rendered by the field that is deemed competent within a culture. To the extent that the field accepts innovation, one (or one's work) can be seen as creative; but to the extent that an innovation is rejected, or not understood, or considered not innovative, it is simply invalid to continue to maintain that a product is creative. Of course, in the future, the field may choose to alter its early judgments.[8]

Gardner further clarifies creativity as a characterization reserved for those whose products are initially seen to be novel within a domain but are ultimately recognized as acceptable within an appropriate community. According to him, judgments of originality or creativity can be made only by knowledgeable members of the field, regardless of whether the field is ancient or newly constituted.

Gardner's definition of creativity runs parallel with his definition of intelligence. Both explanations are geared toward the individual and not toward groups of people. As Gardner explains, "The creative individual is one who *regularly* solves problems or fashions products in a *domain,* and whose work is considered both novel and acceptable by knowledgeable

8. Gardner, *Frames of Mind,* xxxi.

members of a field."[9] To solidify this hypothesis, Gardner researched the creative work of six men and one woman to compile a book entitled, *Creating Minds: An Anatomy of Creativity Seen through the Lives of Freud, Einstein, Picasso, Stravinsky, Eliot, Graham, and Gandhi.*[10] Each of the seven people chosen had a creative strength that was grounded in one of the seven intelligences found within Gardner's Multiple Intelligence theory. For example Sigmund Freud exemplified the intrapersonal intelligence; Albert Einstein, the logical-mathematical intelligence; Igor Stravinsky, the musical intelligence; Pablo Picasso, the spatial intelligence; T. S. Eliot, the linguistic intelligence; Martha Graham, the bodily-kinesthetic intelligence; and Mahatma Gandhi, the interpersonal intelligence.

Gardner's work within the area of creativity extended itself to include early stages of detection within school age children at the ten year old mark. He contends that creativity within children is detected and recognized under very specific conditions and circumstances. Gardner claims, "If creative work is not yet forthcoming, the conditions for a creative (or noncreative) life may already be falling into place: creativity depends heavily on dispositional and personality traits and on the accidents of demography."[11] Gardner believes that youngsters who feel or who are marginal in their culture, those who are ambitious and stubborn, and those who can ignore criticism and remain adamant about their beliefs are "at risk" to live a creative life. However, those children who are comfortable being a part of a group and who advance in their domain with little feeling of pressure or asynchrony are probably headed for a life of expertise within a particular field of study.

When investigating creativity and its usefulness within the fields of education and arts education, numerous questions arise. One mode of inquiry pertains to the imagination. Within the realm of creativity, does imagination have a vital role and, if so, what effect does it have on creativity? Is imagination something that can be developed and, if so, how can it be developed within the educational life of both children and adults? What role does imagination play in the educational constructs of the church? Can imagination be developed inside the realm of religious education and, if so, what tools are needed in order to integrate and implement it successfully? The work of Maxine Greene, Elliot Eisner,

9. Gardner, *Frames of Mind*, xxxi.
10. See Gardner, *Creating Minds*.
11. Gardner, *Multiple Intelligences*, 47.

and Howard Gardner addresses the importance of the imagination, arts education, and the relationship between the two in developing a balanced educational life for the learner and the teacher.

The Wonders of Imagination and Artistic Learning

For Maxine Greene, education—on behalf of both teacher and student—is the breaking of numerous barriers: the barrier of expectation, of boredom, of predefinition, of impossibility, and of smallness.[12] According to Greene, all of these are elements that stop the successful educational interplay found between teacher and student. She purports that it takes imagination to become aware that such interplay is possible and that there are apparent analogies to the kind of learning both teachers and students want to stimulate. Greene declares, "It takes imagination to break with ordinary classifications and come in touch with actual young people to perceive openings through which they can move."[13]

In *Releasing the Imagination*, Greene seeks to remedy the plight of seeing educational concerns as "small" for both teacher and student and, at the same time, to open and validate the passion for seeing educational opportunities "close up and large." It is "this passion that opens the doorway for imagination; here is the possibility of looking at things as if they could be otherwise."[14] Greene contends that it is the releasing of the imagination that can bring about a much-needed educational reform within the public education system.

A continuing concern facing education is the curriculum. Greene, along with other educational reformers, advocates that curriculums be knowledge-based, interdisciplinary, and capable of connecting with students. The call for imaginative capacity, according to Greene, is to work for the ability to look at things as if they could be otherwise. A person's reality must be understood as an interpreted experience; our mode of interpretation depends on our situation and location in the world. She promotes tapping into the imagination to become able to break with what is supposedly fixed and finished, objectively, and independently real. Greene explains this point further:

12. Greene, *Releasing the Imagination*.
13. Greene, *Releasing the Imagination*, 14.
14. Greene, *Releasing the Imagination*, 16.

It is to see beyond what the imaginer has called normal or "common-sensible" and to carve out new orders in experience. Doing so, a person may become freed to glimpse what might be, to form notions of what should be, and what is not yet. And the same person may, at the same time, remain in touch with what presumably *is*.[15]

A major key to Greene's hypothesis is the inclusion of the arts within school curricula. She supplies several reasons for such a proposal. For one, Greene declares that encounters with the arts have the unique power to release our imagination. Stories, poems, dance performances, concerts, paintings, films, and plays all have the potential to provide remarkable pleasure for those willing to move out toward them and engage with them. But it is neither simply the pleasure nor the balance the arts supplies to the rigors of the cognitive, analytical, rational, and the serious found within the standardized school curriculum; the arts should not be used as simply a motivator or an incentive for students to work harder in the areas of science and mathematics. Instead, Greene suggests, participatory encounters with particular works of art may demand as much cognitive rigor and analysis as they do affective response. Works of art cannot be reduced to their beneficent, consoling, or illuminating effects. The role of the imagination is not to resolve, point the way, or improve, rather, it is to awaken and disclose the ordinarily unseen, unheard, and unexpected:

> The arts, as Denis Donoghue says, are on the margin, "and the margin is the place for those feelings and intuitions which daily life doesn't have a place for and mostly seeks to suppress. . . . With the arts, people can make a space for themselves and fill it with intimations of freedom and presence."[16]

Greene agrees with Herbert Marcuse, who states, "The encounter with the truth of art happens in the estranging language and the images which make perceptible, visible, and audible that which is no longer or not yet perceived, said, and heard in everyday life."[17] She contends that all artistic expressions reach beyond what is established and leads those who are willing to risk transformation through the shaping of a new or renewed social vision. Within the school curricula, Greene surmises, if

15. Greene, *Releasing the Imagination*, 19.
16. Greene, *Releasing the Imagination*, 28.
17. Greene, *Releasing the Imagination*, 30.

both teacher and student are to perceive what is presented within the context of subject matter, there must be an answering activity. Regardless of the historical encounter or scientific experiment, if the subject matter is to be consciously realized, there has to be the ability to engage with it fully. It is the imagination, according to Greene, that may provide a new way of de-centering both teacher and learner—of breaking out of the confinements of privatism and self-regard into a space where all can come face to face with others and be presently present in the teaching and learning act.

Greene specifically addresses the teacher and the importance of the imagination within the teaching moment. This emphasis is made because if teachers are incapable of thinking imaginatively or of releasing students to encounter works of literature and other forms of art, then they are probably also unable to communicate to their students what the use of the imagination signifies. She concludes that if the imagination feeds one's capacity to feel one's way into another's vantage point, then these same teachers may also be lacking empathy. Such a quality allows the teacher to encounter the student through their particular situation, circumstance, and worldview, regardless of whether or not that world is filled with poverty, low attention span, or hopelessness.

Greene pushes the use of the imagination further by linking it to how one human being responds to another human being, thereby making community. Describing community, Greene emphasizes process words such as making, creating, weaving, saying, and the like. Like freedom, community is achieved by persons who offer the space to discover what they recognize together and appreciate in common with one another; they have to find ways to make intersubjective sense. She states, "It ought to be a space infused by the kind of imaginative awareness that enables those involved to imagine alternative possibilities for their own becoming and their group's becoming."[18] For Greene, community is not the encountering of social contracts that are the most reasonable to enter, it is the question of what might contribute to the pursuit of shared goods: ways of being together, attaining mutuality, and reaching toward some common world. Community, such as the one described by Greene, is not only easily established within a school but can also be established in any environment that pre-positions itself to educate those who venture inside its walls. Such a place sets itself up to put emphasis not only on the

18. Greene, *Releasing the Imagination*, 39.

individuals and their progress but, more importantly, on a learning space that focuses on the group's becoming as well.

Greene advocates the use of the arts in conjunction with curriculum enhancement through its visions of new perspectives and untapped possibilities. She believes that the arts have the capacity to enable both the teacher and the learner to see more, to discover nuances, shapes, and sounds that would otherwise be inaccessible without them. Greene conceives of the arts in relation to curriculum in the following way:

> To conceive the arts in relation to curriculum is to think of a deepening and expanding mode of tuning-in. There have to be disciplines, yes, and a growing acquaintance with the structures of knowledge, but, at the same time, there have to be the kinds of rounded interpretations possible only to those willing to abandon already constituted reason, willing to feel and to imagine, to open the windows and go in search.[19]

Elliot Eisner, like Greene, finds that the present educational system is in need of a major overhaul to establish methodologies other than the "technicised cognitive culture" and testing modalities that presently dominate public education. Eisner suggests that the aim of education "ought to be conceived of as the preparation of artists."[20] In this case, Eisner is not referring to the creation of artists as referring to those who become professional painters, dancers, poets, and playwrights. He means those:

> individuals who have developed the ideas, the sensibilities, the skills, and the imagination to create work that is well proportioned, skillfully executed, and imaginative, regardless of the domain in which an individual works. The highest accolade we can confer upon someone is to say that he or she is an artist, whether as a carpenter or a surgeon, a cook or an engineer, a physicist or a teacher. The fine arts have no monopoly on the artistic.[21]

Eisner further argues that the distinct forms of cognition needed to create artistically crafted work are relevant not only to what students do in the classroom but also to virtually all aspects of what educators do, from

19. Greene, *Releasing the Imagination*, 104.
20. Eisner, "Artistry in Education," 376.
21. Eisner, "Artistry in Education," 376–77.

the design of curricula, to the practice of teaching, to the features of the environment in which students and teachers live.

According to Eisner, it is the arts that teach students to act and to judge in the absence of rule, to rely on feeling, to pay attention to nuance, to act and appraise the consequences of one's choices, and to revise them and then make other choices. Getting no antecedent relationships to fit is what artists and all who work with the composition of these qualities try to achieve. Eisner believes that we become more qualitatively intelligent as we learn in and through the arts. Students need to be taught to ask not only the "what" questions, but they need to ask the "how" questions, in relationship to the construction of an argument, a musical score, a scientific experiment, or a choreographed dance. For Eisner, it is the curriculum that can be designed to call attention to such matters through activities that refine perception in each of the fields taught.

In the article, "Artistry in Education," Eisner suggests four other lessons that can be gleaned from the arts in the formulation of curricula aims.[22] Within Western models of learning, educational ends are held to be the primary mold for rationalized thinking and the ends always precede the means. However, within this model, a much greater emphasis is placed on prediction and control rather than on exploration and discovery. Although there is an understandable inclination to control and to predict, Eisner believes there is a tendency to only do the things that we know how to predict and control, which leaves the pursuit of uncertainty, journeying, and innovation at a standstill.

The *first* lesson that school reformers can learn is that the arts allow for the means to be the adventurous course pursued in order for the ends to be revealed. Eisner asks how educators can help the classroom become an environment that promotes the element of surprise. How can educators stimulate students to view their work as temporary, experimental accomplishments? How can educators help students work at the edge of their competence in order to find a wider plethora of possibilities?

The *second* element Eisner pursues is the discovery that form and content are inseparable—another lesson best taught through the arts. Developing an awareness of the particular is especially important for teachers since the distinctive character of how we teach is a pervasive aspect of what is taught. The message the current reform movement is sending its students undermines deeper educational values. These values

22. See Eisner, "Artistry in Education."

include the promotion of self-initiated learning, the pursuit of alternative possibilities, and the anticipation of intrinsic satisfactions secured through the use of the mind.

The *third* lesson the arts can teach education is that the limits of cognition are not defined by the limits of language. Eisner quotes John Dewey, who explains that science states meaning while the arts express meaning. Eisner writes that "meaning is not limited to what is assertable."[23] He contends that there is an appeal to the expressive form to say or communicate what literal language can never say, as found in the following examples: some of the most profound religious practices are situated in compositions that have been choreographed; the building of shrines to express gratitude to the heroes of Setptember 11th; and the appeal to poetry when a loved one is buried or gets married. Eisner asks the question, "What does our need for such practices say to us about the sources of our understanding and what do they mean for how we educate?"[24] For Eisner, such questions analyze the present school reform's need to package student performances based solely on standardized, measurable skill sets.

The *fourth* lesson education reform can learn from the arts pertains to the relationship between thinking and the material with which students and educators work. For any work in the arts to be created, one must think within the constraints of the medium in which one chooses to work. Eisner believes that each artistic material—such as a musical instrument, a dramatic play, or a piece of literature—imposes its own distinctive demands and limitations. To use it well, teachers have to learn to think with it. He seeks to find out how teachers can help students become smarter within the media they are invited to use and what cognitive demands different media makes upon those who use them. There are new possibilities for matters of representation that can stimulate the imaginative capacities and generate forms of experience that would otherwise not exist. For Eisner, this leads to the varied ways curriculum is designed and the varied lessons and materials students can experience.

The decisions made about such educational matters have a great deal to do with the kinds of teaching and learning communities develop within schools and within our churches. Eisner argues that schools should

23. Eisner, "Artistry in Education," 380.
24. Eisner, "Artistry in Education," 380.

promote a particular perspective on learning that stimulates profound opportunities of change for both the teacher and student. He states:

> Decisions we make about such matters have a great deal to do with the kinds of minds we develop in school. Minds, unlike brains, are not entirely given at birth; minds are also forms of cultural achievement. The kinds of minds we develop are profoundly influenced by the opportunities to learn that the school provides. And this is the point of my remarks about what education might learn from the arts. The kinds of thinking I have described, and it is only a sample, represents the kind of thinking I believe schools should promote. The promotion of such thinking requires not only a shift in perspective regarding our educational aims, it represents a shift in the kind of tasks we invite students to undertake, the kind of thinking we ask them to do, and the kind of criteria we apply to appraise both their work and ours. Teachers have a critical role to play here. Artistry, in other words, can be fostered by how we design the environments we inhabit. The lessons the arts teach are not only for our students, they are for us as well. . . . Thus it might be said that, at its best, education is a process of learning how to become the architect of our own education. It is a process that does not terminate until we do.[25]

Eisner understands the arts as those special forms of experience that are not restricted to the fine arts. A sense of vitality and surge of emotion is not only touched when one encounters the arts but is also encountered and secured in the ideas teachers explore with their students. They are secured in the challenges both encounter in doing critical inquiry and in the appetite for learning that both stimulate. He asserts that the arts provide a kind of ideal for education that the world needs. His reasoning for this springs from several sources: the increasing ability people must have in dealing with conflicting messages; the making of judgments in the absence of rule; and the coping with ambiguity and the framing of imaginative solutions to the problems people face. Fresh ideas cannot simply be envisioned, but, as Eisner contends, there must be a feel for the situations in which they appear. He states, "The forms of thinking the arts stimulate and develop are far more appropriate for the real world we live in than the tidy right-angled boxes we employ in our schools in the name of school improvement."[26] Therefore, the educational culture

25. Eisner, "Artistry in Education," 380.
26. Eisner, "Artistry in Education," 382.

Eisner endorses is one that has a greater focus on becoming than on being, places more value on the imaginative than on the actual, assigns greater priority to valuing than to measuring, and regards the quality of the journey as more educationally significant than the speed at which the destination is reached.

Curriculum Development and its Effect on Arts Education

According to Eisner, curriculum conception, formation, and construction should stem from a variety of perspectives including that of the educator, the student, the subject matter, the physical learning environment, and the totality of those who make up the entire learning community.[27] He suggests that, through their curriculum, schools teach much more than they intend to teach. Curriculum is the body of material that is planned in advance of any learning event, designed to help students learn specific content, acquire a skill, develop a belief, or have some valued type of experience. Eisner explains that this type of curriculum is known as the intended curriculum. However, curriculum also includes those activities that occur inside the learning event, taking into account the materials, the content, and the events in which students are engaged. Eisner points out that this type of curriculum is known as the operational curriculum. One can approach the intended curriculum by inspecting the materials and plans that have been formulated, while the way in which one approaches the operational curriculum is by directly observing the classroom or learning environment.

It is Eisner's claim that schools provide not one curriculum to students, but actually three.[28] The first is the explicit curriculum, where the learning environment offers the learners educational listings of sorts; it advertises what it is prepared to provide. In response to such a listing, the students have an array of options to choose from as they relate to subject material. The explicit curriculum is the actual subject matter the institution of learning makes readily available. However, numerous questions concerning the explicit curriculum still arise, such as: whose interests are embedded within the subject matter being taught and the texts being utilized? What resources and researchers are being drawn upon in order

27. See Eisner, *Educational Imagination*.
28. Eisner, *Educational Imagination*, 87.

to uphold this curriculum? What voices have been excluded? Are there biases apparent and, if so, what are they and how were they formed?

Kieran Scott elaborates on Eisner's ideas by describing three items that are important in structuring the explicit curriculum.[29] First, the historical resources that pay attention to the past wisdom and practices of the subject being studied. For the curriculum to be rich, liberating, and emancipative, it must dig deep into its historical content in order to glean the richness of its resources and make them applicable for present day learning. The second is the contemporary source of knowledge that must be respected and trusted in its own right while relating insight to the subject at hand. The presentness of the explicit curriculum will add to what was known, yet there must be attention paid to the contemporary human experience of both student and learner. The third is the visionary sources that will pay attention to the curriculum not yet realized. There should be an eschatological sense to the curriculum that stretches the mind to future inquiry.

The implicit curriculum consists of the material and behaviors that are not directly taught within the explicit curriculum, but are definitely a direct result of it.[30] Questions of behavior come into play when the implicit curriculum is addressed. Eisner speaks about the performance behavior of learners—particularly the behavior of children who are rewarded for engaging in school related activity. It is less likely that such an engagement will take place if an extrinsic reward is not provided. The implicit curriculum is composed of the teachings and learnings that underline the subject being taught. They are the learnings attained from the educational environment itself. The outcome of this implicit curriculum should not be considered to be entirely positive or negative, but it does need to be acknowledged and reckoned with if negative behaviors arise as a result.

There are operational patterns of power and decision-making displayed inside the learning environment that come into play within the implicit curriculum.[31] Curriculum designers must pay special attention to what is implied in the implicit and make sure that it complies with the intended explicit curriculum. Critical analysis can assist the curriculum designer in learning how to design and implement adventurous and

29. Lecture notes taken by the author during a class taught by Kieran Scott in the Spring of 2010. See Scott, "Curriculum and Religious Education."

30. Eisner, *Educational Imagination*, 90.

31. Scott, "Curriculum and Religious Education."

experiential learning moments that will benefit not only the individual learner, but the entire educational community.

The null curriculum is the subject matter that is not covered within the explicit curriculum. It is what is purposely left out of the curriculum. Eisner explains the direct results of the null curriculum:

> It is my thesis that what schools do not teach may be as impor-
> tant as what they do teach. I argue this position because igno-
> rance is not simply a neutral void; it has important effects on
> the kinds of options one is able to consider, the alternatives that
> one can examine, and the perspectives from which one can view
> a situation or problem. The absence of a set of considerations
> or perspectives or the inability to use certain processes for ap-
> praising a context biases the evidence one is able to take into
> account.[32]

In identifying the null curriculum, Eisner posits that there are two major dimensions that should be considered. The first is the intellectual processes that schools or any learning environment emphasize and neglect. The other is the content or subject areas that are present and absent within the school. The null curriculum can present the absent subject matter as material that does not exist or is censured, intentionally excluding viewpoints and perspectives not shared by the majority. What is not made available, then, is just as important and crucial to the students as what is made available. Curriculum designers heighten a sense of consciousness when they advocate for topics and subject matter and place them explicitly on the table, when they place subject matter or behavior implicitly under the table, and when they ignore or void out those subjects from being placed on the table. What is essential to the work of the curriculum designer is an awareness that the null curriculum will always exist, and decisions made in the designing of curriculum must warrant such awareness.

Eisner's notions of curriculum are helpful in understanding Gardner's research in arts education and curriculum design that helped format intentional exploration for students K–12. While Gardner explains that there is not a separate artistic intelligence, he does contend that each of the eight intelligences can be directed toward artistic ends. The symbols entailed in a domain of knowledge may but need not be marshaled in an aesthetic fashion. Gardner supports this through an example of the

---

32. Eisner, *Educational Imagination*, 97.

multiple uses of linguistic intelligence. Linguistic intelligence can be used in ordinary conversations or in the composing of legal briefs, with neither using this intelligence aesthetically, or it can also be used in the writing of poetry or novels, where it is employed aesthetically. The same can be explained with the bodily-kinesthetic intelligence. It can be used both aesthetically, by dancers, choreographers, and circus performers, and nonaesthetically, by athletes or surgeons.[33]

In 1976, Gardner's research team devised Project Zero, an experimental and experiential approach to education that included arts education. This program was composed for students who were to be introduced to ways of thinking exhibited by individuals involved in the arts. It included practicing artists as well as those who analyze, criticize, and investigate the cultural contexts of art objects. Unlike the theoretical underpinnings found within discipline-based arts education, Project Zero called attention to ten specific points that separated its core curriculum from that of previous arts-based curricula[34]:

1. Younger children need production activities to be centralized around an art form. Gardner believes that children learn best when they are actively engaged in their subject matter, which, in the case of the arts, will almost always translate into the making of something.

2. Perceptual, historical, critical, and other "peri-artistic" activities should be closely related to and—whenever possible—emerge from the child's own productions. Gardner emphasizes the need for children (this also applies to teens and adults) to be introduced to art objects created by their own hands, allowing them to confront specific elements and problems through personal engagement with the art itself instead of encountering alien art objects created by others.

3. The importance for arts curricula to be presented by teachers and others who possess a deep knowledge of how to think in an artistic medium is highlighted by Gardner. It is not enough to present an art form through language and logic alone. The students must be able to think artistically in the artistic medium they are presenting.

4. Whenever possible, artistic learning should be organized around meaningful projects that are carried out over a significant period of time and allow ample opportunity for feedback, discussion, and

33. Gardner, *Multiple Intelligences*, 150.
34. See Gardner, *Multiple Intelligences*, 153–56.

reflection. Gardner emphasizes that such projects are likely to interest students, motivate them, and encourage them to develop skills
that may well exert a long-term impact on students' competence
and understanding.

5. Within artistic curricula, Gardner affirms, it would not be profit-
   able to plan a strict K–12 sequential curriculum. Artistry involves
   continued exposure at various developmental levels to certain core
   concepts (such as style, composition, and genre) and recurring
   challenges (such as performing a passage with feeling or creating
   a powerful artistic image). For Gardner, then, the curricula would
   need to be rooted in a "spiral" aspect of artistic learning.

6. Assessments in the arts are crucial and must respect the particular
   intelligences involved—musical skill must be accessed by musical
   means and not through intervening screens of language or logic.
   Gardner's theory denotes the error in crafting the curriculum to suit
   the assessment, rather than devising assessments that do justice to
   what is most pivotal in an art form.

7. Artistic learning is not simply a matter of mastering a set of skills
   or concepts; rather, it encompasses deeply personal areas through
   which students confront their own feelings as well as the feelings of
   others. Gardner contends that students need educational vehicles to
   allow for such exploration. Personal reflection should be respected
   and not violated.

8. It is important for students to understand that the arts are permeat-
   ed by issues of taste and value that matter to anyone who is seriously
   engaged in the arts. For Gardner, such issues are best conveyed by
   contact with individuals who not only care about these issues and
   are willing to introduce and defend their perspective but also remain open to alternative views.

9. The arts, according to Gardner, are too important to be left to any
   one group—even to the group designated as "art educators." Rather,
   arts education needs to be a cooperative enterprise, involving artists,
   teachers, administrators, researchers, and the students themselves.

10. Gardner's final point asserts that students should have extended
    exposure to some art form, but it need not be one of the visual arts.
    Gardner would rather have students be well versed in music, dance,
    or drama rather than have a smattering of knowledge across several

lively arts. That way, the students would at least know what it is like to think in one art form and retain the option of assimilating others later in life, rather than being forever consigned to amateur status or even drop out of the art world altogether.

Eisner's theory of curriculum development, Greene's use of the imagination, and Gardner's theory of artistic instruction paves the way to explore the implementation of various art forms as learning tools within educational settings. But can the arts be used to initiate and stimulate the learning of subject matter other than the knowledge that the art form itself possesses? If so, the question still remains as to how this procedure can be developed, processed, and accessed within a regular classroom. These points will be discussed by analyzing dance as an educational tool within the classroom. Dance as a way of knowing and its intrinsic characteristics in developing the educational curriculum, the teacher, and the student learner are considered below.

The Wonders of Dance and Aesthetic Learning

Jennifer Donohue Zakkai's *Dance as a Way of Knowing* offers an approach to learning both academic subjects and movement concepts that have been implemented within the field of education through "The Strategies for Teaching and Learning Professional Library" series, produced by the Galef Institute.[35] Zakkai's research in the field of dance as a way of knowing builds the teacher's knowledge of movement and dance while providing strategies teachers can use to enhance student learning and creativity in the classroom. One of the highlights of Zakkai's work is the inspiration it gives to educators who may not be skilled movers or skilled dancers but can become effective facilitators of movement. She explains it this way:

> You'll use verbal directions to guide most movement activities. That's because our goal is to cultivate children's creativity, not teach them a particular way to move. We want our students to

35. "'The Strategies for Teaching and Learning Professional Library' series was developed to offer educators countless opportunities for professional growth. It's rather like having your own workshops, coaching, and study groups between the covers of a book. Each book in this series invites you to explore: (1) the theory regarding human learning and development—so you know why, (2) the best instructional practices—so you know how, and (3) continuous assessment of your students' learning as well as your own teaching and understanding—so you and your students know that you know" (Zakkai, *Way of Knowing*, 3).

investigate and develop their own movement ideas, not imitate us or others.

> Let's dispel a myth about working with movement and dance. It is not an unstructured experience. Students enjoy solving very specific, challenging movement problems that require the utmost concentration and inspire a high level of personal expression.[36]

The underpinnings of Zakkai's research stems from an understanding that movement and dance are integral tools in the learning process. Exploring a curriculum topic such as letter shapes, formalizing concepts such as cause and effect, and making a dance are all examples of the types of learning that can transpire utilizing movement and dance. Zakkai writes:

> The terms "movement and dance" encompass a full range of motion—from the movement that exists in the natural and human-made worlds around us, to everyday actions we all engage in as human beings, to the carefully crafted movements we know as dance. *Dance as a Way of Knowing* describes how this full spectrum of movement enhances classroom learning.[37]

Zakkai uses movement and dance as umbrella terms for the whole progression of strategies offered in her text. In it, she supplies definitions of dance vocabulary in order to lay down a foundation that is clearly understood by teacher, dancer, and student. Thus, as Zakkai's definition of dance states: "Dance is movement that transcends function and becomes communication. In order to communicate in this way, a dancer or group of dancers come together in an open space and perform crafted movements for an audience."[38]

A major focus in Zakkai's work is the use of everyday actions as starting points for learning explorations. While Zakkai explains that to describe all learning experiences as "dance" alone is not accurate, on the other hand, she points out that "movement" also cannot account for students' emerging creative expression as they learn more about dance and incorporate aesthetic elements into their movement choices.

Greene maintains that the events that make up aesthetic experiences are events that occur within and by means of the transactions with

---

36. Zakkai, *Way of Knowing*, 8.
37. Zakkai, *Way of Knowing*, 9.
38. Zakkai, *Way of Knowing*, 20.

the environments that situate people in time and space. Some say that participatory encounters with paintings, dances, stories, and all other art forms enable people to recapture a lost spontaneity.[39] Greene surmises that if educators are made aware of themselves as questioners, as meaning makers, and as persons engaged in constructing and reconstructing realities with those around them, they may communicate to students the notion that reality is multiple perspectives and that the construction of it is never complete; there is always more.

In his article, "Aesthetic Modes of Knowing," Eisner investigates how the understanding of the aesthetic is found within the realm of learning and knowing all subjects, including the sciences and the arts. He gives three distinct reasons as to how form and the aesthetic are merged into a mode of knowing:

> First, all things made, whether in art, science, or in practical life, possess form. . . . When made well these forms have aesthetic properties. These aesthetic properties have the capacity to generate particular qualities of life in the competent percipient. . . . Second, form is not only an attribute or condition of things made; it is a process through which things are made. Knowing how forms will function within the finished final product is a necessary condition for creating products that themselves possess aesthetic qualities. . . . Third, the deeper motives for productive activity in both the arts and the sciences often emanate from the quality of life the process of creation makes possible. These satisfactions are related to the kinds of stimulation secured in the play process and from the aesthetic satisfactions derived from judgments made about emerging forms.[40]

Eisner aims to find the aesthetic experience in the discovery of and the knowing of any subject matter. Within any subject, there is a particular mode of exploration that encompasses thought, imagination, and eager investigation on behalf of the learner in order to uncover and display not only the rudiments of the subject but also its peculiarities. This sense of commitment in the learning process is itself an aesthetic act that formulates an appreciation for the knowing journey, for the knowing pilgrimage. Eisner promotes a teaching act which can prescribe ways by which teachers can implement aesthetic journeying and aesthetic knowing. He is convinced that this type of appreciation for the aesthetic will change

39. Greene, *Releasing the Imagination*, 130.
40. Eisner, "Aesthetic Modes," 28.

the essence of every teacher who will then discover anew how every subject should be taught. This experience itself is aesthetic in nature and artistic in its undertaking.

Eisner contends that such an absence of the aesthetic mode of knowing has affected the outcome of school curriculum. He writes:

> The absence of attention to the aesthetic in the school curriculum is an absence of opportunities to cultivate the sensibilities. It is an absence of the refinement of our consciousness, for it is through our sensibilities that our consciousness is secured. Attention to the aesthetic aspects of the subjects taught would remind students that the ideas within subject areas, disciplines, and fields of study are human constructions, shaped by craft, employing technique, and mediated through some material. Works of science are, in this sense, also works of arts.[41]

For Eisner, an aesthetic education has two major contributions to make, neither of which, as of yet, is a purposeful part of the educational agenda. First, he suggests, the aesthetic teaches about the world in ways specific to its nature, and second, the aesthetic provides the experiential rewards of taking the journey itself.

Similarly, Greene states that dance confronts the question of what it means to be human. She describes this further:

> Arnol Berleant writes that "in establishing a human realm through movement, the dancer, with the participating audience, engages in the basic act out of which arise both all experience and our human constructions of the world. . . . It stands as the direct denial of that most pernicious of all dualisms, the division of body and consciousness. In dance, thought is primed at the point of action. This is not the reflection of the contemplative mind but rather intellect poised in the body, not the deliberate consideration of alternative courses but thought in process, intimately responding to and guiding the actively engaged body." The focus is on process and practice; the skill in the making is embodied in the object. In addition, the dance provides occasions for the emergence of the integrated self. Surely, this view of the self ought to be taken into account in our peculiarly technicized and academicized time.[42]

41. Eisner, "Aesthetic Modes," 34–35.
42. Greene, *Releasing the Imagination*, 131.

Greene claims there should be a pedagogy that joins art education and aesthetic education together so that teachers can enable students to live within the arts, making clearings and spaces for themselves. There should be a community of educators who are committed to an emancipatory pedagogy, particularly in the domain of the arts. Greene states:

> When students can share in learning the language of dance by moving as dancers move, entering the symbol system of novel writing and story weaving by composing their own narratives out of words, working with glad sounds or drums to find out what it signifies to shape the medium of sound, all these immediate involvements lead to a participant kind of knowing and a participant sort of engagement with art forms themselves. Aesthetic education ought to include adventures like these, just as it ought to include intentional efforts to foster increasingly informed and ardent encounters with artworks. Not incidentally, it ought to include the posing of the kinds of questions— aesthetic questions—that arise in the course of art experiences: Why do I feel spoken to by this work; excluded by that one? . . . To pose aesthetic questions is to make the aesthetic experience itself more reflective, more critical, more resonant. Art education is deepened and expanded by what occurs in answering such questions.[43]

Greene defines art education as the spectrum that includes dance education, music education, the teaching of painting and graphic arts, and, she hopes, the teaching of some kinds of writing. By aesthetic education, Greene means the deliberate effort to foster increasingly informed and involved encounters with art. "The point of enabling our students to both engage in art as maker and experience existing artworks is to release them to be more fully present."[44] For Greene, infusing art education with aesthetic education allows one to understand what there is to be noticed in the work at hand. It releases the imagination to create orders in the field of what is received and allows one's feelings to inform and illuminate what there is to be realized. Greene explains this concept further:

> I would like to see one pedagogy feeding into the other: the pedagogy that empowers students to create informing the pedagogy that empowers them to attend (and, perhaps, to appreciate) and vice versa. I would like to see both pedagogies carried on with

43. Greene, *Releasing the Imagination*, 137–38.
44. Greene, *Releasing the Imagination*, 138.

a sense of both learner and teacher as seeker and questioner, someone consciously "condemned to meaning" and thus reflective about his or her choosing process, turning toward the clearing that might (or might not) lie ahead. The ends in view are multiple, but they surely include the stimulation of imagination and perception, a sensitivity to various modes of seeing and sense making, and a grounding in the situations of lived life.[45]

Before moving forward with this inquiry, some clarifications need to be made. For example, although Zakkai's research in movement and dance is primarily geared toward children in grades K–6, in light of both Eisner and Greene's definitions of art education and aesthetic education (and how both pedagogies feed one another), her findings are applicable to all students and adult learners. The present writing is informed by the combination of these principles.

Zakkai contends that there are seven benefits to inviting students to work with movement and dance.[46] The *first* helps students to focus and engage in learning. By moving the whole body, movement improves circulation and sends oxygen to the brain. It also releases endorphins, which eases stress and promotes a sense of well-being. In movement and dance experiences, Zakkai admits that students always work with specific points of focus as they move. She states, "Because they are focusing their minds as well as their movements, they experience an immediate and simultaneous fusion of intention, action, feeling, and awareness."[47] Thus, total engagement can make learning deep and memorable. In this way, moving to learn can be highly motivating and have a long-lasting impact. This first benefit is an example of Greene's emancipatory pedagogy, that is, the infusing of dance education (the actual encounter a student has with dance) with aesthetic education (the reflective and contemplative feeling and awareness a student gains as a result of the encounter).

The *second* benefit is the application of the kinesthetic intelligence. Zakkai's work leans heavily upon Gardner's Multiple Intelligence theory, and yet she adds to the benefits of using the bodily-kinesthetic intelligence within the classroom by suggesting that, "together with more traditional ways of receiving, recording, and reflecting knowledge, students can also use their bodily-kinesthetic intelligence to learn and show

45. Greene, *Releasing the Imagination*, 138.
46. See Zakkai, *Way of Knowing*, 10–25.
47. Zakkai, *Way of Knowing*, 10.

what they know about different topics, concepts, and processes through movement."[48] She gives the following example:

> For example, in language arts, we can put action words into motion to reinforce and demonstrate comprehension. Let's see how this would work. Begin by reading this paragraph:
>
>> Human beings are in constant motion. Even when we sit completely still, lost in thought, our hearts are pumping, our lungs are expanding and contracting, our chests rise and fall. Soon we blink, shift our weight, unclasp our hands, turn our heads, stand up, and walk across the room.
>
>> Now, let's highlight the action words. Move your hands and create your own way of understanding what we mean by *expand, contract, rise, fall,* and *walk.* Give this a try with your students. You'll discover that they'll enjoy exploring the meaning of action words from any text with their hands and whole bodies.[49]

Learning through moving is highly motivating for all children, especially for those children who demonstrate a strong bodily-kinesthetic intelligence. The success they experience as creative movers can also help them access other skills.

The *third* benefit is the ability to understand concepts and themes. Zakkai gives the example of second language learners who can understand the meaning of words through movement. A movement lesson is a perfect opportunity to build student's basic vocabulary. Zakkai explains how this can be demonstrated.

> As they label all the different ways the body can move, students learn action words like *stretch, turn, skip.* They also discover such spatial concepts as *high, low, circular.* Adverbs—*lightly, powerfully, quickly*—come to life as well. Second language learners who are not yet speaking and writing in English will appreciate movement as a way to learn and demonstrate what they know.[50]

The *fourth* benefit develops and refines the student's higher level thinking skills by engaging them in exploration, creative problem solving, and decision-making. Zakkai submits that students learn about key components of dance through movement exploration that involves students

---

48. Zakkai, *Way of Knowing,* 11.

49. Zakkai, *Way of Knowing,* 11–12.

50. Zakkai, *Way of Knowing,* 12.

in a structured yet open-ended process of investigation. This type of exercise affords students the ability to discover inventive movements as they explore specific dance ideas. Creative problem solving is the ability to confront a problem and to discover a creative solution to the problem. Zakkai contends that creativity is like a muscle that must be used and exercised in order for it to be developed and strengthened. Movement and dance encourages students to explore a variety of solutions to a movement problem. Zakkai points out that "once students realize that there is not just one correct answer, but a range of more and less effective choices, students are inspired to take greater risks and invest themselves more deeply as learners."[51] As they learn new skills and discover that their individual choices have value, they can grow in their self-confidence and productivity. To foster decision-making, the students are asked to create sequences of movement which can range from simple juxtapositions to a complete dance. Zakkai suggests that the selecting, sequencing, and revising of movement choices into a whole enables students to think with discernment as they transform movement into effective communication.

The *fifth* benefit is the ability to communicate in unique ways and to appreciate the artistic expression of others. Zakkai proposes that there is a special kind of human communication by which people speak the same language even though no words are exchanged. She describes it this way:

> Sometimes artists invite us to look at people, issues, and designs through a "different lens." This process can be so powerful that we enlarge or dramatically alter the way we view ourselves and others who may have lives completely different from our own. Therefore, it is important that students not only learn how to communicate their ideas through movement and dance but also learn to experience the kinesthetic expressions of others as observers. As students view each other's efforts as well as the work of dance artists, they can develop their aesthetic awareness and critical thinking skills. This learning can sharpen their assessment of their own work and inspire them to a higher level of achievement.[52]

Students investigating dances from different times and cultures can benefit from a different way of knowing a historical era or group of people. To learn more about dance, Zakkai recommends that teachers invite artists and dance groups from the community as well as those who travel,

51. Zakkai, *Way of Knowing*, 15.
52. Zakkai, *Way of Knowing*, 15–16.

perform, and teach throughout the United States to perform and work with their students. This way, students can reach outside their immediate environment and extend their learning into a larger artistic community.

The *sixth* benefit is spatial awareness, which allows students to become more aware of the space they are moving in, their personal space, and the space of others. Regardless of how large or small the workspace is, Zakkai claims that students can learn to move within clearly defined parameters while enjoying the challenges of how to move freely without bumping into one another. Whether moving in place or moving through space, students will learn to look where they are going and remain sensitive to the parameters of their personal space and that of others. Zakkai specifies key benefits for teachers:

> Spatial awareness has enormous benefits. Rambunctious students develop more self-control and respect for others, while quieter students feel it's safe to move and take risks. Then, as the facilitator, you can concentrate on how students are moving, rather than on traffic problems.[53]

The *seventh* benefit of inviting students to experience movement and dance is the invitation to work together with one another, as either fellow movers or collaborators. In the beginning, students explore movement problems as a whole group, since it takes a while for everyone to get familiar with this new way of learning. From there, students begin to break into smaller groups to share their ideas and solve problems together. As viewers or participants, they learn to respect the creative efforts of others. The experience of envisioning and realizing a project together can lay the foundation for becoming effective workers and responsible community members once they leave school.

Zakkai uses the concepts and vocabulary of modern dance as a staple for her movement and dance curriculum. The elements utilized within modern dance are some of the key learning concepts that comprise her curriculum. Space, energy, and time are investigative tools that help a dance artist discover movements which are expressive and unique. For Zakkai, space is that which encompasses the overall design of movement, including where it takes place, its size and shape, its energy, and the flow of motion. Movements are animated by kinetic energy in distinct ways. Time includes how fast or slow a movement is and whether it unfolds with its own natural rhythm or is tied to a steady beat.

53. Zakkai, *Way of Knowing*, 16.

One of the last components of Zakkai's *Dance as a Way of Knowing* curriculum is a progression of facilitation strategies used by teachers to engage students in a three-phase learning continuum. The first is the *natural movement phase*, which helps students to establish their spatial awareness and become responsible movers. The students learn and show what they know through ordinary actions. Zakkai believes this is both an enjoyable and focused way to begin working with movement in the classroom. Examples of this would be students creating gestures while singing a song, moving as quietly as possible from one work area to another, exploring movements associated with work, and putting verbs, adverbs, and prepositions into action. The second is the *creative movement phase* which, for Zakkai, is the heart of the movement and dance process. It is here that students focus on the process of exploration and creative problem solving. Zakkai indicates that this is done by learning about the dance elements of space, energy, and time, moving beyond the limits of natural movement, making in-depth connections across the curriculum, and creating short movement sequences in group studies. The third strategy is the *artistic movement phase* in which students focus on making dances. They relate their efforts to the work of various dance artists, either through live performances or videos, to deepen their understanding of the discipline.

The work of Jennifer Donohue Zakkai, Maxine Greene, Howard Gardner, and Elliot Eisner have been juxtaposed and combined to formulate sound theories in the areas of learning abilities, imagination and creativity, arts and aesthetic education, dance education, and education curricula. They pave the way for a type of educational approach that stresses the continual becoming of an individual, both as a teacher and as a student learner. These principles can be applied to places of learning outside the public and private school arena, such as the church. Imaginative religious education can bring creativity, imagination, as well as diverse learning opportunities within the life and breath of the church. The church can become a place of sincere nurturing and faith-building. The Christian community can be enhanced as living witnesses of the love of Christ displayed both inside and outside the walls of the church. The last section of this chapter focuses on the importance of the imagination and the use of dance as instructional tools within the church and religious education.

The Wonders of the Imagination inside Church Teaching

The work of Maria Harris relates to a variety of categories within the field of religious education, one of which is the use of religious imagination in the act of teaching. In *Teaching and Religious Imagination*, Harris describes teaching as an activity of religious imagination:

> Teaching, when seen as an activity of religious imagination, is the incarnation of subject matter in ways that lead to the revelation of subject matter. At the heart of this revelation is the discovery that human beings are the primary subjects of all teaching, subjects who discover themselves as possessing the grace of power, especially the power of re-creation, not only of themselves, but of the world in which they live.[54]

Harris's definition of teaching through religious imagination exposes the direct relationship a teaching subject has to human life. This activity allows for the manifestation of the subject to be witnessed in and through human beings who become the primary objects of every teaching moment. In this teaching moment, the state of becoming is witnessed personally in the interactions one has with the other.

Harris identifies imagination as "all the faculties of human beings, all our resources, not only our seeing and hearing and touching, but also our history, our education, our feelings, our wishes, our love, hate, faith, and unfaith, insofar as they all go into the making of our image of the world."[55] She looks at reality from the reversed, unnoticed side, suggesting that imagination is the mind's glory, the ample fullness of intelligence, rather than the thinness of reason alone. At the same time, since imagination is always a human power, rooted in body and biography, it continually spills over the boundaries of mind so as to be always more comprehensive and comprehending.

Harris clarifies that the teaching that one is perhaps more affected than one realizes is by the way one thinks about, conceptualizes, and mentally envisions one's own teaching. At the same time, teaching is essentially an embodied, incarnate act, carried on in a situation where human beings are physically present to one another. It is dependent on the total resources a human being possesses in the students and in the environments, all of which go into the making of our worlds.

54. Harris, *Teaching*, xv.
55. Harris, *Teaching*, 9.

Harris contends that the thinking and knowing of those who teach is shaped by the metaphors they employ, so it matters which words they choose when they instruct or instruct others to teach. The metaphors teachers choose can catalyze or paralyze one's capacity to perceive and receive what is being taught, no matter how plain or abundant the evidence. While the words a teacher uses can indeed paralyze and stifle a person's growth, they can also transform and redeem a person's life. The verbiage a teacher uses is crucial in all areas of teaching, especially when teaching religion. According to Harris, people are moved by experiencing their imaginations touched by someone or something that excites them into hoping and acting. When the word is made flesh, redemption is at hand; it is the vocation of the teacher to give flesh to language and make metaphor incarnate.

From the Christian tradition, Harris draws on the terms contemplative, ascetic, and creative to expand and give new religious meaning to imagination. The notion of the imagination as contemplative draws on the active intensity of the contemplative life, which calls for a totally engaged bodily presence. Words such as attending, listening, being-with, and existing fully in the presence of being all come into formation, especially for the teacher. When the teacher is fully present in all matters related to teaching, students are encouraged to mirror such an approach as well, being fully present in the learning environment. Ascetic imagination brings the understanding associated with religious discipline and discipleship to the surface, including the need for detachment in the presence of the other, the letting be of being, and the standing back in order not to violate.[56] The ascetic imagination helps teachers teach to exercise respect and restraint toward both students and subject matter and to avoid the danger of being too distanced and too removed from daily life. The ascetic imagination, according to Harris, helps teachers teach sympathetically and empathetically, but always with the reverence and respect people need.

Drawing on the creative imagination and theology of creation embedded in the Christian tradition, teachers can work with students in ways that create new possibilities within every teaching occasion, offering students the opportunity to take the material presented and to reform and recreate it in and through themselves. Those who believe human beings are made in the image of a Creator God can use this aspect of

56. Harris, *Teaching*, 21.

imagination to tap into their own creative and aesthetic potential. Such potential welcomes both teacher and student to become creators in the midst of their religious learning.[57]

The connection between dance, religious education, and worship is described by Carla DeSola and Arthur Easton in "Awakening the Right Lobe through Dance."[58] They discuss how such a connection provides a more personal, vivid experience between the dancer and God through the avenues of liturgy and prayer. According to them, the dancer is neither just involved with the body nor is the body used solely to gain awareness of the self; rather, the body also gains a greater awareness of the self in relation to space and to the Spirit which fills that space in an unseen, intuited way. Like Zakkai's explanation of the importance of using the elements of space, energy, and time as concepts in teaching and learning dance, DeSola and Easton understand the use of space and sound for the dancer within the sanctuary. They describe how, "the dancer relates to the surrounding space with a variety of rhythms and dynamic changes. . . . In the artistic process, one is interested in the creation of beauty and in the unveiling of what is real but not normally perceived."[59] In terms of sound, the dancer listens in the quiet and becomes aware of a new speech or language. DeSola and Easton point to the dancer's alphabet as containing the elements of silence, space, stillness, rhythm, textures, and flow, declaring that the speech is apprehended in the "silent" areas of the brain, which recognize beauty, music, song, truth, and patterns of the unrecognizable and unknown. All of these concepts are the fundamental elements of dance that present possibilities for teaching and learning to both the dancer and the congregation.

For DeSola and Easton, religious dance is that which connects dance with religion.[60] Since the movement's source comes from the heart's response, in an overflowing of gratitude or speech, to God, religious dance can be assumed to be the result of a personal, meditative experience of God:

57. Harris, *Teaching*, 21.

58. See DeSola and Easton, "Awakening."

59. DeSola and Easton, "Awakening," 72.

60. Religious dance is a term that DeSola and Easton use to refer to the association and relationship between dance and religion. There are many terms, however, used to describe the affiliation dance has with Christianity. DeSola and VerEecke use the term "liturgical dance prayer," while others use the term "liturgical dance."

In Christian terms, one could speak of Christ as the partner in an ever-new dance which is inspired by the Holy Spirit and offered to the Father. The highest level, point, or state would be a contemplative absorption, moving in a reality filled with God's love, realizing the words of Scripture: "In Him we move and live and have our being." . . . The corresponding spirituality for the dancer would be a total union of body, spirit, music, and space, forgetting the self in actualizing the dance (this is easier said than done). When this is successful, those who view the dance also become at-one and also forget themselves. For they are equally absorbed in the *aesthetic* spirituality of the prayer-dance.[61]

According to DeSola and Easton, dance is a bridge from the world of intellect to the world of the imagination. Through dance, one can grasp the meaning of religious concepts in a deeper way. As explained earlier, through the work of Zakkai, Eisner, Gardner, and Greene, both art and aesthetic pedagogies within the explicit, implicit, and null curricula push the educational process forward.[62] Personal and collective growth is transpiring for both teacher and learner or, in this case, for both dancer and congregation. By engaging the teacher and the student to become more fully present and alert to the subject, to themselves, and to the others who are learning with them, one of the major goals of aesthetic education is accomplished. In grasping the deeper meaning of religious concepts, DeSola and Easton affirm the use of the imagination, as does Harris. DeSola and Easton recall such an experience:

When a prayer during liturgy is offered with movements of arms, hands, and torsos, a new energy seems to enter the sanctuary. The movements may include simple hand gestures, lifting the arms in praise, or lowering the torsos in deep bows. These movements are done reverently and as the Spirit suggests. On a number of occasions, people reported 'seeing' the waves of arms lifting even though their eyes were closed. It was as though layer upon layer of branches in a forest, or stalks of wheat in a field, were swaying to the movement of the wind and a healing power seemed to flow from the tips.[63]

---

61. DeSola and Easton, "Awakening," 73.

62. For the benefit of this writing, it is acknowledged that, within art and aesthetic educational paradigms, the explicit, the implicit, and the null curriculums are present and operating within all educational environments.

63. DeSola and Easton, "Awakening," 77.

In her essay, "A Model for Aesthetic Education," Harris writes about a course she taught for a number of years and in a variety of seminaries entitled, "The Aesthetic and Religious Education." The starting point of the course was the notion that religious education is a field where the religious intersects with education—and that the aesthetic is a dimension of both.[64] Religion, with its ties to creativity and feeling, has always been the vehicle through which people have expressed their relationship to the divine. Education, with its focus on the intentional reconstruction of experience, has strongly relied on the creation of conceptual forms, but is also in need of a perceptible form more proper to art. Thus, for Harris, the field of religious education can only be enhanced by the inclusion of the aesthetic.

Harris points out that, in religious education, developmental theorists have not generally studied aesthetic or artistic developments in adults as much or as carefully as topics like faith formation and the psychology of adult learning. Therefore, Harris suggests, religious education theorists are in danger of assuming that they have a firm understanding of the nature of adulthood. This is especially true in light of the aesthetic, which is more open to multiple interpretations. Harris also speaks of the need for a special kind of healing in religious education. She writes, "Just as there is a possible over-reliance on psychology, there is a possible danger in all educational circles of separating such persons as artists and poets from others who come to be referred to as scientists and thinkers."[65]

Finally, the philosophy of the course is based on a set of assumptions about adult students in theology and/or religious education. Harris recognizes there are some students who are afraid of the artistic; while others are especially sensitive to the aesthetic and are in need of artistic expression; while still others may not feel either extreme but are just seeking a different type of learning space. These types of students demonstrated a personal, religious, and educational need for a place within the curriculum where they can simply integrate what they are learning.[66] Harris asserted that the course, "provides an oasis where people can, in stillness, let their understanding, their intellect, and their feelings come

64. Harris, "Aesthetic Education," 143.
65. Harris, "Aesthetic Education," 143.
66. Harris, "Aesthetic Education," 144.

together without pressure, but with support from within the institution where they are learning."[67]

While the design of the course has been varied, one aspect remains constant, namely, everyone participated in the art forms at some point. This participation is essential to the understanding of the aesthetic. There is a foundational blending of two modalities within the course structure—participation and reflective discussion—reflected in the course description:

> The purpose of this course is to provide understanding of, participation in, and expression through various art forms. Class members will be required, either individually or as a group, to choose an artistic form, research it, and develop a process which will engage the other class members in this form. At various times, class members will act as creators, performers, audience members, and critics. Actual attendance at class sessions is expected, since these form a key part of the course and are its focal point. Class members with expertise in various forms may be called on as resource persons in these forms, but are encouraged to choose for presentation an area with which they are not familiar. It is strongly recommended that all class members keep a journal to record their impressions for themselves as the semester progresses.[68]

From this description it is clear that Harris supports an integrative curriculum by which the body, mind, and spirit of both teacher and student are very much present in the learning process. It also affirms a community whose central focus is not simply on academic learning but also nurturing and ever-becoming—as both separate individuals and as a community of learners.

There are three conceptual poles that have anchored the course for Harris. They are word, world, and wisdoms. *Word* is an appropriate starting point because of the heavily verbal nature of all education, particularly the teaching act.[69] For religious education, Harris explains, that word can be understood as both discursive and presentational. The aesthetic form of words—in poetry, drama, literature, and fairytale—are studied as educational vehicles. Especially in the Christian religious tradition, the "Word" is central. The word is not only that which humans

---

67. Harris, "Aesthetic Education," 145.
68. Harris, "Aesthetic Education," 145.
69. Harris, "Aesthetic Education," 147.

speak, through which they communicate, in which they dwell; rather, more importantly, it is the metaphor for the divine—the Word which becomes flesh.[70]

Harris uses *world* as that of the earth, the stuff of which the world is made. The aesthetic is the human way of establishing relationship with this world-stuff: clay, paint, water, color, line, point, sound, and body.[71] Harris suggests:

> In our everlastingly talkative ecclesial circles, the bodiliness we must call on in order to shape and mold clay, to dilute and mix color, to harmonize and project sound, and to freely and ecstatically dance is often minimized. A course such as ours has always had a heavy emphasis on world and our relationship to it, and this is manifested not only in the times we remain indoors and design form together, but in the yearly experience . . . of going outside the classroom, to sketch, to do rubbings, to find a sound, to fill a silence.[72]

Wisdoms is the third and final element of the course. In other environments, this might be called learnings, results, or conclusions. Harris prefers the notion of wisdoms because of its rich and multi-layered meaning. Wisdom does indeed mean learning as well as the understanding of what is true, right, or lasting. Harris pursues the answers to such questions as what does one see after a course like this; what takes form, takes shape; and what becomes clearly visible. According to her, four wisdoms stand out from experiencing such a course; foolishness, creativity, a sense of wholeness, and the wisdom of worship.

Foolishness comes as a result of spending an entire semester on the aesthetic. It serves as a reminder that not all knowledge is for use and, in our Western culture, the aesthetic is undoubtedly foolish to many. Harris asserts that the aesthetic is a reminder that the more-than-rational exists and that, if allowed, it nurtures and feeds the human spirit: "There is also the foolishness in this course of making a fool of oneself in the sense of trying something in front of others where we do not come off as experts."[73]

70. Harris, "Aesthetic Education," 147.
71. Harris, "Aesthetic Education," 147.
72. Harris, "Aesthetic Education," 147–148.
73. Harris, "Aesthetic Education," 149.

One's own creativity is the second wisdom, and this is given possibility by the absence of the pressure to win. Harris reports that a shared
commitment grows in order to allow creativity to grow as the course continues. A particular climate must exist to cultivate creativity which Harris
describes as including:

> the *detachment*, the willingness to accept any outcome; the
> *passion* that can be expressed in an unthreatening atmosphere;
> the *immediacy* of involvement in a process, with the *deferral* of
> satisfaction almost always present in a two-hour segment; the
> *letting the artwork*, art object, art process *take over*, or the letting
> of the internal drama unfold so that one can *let the material be*
> what it must be; the relinquishing of the urge to control and to
> be in charge. And, in doing so, coming to a new seeing, a new
> understanding of oneself.[74]

A third wisdom is the sense of wholeness, which feeds students in
theology or religious education because of their work with words and
books.[75] Harris emphasizes that dealing with the aesthetic, the artistic,
and the non-discursive is not a denigration of the world of discourse and
rationality but rather a complementing of it. The sense of wholeness becomes more evident by encountering the material universe and working
in the intuitive, the imaginative, and the perceptual modes more proper
to art.

The fourth is the wisdom of worship. Harris points out that the
course is not a course on or about worship, however, the topic of worship steals into the curriculum each time she has taught the course. This
comes about when someone chooses to conduct a class on prayer, or on
a liturgical celebration, or in choosing the form of worship as a closing to
the semester's work.

Teaching this course and courses like it affords Harris the opportunity to venture into educational modalities that combine the various
ways people learn. From such experiences, her research proves to be not
only vital but necessary—particularly in our post-modern world of individualism, absoluteness, and the continual disintegration of the value of
time. It is time that is needed for instruction; time for nurturing, time for
absorbing, and time for transforming. Harris concludes her essay with a
plea:

74. Harris, "Aesthetic Education," 149.
75. Harris, "Aesthetic Education," 150.

In describing a course that is now almost a decade old, I have shared the best moments and those experiences and insights which have proven most satisfying and most enriching for me and for the students. I have done so in the belief that what is done in a course like this is enormously important, and with the hope that others will try something similar. I am not an artist by training; I am a teacher, a religious educator, and I am convinced that what I have done, others can do, and do better. My essay is a challenge and an invitation to make that attempt, and an affirmation that to do so is to enter a world of words and wisdoms yet to be named.[76]

Conclusion

The challenge and invitation Harris presented over more than three decades ago is still a summons to current theological and religious studies departments—as well as the church itself. Such a venture permits the learning and educational processes of religious institutions to value the use of multiple intelligences. These intelligences are evidenced in domains where alternative crafts, disciplines, and learning activities foster their development.

The invaluable use of the imagination enlarges the possibilities for instruction and learning to transform educator, learner, religious departments, and church congregations. Aesthetic learning opens up the senses and heart of all human life to discover how expansive, creative, and intrinsic learning engagement can be. Dance as a teaching tool is able to educate both teacher and student in ways that are not only creative and imaginative but are mentally stimulating and emotional satisfying. Finally, such educational opportunities bring attention to a creative God who has formulated a creative and nurturing people.

The next chapter draws upon John Dewey's theories of education and aesthetic education through and by experience. In helping to describe the church as a community place of learning, it examines multiple ways by which the church can become a place of nurture for all who make up its congregational body. Through the exploration of Dewey's theories, church-related activities such as worship propose ways by which Christian education can be both taught and learned. Finally, it examines an in-depth view of the use of the arts as a teaching methodology within the church setting.

76. Harris, "Aesthetic Education," 150–51.

Chapter 3

Teach Me and Give Me Understanding

Experiential Learning and the Church Community

Introduction

This chapter addresses how John Dewey's ideas on education and aesthetic education through experience can assist faith communities in those teaching, learning, and living experiences that are also religious. It shows that Dewey's work in this area provides a plethora of possibilities for the field of religious education.

The work of John Dewey is unique in the development of education within the United States, and his influence has affected institutions throughout the world, especially religious education institutions. This influence was highlighted in his 1903 address at the First Annual Convention of the Religious Education Association, in which he states:

> Many persons whose religious development has been comparatively uninterrupted find themselves in the habit of taking for granted their own spiritual life. They are so thoroughly accustomed to certain forms, emotions, and even terms of expression that their experience becomes conventionalized. Religion is a part of the ordinances and routine of the day rather than a source of inspiration and renewing of power. It becomes a matter of conformation rather than of transformation.[1]

1. Dewey, "Psychology, Pedagogy, and Religion," 9.

Dewey's concern that religious experience should be transformative and not conventionalized remains a relevant concern for those presently involved in the field of religious education. All education for Dewey transpires through the explorations of touching, feeling, and thinking, reinforcing the notion that all education begins with experience. Indeed, personal experience is important for all concerned within the context of the learning community.

There are several implications of this principle for religious educators—it is essential to view religious experience as the centerpiece of their work with learners. If this premise is to be taken seriously, then the religious educator must find ways through which the religious experience can be identified, fostered, encouraged, and made applicable for all members of the congregation within a variety of religious learning experiences. Then, the church can be defined as a community of learning, and a variety of religious experiences can emerge in a way that fosters critical reflection and application in a variety of venues—both individually as well as corporately—for all members of the congregation. Within this context of religious experience, however, learning is not limited to those directly engaged with the religious experience. Learning also takes place for those with whom the congregation engages—those found outside the walls of the church, residing in both the surrounding and distant communities. This chapter is concerned with how Dewey's ideas on experience can assist faith communities through experiences within the context of the church as a community of learning.

John Dewey's theory of education is explored through the following four themes: (1) seeing education as a necessity of life, (2) education as a social function, (3) education as experiential, and (4) the aesthetic aspects of education. This is followed by a consideration of C. Ellis Nelson's notion of the value of experience in understanding congregational life. Finally, Dewey's theories are examined through the views of three religious educators: Charles Foster, Norma Cook Everist, and Anne Streaty Wimberly. While Charles Foster explores congregational learning from a variety of perspectives, this chapter discusses how Foster's notions of meaning making and teaching for meaning help create an educational, operational, and functioning Christian congregation. Norma Cook Everist presents the curriculum as a module that encompasses the entire life of the church. From this perspective, the elements of re-membering and a communal curriculum are explored. Anne Streaty Wimberly points to the nurturing experience found within congregational worship as a model for Christian Education within the Black church. A closer look at the nurturing components of faith and hope as found in the worship elements of preaching, music, and prayer are examined. Since a merging of Dewey's philosophy of education with and through experience is presented, it is proposed that it can continue to enrich religious education as a way to teach, foster, and give understanding to religious experience for the church as a community place of learning.

John Dewey's Theory of Education

Although Dewey's work pertains to the teaching environment of the public school classroom, it also has import and relevance for all educational settings. Dewey pressed to establish a school environment where education takes place without rigidity, legalism, and the absence of human imagination and creativity. He viewed education as a process of effective, transformational moments for the individual as well as for the community at large. In looking at both the individual and the community in which the individual is situated, Dewey discovered several important dynamics concerning the formation of community.

Before education could transpire within a particular community of people, Dewey held that there had to be a certain key understanding of what formulates a community first. He writes:

> Society not only continues to exist *by* transmission, *by* communication, but it may fairly be said to exist *in* transmission, *in* communication. There is more than a verbal tie between the words common, community, and communication. Men [humanity] live in a community in virtue of the things which they have in common; and communication is the way in which they come to possess things in common. What they must have in common in order to form a community or society are aims, beliefs, aspirations, knowledge—a common understanding— like-mindedness as the sociologists say. . . . The communication which insures participation in a common understanding is one which secures similar emotional and intellectual dispositions- like ways of responding to expectations and requirements.[2]

What links a people together to form a community is the commonality found within the shared knowledge, aims, belief systems, and growing

2. Dewey, *Democracy and Education*, 4.

aspirations of the people themselves. Regardless of the context, a community is only formed once all of its members recognize their shared common end and make an effort—through communication—to regulate specific activities in view of this common end.

Dewey distinguishes what makes a group function socially as oppose to functioning like a "machine-like plane."[3] He claims that individuals use one another so as to retain desired results without any reference to the emotional and intellectual disposition and consent of those being used. For example, he states:

> So far as the relations of parent and child, teacher and pupil, employer and employee, governor and governed, remain upon this level, they form no true social group, no matter how closely their respective activities touch one another. Giving and taking of orders modifies action and results, but does not of itself effect a sharing of purposes, a communication of interests.[4]

Therefore, it is the mutuality of shared purpose and a communication of interests that help to formulate and nurture a socially functioning community.

In viewing the church as a socially functioning community of people with specific aims, knowledge, aspirations, and beliefs that are shared in like-mindedness, those congregants who participate in it are made to discover the deep meaning of Christianity and the deeper meaning of what it means to be Christian. Such discoveries are examined by focusing on the life, teachings, death, and resurrection of Jesus Christ, the acclaimed son of God as revealed in the Holy word of God, the Bible. Through reading, critical reflection, prayer, and the physical activities of the people of God, a commonness of belief is discovered, finding the meaning of how one loves God and neighbor within the context of living life one day at a time. This is consistent with Dewey's notion that any social arrangement that remains vitally social or vitally shared is educative to those who participate in it.

Dewey's theory of education expands as a social function, where education is seen as a process that fosters, nurtures, and cultivates growth. Thus, education, for Dewey, means a process that leads or brings up; it is an activity that shapes, forms, and molds, "that is, a shaping into

3. Dewey, *Democracy and Education*, 5.
4. Dewey, *Democracy and Education*, 5.

the standard form of social activity."[5] As Dewey asserts, environment plays an essential role in the education process, as it consists of those conditions that promote and stimulate or inhibit and hinder the characteristic activities of a living being. The first step is to set up conditions that stimulate certain visible and tangible ways of acting within the social activity. He emphasizes that the individual should be made to be a sharer or partner in the associated activity so that individuals feel the activity's success as their success, and its failure as their failure. The individual's beliefs and ideas will take a form similar to those of others within the group. Achievement of the same stock of knowledge will be attained since that knowledge is an ingredient of their habitual pursuits.[6]

Dewey's definition of education helps to identify the church as a community that fosters, nurtures, and cultivates Christian faith. It is one that brings up everyone—male and female, children, teens, and adults, those with diverse learning styles, from diverse cultures, and from diverse economic backgrounds—with the understanding of the visible and tangible ways of being Christian. Such an understanding of religious education can be nurtured within the corporate worship setting of the Sunday church service, within individual group settings of bible study and Sunday school classes, as well as through interactions and activities that take place both inside and outside the church. For example, the ministry of "helps" allows church members, both young and old, to partake and share in a variety of activities to assist those within the congregation who are in need. Regardless of how big or small the need is, this very work educates both the helper and the helped. As congregants invest their time and effort in such educational activities, shape is given to the meaning of being Christian. This shaping is not static, but it is constant—as the ideas and beliefs of each church member take on a form similar to those with whom they worship.

Craig Dykstra contends that there is great understanding between Christian education and the spiritual formation of the congregation.[7] It is Dykstra's view that Christian education is dependent upon the church; it does not create the church. Christian education, according to Dykstra, depends upon both the church already being there and for it to

---

5. Dewey, *Democracy and Education*, 10.

6. Dewey, *Democracy and Education*, 14.

7. See Dystra, "Formative Power."

understand its own experiences through the movements and activities that identify them as Christian. He declares:

> If there are congregations where there is absolutely no move-ment toward confession, repentance, proclamation, and prayer, and no one who has experienced to any degree or any way some release from the mutually self-destructive dynamics of personal and social life that comes by God's grace, then, in that congrega-tion, there is no possibility of Christian education. For Christian education is the church's attempt to *understand its own experi-ence*. When a congregation has absolutely no experience as a church, there is nothing, Christianly speaking, to understand.[8]

Dykstra affirms that Christian education is the church's attempt to help its people see and grasp the inner character and hidden nature of its own experience as a confessing, repenting, proclaiming, and praying commu-nity in response to God's gracious, redeeming activity in the world.

Dewey's Theory on Education and Experience

Dewey's formal definition of education is: "That reconstruction or reor-ganization of experience which adds to the meaning of experience and which increases ability to direct the course of subsequent experience."[9] Education is aimed at human flourishing when each subsequent expe-rience becomes a more enriching experience than the previous one. A genuinely educative experience is one in which the instruction is appro-priately conveyed and our ability is increased. It is contradistinguished from a routine activity, on the one hand, and an impulsive activity on the other. A routine action is one which is automatic. It may increase skill to do a particular thing over and over again, but it does not lead to new perceptions of bearings and connections. An impulsive action is one where learning is achieved by doing something which was not previously understood. This learning, however, is only achieved after the act is per-formed, because there are results which were not noted before.

For Dewey, a key aspect of education as continuous reconstruc-tion is that it identifies both the process and the end result. This means that experience as an active process occupies time and that its later pe-riod of reconstruction completes its earlier portion. It brings to light the

---

8. Dystra, "Formative Power," 263.

9. Dewey, *Democracy and Education*, 76.

connections that are involved—yet were not understood—in the prior experience. The later outcome thus reveals the meaning of the earlier one, while the experience, as a whole, establishes a bent or disposition toward the things possessing this meaning:

> To "learn from experience" is to make a backward and forward connection between what we do to things and what we enjoy or suffer from things in consequence. Under such conditions, doing becomes a trying; an experiment with the world to find out what it is like; the undergoing becomes instruction—discovery of the connection of things.[10]

Experience is primarily an active-passive affair; it is not primarily cognitive. The measure of the value of an experience, however, lies in the perception of relationships or continuities to which it leads. It includes cognition to the degree in which it is cumulative, that it amounts to something, or that it has meaning. As it relates to the senses and those lessons learned with the application of the mind, some bodily activities have to be used. In this regard, the senses are regarded as a kind of mysterious conduit through which information is conducted from the external world into the mind. They are considered gateways of knowledge.

According to Dewey, thinking is the intentional endeavor to discover specific connections between something that we do and the consequences which result from it, so that the two become continuous. It is the accurate and deliberate instituting of connections between what is done and its consequences. Within the context of religious education, an example of this would be teaching the topic of prayer and its value to an adult class. The lesson may first warrant that the adult class first learn and understand the components of prayer, which can be done through the reading, examination, and deciphering of a particular biblical prayer—for example, the Lord's Prayer. After such an investigation, a variety of prayers can be considered, including intercessions, laments, salutations, and blessings. As the adults experience praying in ways that are personal, revelatory, and self-reflective, this type of activity necessitates reflective thinking. Learning biblical prayers can lead to writing and composing prayers for the class, family, church, community, and world. Sharing their personal findings with one another on a weekly basis helps them to discover the connections between prayer, creation, and faith. Reflection could be further engendered when the adult class is assigned to assist

10. Dewey, *Democracy and Education*, 140.

those who regularly do sick visitations. The adults could travel, two by two, to either the member's home or hospital, and each week record and share their impressions concerning the connections found between the effectiveness of prayer and faith while learning the primary lesson of loving God and loving neighbor. As they reflect, the use of the senses will help them to decipher more closely what they see, hear, feel, speak, and touch during these encounters. Because of the experiences encountered, the value of prayer will never be the same again. Critical reflections help to give genuine identity and meaning to the teaching and learning act, and its application will continually define what Christianity is and the true meaning of being Christian.

According to Dykstra's understanding of spiritual formation within the worshipping community, Christian education is a deepening and broadening of the church's experience as they come to understand it more and more and take more responsibility for it. He explains that Christian education itself:

> is an investigative process, which guides people in the explora-tion of this experience, a critical process which jars people out of the patterns of thinking, feeling, valuing, and behaving that make it difficult for them to participate in this experience, a hermeneutical process which aids people in the interpretation of this experience, and a caring process which invites people continually more deeply into this experience in freedom.[11]

Thus, Christian education helps the Christian community see and grasp the inner character and hidden nature of the mutual self-destruction and redemption that goes on in its own experience in order that, in its whole ministry, it may participate less and less in its own destructive patterns and those of the broader society and may be open more and more to the redemptive activity of God. It is through such an investigation that instruction and understanding are formulated.

Dewey's Challenge to Contemporary Education

Dewey continually challenged the educational system regarding the rela-tionship between education and experience. For example, since all genu-ine education comes through experience, are all experiences genuinely or

11. Dykstra, "Formative Power," 264.

equally educative? He responds that experience and education cannot be directly equated to each other:

> Some experiences are mis-educative. Any experience is mis-educative that has the effect of arresting or distorting the growth of further experience. An experience may be such as to engender callousness; it may produce lack of sensitivity and of responsiveness. Then, the possibilities of having richer experience[s] in the future are restricted.[12]

The educator must not only rely on the principle of shaping experience by its encircling conditions but also recognize what types of surroundings are conducive to having experiences that lead to growth. Dewey contends that the educator should know how to utilize their existing physical and social surroundings so as to extract from them all that they have to contribute to the building up of experiences that are worthwhile, positive, and continue in the growing of more experiences. Therefore, the educator needs to have an appropriate philosophy of education.

> A philosophy of education, like any theory, has to be stated in words, in symbols. But so far as it is more than verbal it is a plan for conducting education. Like any plan, it must be framed with reference to what is to be done and how it is to be done. The more definitely and sincerely it is held that education is a development within, by, and for experience, the more important it is that there shall be clear conceptions of what experience is.[13]

For the religious educator, this clarity is essential in developing an understanding of how education can be shaped by those experiences that teach and foster new ways of understanding the meaning of Christianity and how one lives a Christian life.

Dewey maintains that continuity and interaction are two principles that intercept and unite, therefore providing the measure of the educative significance and value of the experience. The immediate concern for the educator is those situations in which interactions take place. First, there is the individual or student in the interaction, and then, the objective conditions that are somewhat regulated by the educator. Such conditions involve the educator's preparations: the "what" and the "how," the equipment and materials utilized for engaging the student, and, most importantly, the total social set-up of the situations by which they are engaged.

12. Dewey, *Experience and Education*, 25–26.
13. Dewey, *Experience and Education*, 28.

Dewey explains that the objective conditions are within the influence of the educator so as to directly regulate the experiences of the students and the education they obtain. The educator must determine the type of environment most conducive for the interaction between the student, the materials, and their surroundings to take place so that worthwhile experiences can be formulated and made manifest.

The principle of continuity within the educational application must take into account "the future at every stage of the educational process."[14] Dewey contends that every experience should do something to prepare a person for later experiences of a deeper and more expansive quality. For Dewey, "That is the very meaning of growth, continuity, [and] reconstruction of experience."[15]

As stated earlier, the example of teaching about prayer to an adult class can present prayer in three situational settings. The first is within the classroom, where prayer is defined, classified, and examined by the class both individually and collectively. The second extends the teaching objective further, by engaging each adult in the activity of creating prayers. The third affords the adult class the opportunity to physically participate in praying for the sick for one month. Each of these three educational settings is connected with an ascending pattern of instruction that paves the way for a deeper, more expansive understanding of the topic of prayer. Within this example, continuity, interaction, and sound objective conditions undergird the lesson, thereby promoting education as a lived experience that is both continual and always reconfiguring itself.

The Aesthetic Experience

The educational experience of the artistic and the aesthetic is essential for the learning process. Dewey ventures into this field of inquiry through the lens of the educator, the artist, and the perceiver. He maintains that, when one has an experience—particularly when it relates to an aesthetic experience—the material experienced runs its course to fulfillment.[16] In this case, experience is defined by those situations and episodes that are spontaneously referred to as "real experiences."[17] In an experience, flow

14. Dewey, *Experience and Education*, 47.
15. Dewey, *Experience and Education*, 47.
16. Dewey, *Art as Experience*, 35.
17. Dewey, *Art as Experience*, 36.

is from something to something. As one part leads into another and as one part carries on with what went on before, each gains distinctness in itself.[18] For Dewey, this type of experience has a unity that gives it its name. An example of this could relate to a particular meal, a particular song, or a ruptured friendship. Dewey writes:

> The existence of this unity is constituted by a single quality that pervades the entire experience in spite of the variation of its constituent parts. . . . In going over an experience in mind, after its occurrence, we may find that one property rather than another was sufficiently dominant so that it characterizes the experience as a whole.[19]

Dewey asserts that there are conditions to be met without which an experience cannot come to be: "The outline of the common pattern is set by the fact that every experience is the result of interaction between a live creature and some aspect of the world in which [one] lives."[20] An experience also has pattern and structure; it is not just doing and undergoing in alternation but also consists of them in relationship. The action and its consequence must be joined in perception. This relationship, for Dewey, is what gives meaning to the experience; to grasp it is the objective of all intelligence. The scope and content of the relations measure the significant content of an experience. According to Dewey:

> It is not possible to divide in a vital experience the practical, emotional, and intellectual from one another and to set the properties of one over and against the characteristics of the others. The emotional phase binds parts together into a single whole; 'intellectual' simply names the fact that the experience has meaning; 'practical' indicates that the organism is interacting with events and objects which surround it.[21]

Dewey attempts to show that "the [aesthetic] is no intruder in experience from without, whether by way of idle luxury or transcendent ideality, but that it is the clarified and intensified development of traits that belong to every normally complete experience."[22] The artistic expression is one that unites the same relation of doing and undergoing, outgo-

18. Dewey, *Art as Experience*, 36.

19. Dewey, *Art as Experience*, 37.

20. Dewey, *Art as Experience*, 43–44.

21. Dewey, *Art as Experience*, 55.

22. Dewey, *Art as Experience*, 46.

ing and incoming energy that makes an experience to be an experience. Artistic expression of any kind not only does the actual creation of the art but also embodies within itself the attitude of the perceiver as the work is being created. This incorporation allows the art to be a work of the aesthetic. For Dewey, one who perceives is one who must create one's own experience:

> [The perceiver's] creation must include relations comparable to those which the original producer underwent. They are not the same in any literal sense. But with the perceiver, as with the artist, there must be an ordering of the elements of the whole that is in form, although not in detail, the same as the process of organization the creator of the work consciously experienced. . . . The artist selected, simplified, clarified, abridged and condensed according to his interest. The beholder must go through these operations according to his point of view and interest. In both, an act of abstraction that is an extraction of what is significant, takes place. In both, there is comprehension in its literal signification—that is, a gathering together of details and particulars physically scattered into an experienced whole. There is work done on the part of the percipient as there is on the part of the artist.[23]

A Practical Example

An example of putting Dewey's theories into practical perspective is a summer enrichment project in which a group of teens came to visit Camp Kingdom. Camp Kingdom was not classified as a Christian camp, and its enrollment was not limited to those who are Christian. Christian moral principles were taught, however—particularly how to love God and one's neighbor through song, dance, sports, education, community service, and drama. On one particular day, a group of about seventy-five teens from across the country and the world were in New York to attend a liturgical dance conference, entitled "Purify...," sponsored by The Greater Allen AME Cathedral of New York. They were scheduled to visit Camp Kingdom in order to dance and participate with the campers during a morning gathering. About twenty volunteers from both the camp and the conference were asked to share their faith by dancing to a song entitled,

23. Dewey, *Art as Experience*, 54.

"Never Would Have Made It."[24] This invitation came immediately after one of the dance facilitators and a group of teens from the conference had just finished performing a gospel and hip-hop dance to the same song. The invitation asked more teens to tell their faith story through movement voice, an artistic endeavor most young people would consider challenging, yet not impossible, to achieve:

> There were about thirty volunteers who took their places on either the school stage or in one of the three aisles of the auditorium and proceeded to dance their life of faith to the song. Boys, girls, [and] teens from both the camp and conference were among those who danced their testimony, which encapsulated every adult, teenager, and youth in attendance. Even the few public school security guards who were on duty found themselves coming inside the auditorium and all were brought to a level of faith that indeed made everyone confront who and what they believed. A pregnant hush fell over the entire auditorium as tears flowed down the cheeks of onlookers; arms linked and hugged, bringing the hearts and minds of those sitting next to each other closer together. Some sat silently with hands placed over their mouths; however, eyes were clearly fixed upon the dancers, both those in nearby aisles and those situated on the stage.[25]

This challenge had a pattern and structure that gave life to an experiential moment. This was a living experience for all, both the dancer and the observer. For the more than 300 people who were watching this on-the-spot dance improvisation, the actions and consequences were joined together to formulate meaningful perceptions that gave direct and personal meaning to everyone's experiences. People were joined by this experience, uniting personal experiences of faith regardless of age, gender, culture, and belief. It seemed the scope and content of the relations measured how significant an experience this truly was. Learning took place on a practical, emotional, and intellectual level for all of those who were in attendance.

This experience was consistent with Dewey's notion of education as the reorganization of experience, giving every subsequent experience a clearer perspective through which the individual can arise and grow in learning capacity and comprehension. Experience allows instruction

24. Sapp, "Never Would Have Made It." For the full song text, see Appendix H.
25. Turner, Curtis, director of the camp, in an interview with the author, 2010.

to take center stage on its own terms in order for the individual to fully engage as a learning participant. Allowing the subject material to run its full course within the experience affords the practical, the emotional, and the intellectual aspects of the educative act to gain momentum within the individuals participating in the experience. Perception occurs once an action and its consequence are joined in union together. Continuity, interaction, and sound objectives undergird the relationship found between education and experience.

Dewey's theory of education through experience lays a foundation for religious education and its role in presenting monumental opportunities for learning and developing faith within the church as a community of learning.[26] Every individual who regularly attends church service, regardless of age, should be given multiple opportunities to discover and learn the meaning of Christianity as well as what it means to be Christian. The church represents a type of microcosm of the world in which one lives, where generations of people—young or old, male or female, and with diverse learning styles, cultures, and economic backgrounds—come together to learn how to worship and love God while experientially learning what it means to love one's neighbor. This type of religious setting can utilize Dewey's educational theory in ways that are insurmountable for the congregation as a collective community—where learning transpires and growth for the heart, mind, and spirit never ends.

The work of religious educators Charles R. Foster, Norma Cook Everist, and Ann Streaty Wimberly promotes religious education in the context of the church as a community of learning. The understanding of experiential learning and aesthetic education in the work of these three religious educators reveals a strong Deweyan influence. My examination of their work will be done through the lens of John Dewey's educational theories. First, however, the meaning of congregation and community is clarified through C. Ellis Nelson's definition of what church is and how it is composed.

26. See Dewey, *Experience and Education*.

The Value of Experience in Understanding
Congregational Life

The term congregation is defined within the context of church life. The use of the term congregation is a way to define what church is and what the church does. How congregation is defined will be addressed through the work of C. Ellis Nelson. Nelson defines congregation in the following way:

> A congregation is the place where the Christian faith is communicated from past to present, where the faith is interpreted for the needs of the day, and where the faith might grow stronger by exercising it with people who share the faith.[27]

According to Nelson, a congregation is the place where Christian faith is communicated to those individuals who come together to learn of its effectiveness—from its very beginnings, to the present, and in its relevancy for the years to come. Faith is interpreted and explained according to the spoken or unspoken needs that presently confront the congregation. Just the same, faith is also explained as a growing process that exhibits its strength to the congregation as they share their faith with one another.

Nelson writes that "the *particular* congregation is the community in which persons experience the meaning of the Christian faith and the community to which they refer mentally as they make decisions in all the circumstances of their lives."[28] The term community means "fellowship," "common," "a group of people residing in the same locality and under the same government," "a group or class having common interests," and "likeness or identity."[29]

Similarly, for Dewey, there is a likeness, a fellowship, and a coming together of common interests that formulate the classification of a people who form a community. Nelson defines congregation as that community of people who experience the meaning of the Christian faith. It is this same community that helps the individuals within the community make decisions of faith concerning the life circumstances they each confront.

In order to understand the congregation as a community for learning, experience must be seen as the way it develops its own understanding of congregational life. For pastors, ministerial or church leaders,

---

27. Nelson, *Congregations*, 6.

28. Nelson, *Congregations*, 18.

29. Pickett, *College Dictionary*, 233.

religious educators, and lay persons, experience is a valuable tool when it is utilized and reflected upon. Experience needs to be placed in a larger perspective where it has a rightful place. Nelson contends that to understand the dynamic of the congregation it must first be understood as being more than simply the sum of its parts:

> It is more because the whole includes all ages and conditions of members; therefore, it represents the body of Christ and reminds us of our obligation to each other. It is *different* because the promise of God's Spirit is to be present in the community of believers; therefore, there is a need to search for God's will for the *whole* congregation. . . . The whole congregation should be the reality about which we must think if we are to bring about significant change.[30]

Education is an important necessity in the dynamic growth and development of the congregation as both its parts and as a whole. Purposeful educational strategies can affect the dynamic interaction that goes on continuously within congregations. Purposeful and critical reflective conversations about faith and moral choices among church members is just one way religious education can assist the experiential process of faith growth and formation. The work of Charles R. Foster attempts to construct ways by which a vibrant and faithful education encompasses the entire congregation. It is this type of education that is not only formational but also transformational.

Charles Foster and the Importance of Meaning Making in Educating Congregations

The work of Charles Foster may appear to be rather straightforward. When it is examined more thoroughly, however, it is quite profound. His goal is to develop a format for Christian religious education that is both emancipatory and transformational in nature.[31] Foster does this by emphasizing three specific tasks. The *first* is to build up congregations—as communities of faith—to be the body of Christ in this fragmented world. The *second* is to develop the ability to identify and articulate the relevance of the gospel in an age inundated with information and confused by new knowledge. The *third* is to nurture hope among people overwhelmed by

---

30. Nelson, *Congregations*, 4–5.
31. Foster, *Educating Congregations*, 13.

wars, natural disasters, and social, economic, and health crises. Foster sets out to discover how the church can participate in the "formative and transformative events of Christian tradition and witness."[32] Foster's research goes hand in hand with Dewey's understanding of community as communication—where the participation of people within the learning process is assured due to a common understanding.

Meaning making for Foster "involves the interplay of cognitive and affective activity."[33] He believes that knowing and doing are intensified by feelings, and feelings enlightened by knowing. Something has meaning when it reveals both the significance and purpose it has for the individual. For religious meaning to make itself significant and purposeful for the congregation, it must first establish a communal bond, thereby facilitating conversation. If the church community is culturally and economically diverse, the significance and purpose of Christianity would need to be developed through a common interpretation and understanding that allows for its deeper meaning of love to transpire. Foster clarifies this point as follows:

> Something has significance if we "think" it is important. But its significance is enhanced if we also "feel" it is important. In a similar fashion, we may discern the purpose of something intellectually. But our relationship to that purpose has to do with its potential to motivate us—a willful and affective process.[34]

Another aspect of meaning making is the fact that the individual feels a sense of being at home with the subject. People find comfort within meaning. Within Christianity, the meaning of salvation, repentance, and love from a historical, biblical perspective must also provide comfort to every member of the congregation, despite their gender, culture, class, learning capacities, age, and denomination. This can only be done if the educational act of sharing faith is conceptualized and allows space for the comfort of all who reside within the congregation.

Foster further explains that meaning making brings insight. In this case, Foster defines insight as "the capacity to see from the inside of something. One knows more than the information on the surface of things. We participate in its possibilities."[35] Another characteristic of

32. Foster, *Educating Congregations*, 8.
33. Foster, *Educating Congregations*, 89.
34. Foster, *Educating Congregations*, 89.
35. Foster, *Educating Congregations*, 95.

meaning for Foster lies in the human quest for intellectual freedom. He claims that one is not "truly free to think until one has both a basic grasp of the correspondence of words and facts and enough familiarity with that interaction to begin to play with its possibilities."[36] An example of this is in discovering the meaning of the Christian concept of grace from an internal perspective taken from Romans, which states:

> But the gift is not like the trespass. For if the many died by the trespass of the one man, how much more did God's grace and the gift that came by the grace of the one, Jesus Christ, overflow to the many! (Rom 5:15)

An understanding of grace can become more effective and more insightful from an experiential type of teaching. A church-wide teaching based on this verse on grace from the Letter to the Romans can stimulate the hunt for its application in many ways and through many channels. From the youth in Sunday school to the worshiping community during Sunday service, the entire congregation could be challenged to understand the depth of the meaning of grace as defined in Romans through exercises that focus on grace as being both granted and received. To highlight the topic of grace, choir songs might have grace as their theme for the time period of this study; the weekly bible study classes might emphasize grace as the study topic; and sermons on grace might complement the congregational teachings on the subject as well. A church-related assignment could also ask the congregation to work on granting a person or persons grace over a period of about two to three weeks. The significance of this assignment would be to grant grace to someone who did not warrant or deserve it. This type of exercise might help the congregation to gain a deeper insight into the type of grace God truly bestowed upon fallen humanity through the death and resurrection of Jesus Christ. This type of grace is motivated by a supernatural understanding of love—God's love—and would also undergird the theological education the entire congregation would embark upon.

Conversations between church members can begin during the course of the first week, whether between neighbors, teens at school, or simply those who meet one another throughout the time frame. Such conversations would not only begin to add insight but also introduce a plethora of conversations that might become emancipatory and transformative for those participating as well as those who choose to listen. If

---

36. Foster, *Educating Congregations*, 96.

theological conversations could take place outside the walls of the church, these conversations would be all the more fruitful once the members of the congregation come together during the course of the week. This notion supports Dewey's understanding of the educational process as one that functions socially. It is within this context that education fosters, nurtures, and cultivates the possibility of changed behavior. This type of education leads and brings forth a comprehension that shapes, forms, and molds new behaviors for the good of the self, the church, and humanity. Instruction such as this can give clear and attainable understanding to the individual members as well as the collective church body.

Meaning Making and the Church as a Disciple Community

Foster expands his understanding of meaning making by seeing the church as a disciple community. This is an adaptation from the work of Douglas John Hall, who explains that when congregations facilitate the quest for meaning, they also engage in theological education:

> A disciple community is a community engaged in and committed to theological self-reflection. Christian meanings emerge from the reflection of the church on the "subject matter of the Christian faith" with those "who struggle with this subject matter and live in the sphere of its influence."[37]

Foster identifies six characteristics of a disciple community. The *first* focuses on particular events that highlight the life of the church. An "event-full" education, Foster suggests, gives foundation to the formational growth of the church.[38] Event-full education is comprised of seasonal events that encourage and foster congregational participation. Therefore, if the church focuses its energies on one of these events, this action emphasizes congregational mutuality in its education.

The *second* characteristic promotes the partnership between clergy and laity. Using the example above, the clergy could participate with the laity in not only the teaching and theological preparation for such an exercise but also in the artistic endeavors that could emerge out of such a teaching. Artistic examples such as poetry, song, and artwork can be created from the perspective of the congregation that places grace as its

37. Foster, *Educating Congregations*, 100.
38. Foster, *Educating Congregations*, 102.

theme. During the course of a Sunday service, poetry can be shared or a song can be sung by the young people based upon their "grace" experiences. A short scenario can be presented during one of the bible study sessions which captures the challenges members of the congregation faced in learning how to grant grace to those who may not have deserved it, but were granted grace through God's love. Artwork can be created by the youngsters during their Sunday school class which may reveal their impressions of what took place during their encounter with the grace exercise.

The *third* characteristic presents the local congregation as the primary context in which theological reflection takes place. This is shown as the example of grace applied by the members of the congregation themselves. Grace is granted to anyone God deems fit—not simply on those who are within the walls of the church. Therefore, the congregational members would learn how to rely on the movement of the Holy Spirit to lead them to the people who would receive the unmerited favor of grace.

The *fourth* allows for theological meanings to emerge from negotiations among a variety of perspectives. A variety of meanings could emerge from this congregational exercise on grace. Depending upon the gender, age, culture, learning abilities, and economic status, variations of meanings may emerge that give foundation and identity to the congregation during this time. This type of development supports Dewey's premise that our environment plays an essential role in creating conditions that promote and stimulate certain visible and tangible ways of acting within the social context and activity. Dewey affirms the sharing and partnership the activity grants the participant. In this case, the entire church environment stimulates a feeling of compatibility between the community members, laity, ministerial staff, and those they will encounter who are located outside the peripheries of the church. Among the ages found within the congregation, the individual's beliefs and ideas within the congregation will take on a form similar to those of others found within the congregation.

The *fifth* pushes meaning to emerge out of a struggle against irrelevant meaning and application. This characteristic will probably be one of the most challenging, as it presents an "alienation of spirit," caused by texts and practices that people do not understand, appreciate, or trust.[39] For example, referring to the above theological exercise on grace,

---

39. Foster, *Educating Congregations*, 103.

teaching will have to go forth in understanding what grace is and how grace is not deserved, is not earned, and yet is granted from the only perspective that can tolerate such a position—and that position is love. Such an understanding of love would have to be explained and spoken about from a variety of perspectives for true understanding to emerge. This understanding of love, however, will also have to be demonstrated— not just in granting grace but also in loving one's neighbor, family, and even self when it appears impossible to do so. This lesson on love will have to translate and affect all aspects of life, within every member of the congregation, in order to comprehend the full meaning of God's unmerited favor.

The *sixth* and final characteristic calls for disciplined reflection that promotes a better comprehension of the event and the implications of the event upon the lives of the congregation. The ability to honestly reflect on the struggles and the new understandings requires a pure approach to the theological educative exercise. Dewey presses this point in his understanding of experiential learning.[40] Learning does not take place when a routine action is done in which the action is automatic. As explained earlier, it may increase skill to do a particular thing, and although it may be classified as educative, it does not lead to new perceptions, connections, or bearings. This also holds true for an impulsive action, where learning may be achieved by doing something which was not necessarily understood. Here, learning is only achieved because, after the act is performed, there are results which were not noted previously. For Dewey, then, the essential idea of education as continuous reconstruction is that it identifies both the end result and the process. This can also transpire in the reflective, theological exercise on grace. After experiencing such an exercise, taking the time to explain the true meaning of grace theologically can only bring deeper meaning to understanding what Christianity is and to the meaning of being Christian in a world of pluralities and differences. Norma Cook Everist examines the task of the faith community in developing a curriculum of learning that is worldwide in its scope. In exploring the concepts of "re-membering" and "differently-abled" as they apply to the ministry for teaching, Everist seeks to define what community learning truly is in the life of the church and all of its membership.

40. See Dewey, *Democracy and Education.*

Norma Cook Everist's Understanding
of Community Learning

Norma Cook Everist contends that the faith community's curriculum is much more than material on paper to be read and recited. She firmly believes that it embraces all of the people in this time and context as well as people in God's global and historic community.[41] Everist states that:

> religious education is the ministry of all teaching activities, verbal and nonverbal, including cognitive, affective, and life activity. The Bible is a living reality which includes the account of God's interactions with people in biblical times, but also God existentially interacting with all those who encounter Scripture. What is important is not teaching *about* the Bible, trying to prove what it is or is not, but, insofar as it is inspired revelation and God's outpouring of love, making it the solid foundation for religious education, which is encounter with the living God. The church as learning community becomes an arena for such an encounter.[42]

With this definition, Everist seeks to fashion a methodology of religious education that encounters two aspects of God: first, the inspired revelation of God, and second, the outpouring of God's love. Therefore, for Everist, religious education sets a platform whereby the teacher and the learner encounter the living God with fluidity, and the church is one place in which this encounter materializes.

Drawing on the epistles, Everist further attests that, within Christian religious education, we teach "so that the cross of Christ might not be emptied of its power."[43] This scriptural text highlights both the inspired revelation of God and the outpouring of God's love.[44] Everist contends that God gathers God's people so that they are rooted in the wisdom of the cross. Using this theme as the highlight, there are potential Christian communities all around us; it is the task of the religious educator to recognize them, gather them, and affirm them.[45]

---

41. Everist, *Church*, 9.

42. Everist, *Church*, 22.

43. Everist, *Church*, 29.

44. "For Christ did not send me to baptize, but to preach the gospel not with words of human wisdom, lest the cross of Christ be emptied of its power" (1 Cor 1:17).

45. Everist, *Church*, 29.

Everist's theory of the community curriculum is in agreement with Dewey's theory of education as a social function, where education is seen as a process that fosters, nurtures, and cultivates. Everist seeks to allow the opportunity for learning to transpire for every church member socially within every aspect of church life. These moments must be sought after and found by the religious educator. These moments are not simply restricted to the confines of classroom instruction, but are present within any activity that fosters, nurtures, and cultivates knowledge of the revelation of God. Christian communities can be recognized, gathered, and affirmed within the settings of congregational worship, membership nurturing, ministry outreach, and congregational fellowship. It is here that education, for Dewey, is a process of activity that shapes, forms, molds, and, as stated earlier, "is a shaping into the standard form of social activity."[46]

Re-membering, Differently-Abled, and the Utilization of Resources

Everist suggests that the religious educator can compile an enriching curriculum if it flows from several vantage points. Three that are highlighted here are the ministry of re-membering, the understanding of the term "differently-abled," and the successful utilization of resources, including the artistic. Everist states:

> The community engages in its ministry of re-membering the body of Christ, literally incorporating all the differently abled people in the parish. Thus the curriculum is formed, God and God's people in this time and place. All else is resource, but substantial resource it is. The community needs to learn how to utilize who they are and who they are becoming, adding appropriate curriculum resources, developing a mutual accountability to sustain and cultivate the entire community.[47]

The ministry of re-membering emphasizes the belonging element people wish to feel within any organization, but particularly within the faith community of the church. Everist believes that the need to be re-membered can strengthen a person's sense of identity and purpose as members of the church who work and care for each other. Everist relies

46. Everist, *Church*, 10.
47. Everist, *Church*, 23.

on the twelfth chapter of 1 Corinthians, where the church is illustrated as one body with many parts that are different in size, function, and ability, yet function together in a unique and cohesive way.[48] This type of body cannot be dismembered because it is the church community who is called to care, suffer, and rejoice with one another. For Everist, this is the call to re-member what Christ has joined in this rich unity of the church that is situated within a great sea of diversity.

Within this body, all members have unique gifts that are united in the one call to discipleship.[49] Discipleship is not an individual endeavor but rather one that calls forth the gifts that have been given to every Christian believer to be made manifest during their joining together as a church community of learning. There are a variety of gifts found within the New Testament that are given to the church to utilize and build up the body of Christ. Everist emphasizes the gifts found in the Christian Scriptures of 1 Corinthians 12:7–11, however, those recorded in Romans 12:6–7 can also be cited here.[50] These gifts of the Spirit highlight prophesy, serving, teaching, encouraging, contributing, leadership, and showing mercy, which are gifts for use in the edification and instructional well-being of every member within the church community. Religious educators need the leadership and the encouraging skills offered by the text in Romans to fulfill the call in developing a re-membering congregation of disciples who follow the teachings of Christ and the power of the cross in order to love God and one another more sincerely and effectively. According to Everist, this means that all gifts are necessary for this to be a learning community in mission.[51]

Everist's use of re-membering clarifies Dewey's understanding of education. Dewey contends that educative experiences that are mis-educative promote stunted, stifled, and distorted growth, whereas educative

48. "The body is a unit, though it is made up of many parts, and though all its parts are many, they form one body" (1 Cor 12:12).

49. Everist, *Church*, 35.

50. "Now to each one the manifestation of the Spirit is given for the common good. To one there is given through the Spirit the message of wisdom, to another the message of knowledge by means of the same Spirit, to another faith by the same Spirit, to another gift of healing by that one Spirit, to anther miraculous posers, to another prophecy, to another distinguishing between spirits, to another speaking in different kinds of tongues, and to still another the interpretation of tongues. All these are the work of one and the same Spirit, and he gives them to each one, just as he determines" (1 Corinthians 12: 7–11).

51. Everist, *Church*, 35.

experiences that are worthwhile develop a positive *hunger* for the furthering of more growing experiences, as mentioned earlier. Dewey's concept
of continuity, interaction, and objective conditions allows Everist's use
of re-membering to restate the learning stream of the church as a community where the gifts of each member are allowed to grow, influence,
comfort, and care for all persons. The social set up by which interactions
and learning situations transpire are made available through the process
of re-membering. It allows the community of believers to understand
the true definition of being Christian, not only in word but also in deed,
producing a furthering of educative experiences.

A useful term that Everist develops is "differently-abled."[52] Everist
implies that "by virtue of being a diverse creation and reassembled into
one body of Christ, suffering and rejoicing together, the gifts of the Spirit
can all be used."[53] Differently-abled is a term that allows people to see how
they view one another regardless of their physical, mental, and emotional
well-being. Everist explains that each person, in some way, is able, and
each person is disabled, regardless of whether the disability is hidden (as
in heart disease or lupus) or revealed (as in cerebral palsy or deafness).
The goal is not to change, or even to "cure" certain "disabilities" but rather
to care in a way which gives attention to each person individually.[54]

While the term disability does not discriminate, people do discriminate against those who are disabled. As Everist puts it, "The problem is not
the ability of people with disabilities to learn and to teach, but attitudes
on the part of the temporarily abled which 'handicap' their learning."[55]
Everist asserts that each member of the congregation is differently-abled
to some degree, so humans are placed on a playing field that is not only
even, but is also one that should openly respect God's human creation
and the gifts that have been bestowed upon each. Individuals are to rejoice in remembering each person as one who is capable of both learning
and teaching. People are all differently-abled creatures who are seen as
equal in the sight of God.

The gifts that are given by God are gifts for the kingdom to be utilized for the good of all. Everist's strategies push the religious educator to
brainstorm on how such a stance and method of re-membering can be

52. Everist, *Church*, 29.
53. Everist, *Church*, 29.
54. Everist, *Church*, 36.
55. Everist, *Church*, 36.

incorporated within the church community. One question addresses the "other" within the complexity of the congregation: how can the learning community of the church prove instrumental for those who have special needs? All differently-abled persons live with special needs; therefore, the church should be open and aware of how their attendance teaches the entire church body to grow further as a result of their presence and their gifts. How can the worship service adopt an awareness and appreciation for all differently-abled people? In addition, the "other" examines the elders who live with special needs. What role does reception play in recognizing the situations and presence of the elders?

Everist believes that curriculum, broadly speaking, is an inclusion of all learning experiences, beginning with God and God's people, in time and place. She states:

> In the complexity, even in the midst of the confusion and controversy of diverse people who do not understand one another, God has created and will sustain community, thereby creating living curriculum—one which we will never complete but one which is real. God is in the center of this concept of church as a learning community with all of God's creating, redeeming, and liberating activity.[56]

This living curriculum is one that encounters both the word of God and the people of God with the presence of God in a complexity of learning experiences and applications that sustain, heal, and transform the life of God's people in ways that are concrete yet creatively imaginative. God is a God of great imagination and wonder, endowed with great resources. In response, religious educators have to learn how to be exposed to such creativity as it relates to the artistic and the teaching resources found within this area of expression.

The aesthetic is not an intruder that comes from outside of experience—and especially not from the outside of the educative act of experience. Rather, the aesthetic is the clarified and intensified development of the traits that belong to every normal experience. Artistic expression unites the same relation of doing and undergoing, outgoing and incoming energy that makes an experience to be an experience. Dewey contends:

> The conception of conscious experience as a perceived relation between doing and undergoing enables us to understand the

---

56. Everist, *Church*, 46.

connection that art as production and perception and appreciation as enjoyment sustain to each other.[57]

Artistic expression of any kind results in the actual creation of art
and embodies, within itself, the attitude the perceiver has while the work
is being created. Perception is an act of the going out of energy in order to
receive—not a withholding of energy. Although this experience is not the
same as what the artist has undergone, perceivers must create their own
experience. There must be a process of organization, however, for acquir-
ing what is witnessed, what is perceived. Without the act of recreation,
the object is not perceived as a work of art.

When incorporating the artistic in instructional teaching, the
educative relationship between the lesson and the learner is incorporated, comprehended, and implemented. The artistic is solely a tool to
experience for learning and instruction to transpire between teacher
and learner. Yet it also means that the choice of the artistic—whether it
is music, drama, dance, or art—is the most concrete of choices for the
lesson to be taught, understood, and grasped by the learner. When the
lesson is being conceived and created, it is the learner which occupies the
teacher's mind first, the lesson second. Therefore, when the arts are used,
they are to be made effective in the teaching of biblical and faith concepts
and not simply as extra, added attractions. The arts are inspirational as
educational resources; for the religious educator to explore and awaken
the voice of the artistic within every individual in learning about a God
who is also artistic.

For Everist, there are four essential elements that shed a concern on
the caring of the learner within the aesthetic learning experience.[58] She
purports these four elements of care will assist the religious educator in
curriculum building, resource development, and teaching opportunities
that are imaginative and effective in developing the church community
in ways that will lead to learning experiences that are aesthetic in nature.
The four elements are described below.

The *first* is the caring about the learner, which is the caring for the
learner's imaginations. This pertains to the many ways in which lessons
are presented utilizing the arts. The *second* is the caring about the content
where the religious educator's belief in the Christian faith is strong. Lively
lessons and artistic presentations can reveal the obvious affirmations

57. Dewey, *Art as Experience*, 48.
58. Everist, *Church*, 112.

as well as the critical questions the teacher themselves may have. Such honesty can bring about a positive and reflective enthusiasm about the content within the student. The *third* deals with the selection of the appropriate teaching style within the artistic, where the goal and function is to stimulate and ignite the imagination of the learner. The *fourth* focuses on how well the artistic presentation is done in order to allow the content, interaction, and experience to stretch both the instructor and the community of learners.

To fully comprehend Everist's four essential elements in terms of aesthetic learning, liturgical dance will be used as an example. Within the worship setting, there is already found gestural movements in motion. These include the gestures of sitting, standing, walking, praying hands, kneeling, and the lifting up of hands. For some churches, these gestures extend to include the clapping of hands and the waving of hands which are all gestures that appear in the Book of Psalms as physical directives for the reader to do in the presence of God. Liturgical dance is the physical movement responding to the spiritual and gestural directives found in the Psalms. These gestures can simply remain as they are given or they can develop artistically to become more complex movements depending upon the teaching and occasion.[59]

An example would be a Sunday morning service where the congregation sings a song of praise that is accompanied by simple movement gestures. The song, "Welcome into this Place," is classified as a song of adoration and praise.[60] It is inspired by the Psalm, "I was glad when they said to me, 'Let us go to the house of the LORD'" (Ps 122:1).[61] Once again utilizing the theme of grace, the gestures to this song can be done by the entire congregation, helping to internalize the meaning of both the scriptural text and the song text while also gaining further understanding of the meaning of grace. In this case ,the meaning of grace is twofold. First, grace is extended by God to God's people, who are invited to worship God with their entire being. The second meaning of grace is the acknowledgement and acceptance of God's grace by the congregants themselves, who sing with the awareness that God's unmerited favor is being extended to them.

59. Turner, "If David had not Danced," 49–58 and 80–91.

60. The text of the song, "Welcome into this Place," written by Orlando Jaurez and arranged by Jimmie Abbington, can be found in Appendix F.

61. Carpenter and Williams, *African American Hymnal*, 114.

The purpose of doing movement gestures by the congregation is to internalize the meaning of the words of the song. For learning to be internalized, for most people, the repetition of meaning must take place, so that they can fully understand what is being conveyed. Within the worship setting, a selection of prayers or songs can incorporate movement gestures in order to critically reflect upon the theme of either prayer or song.[62] This particular example utilizes the entire congregation as a community of learning where the participation is done by all.[63] In like manner, all parishioners in attendance can participate in this movement of praise, regardless of ability. Depending upon the individual or disability, it may be necessary for some of the movements to be slightly altered, but the invitation for all parishioners to participate is both essential and central to support the understanding that the church is truly a community place of learning.

The first line of the song is, "Welcome into this Place," which can call for the simple gesture of having the congregation open up their arms as if to welcome the presence of the Holy Spirit into their hearts, both individually and collectively. The second line is, "Welcome into this broken vessel," which can call for the congregation to open their arms once again, but then to cross their hands, bringing them inward, to acknowledge their brokenness. The next line is, "You desire to abide in the praises of your people," where the congregation can bring their arms upward, toward the ceiling, and then wave them from side to side, signifying the presence of God and, with the waving of their arms, the praises of the people. The last line of the song is, "So we lift our hands and we lift our hearts as we offer up this praise unto your name." After the waving of the arms, the congregation can bring their arms down to raise them up again, demonstrating the lifting up of their hands. Then they can bring their hands to their hearts and extend them upward, demonstrating the lifting up of their hearts. The offering of their praise unto the Lord can be signified by the waving of their hands, from side to side, and then bringing them back down again.[64]

In order to help the congregation learn the words and movement, this song of adoration can be repeated a number of times. Again, this artistic exercise can be carried out by every differently abled person in

62. Turner, "If David had not Danced," 49–52.

63. DeSola, *Spirit Moves*, 13–14.

64. Carpenter and Williams, *African American Hymnal*, 114.

the congregation. The movements can simply be adopted for all, to execute them in their own way while still feeling directly connected to both song and movement. Once this is done, the internalization of the song's meaning and the congregation's critical reflection upon that meaning transpires accordingly. A further learning on the subject of grace takes place both corporately and individually through an aesthetic experience.

The work of Anne Streaty Wimberly in the nurturing of faith and hope illustrates worship as a teaching arena. The effectiveness of the worship gathering as an essential teaching methodology for the religious educator is seen through the insights of Jeff Astley as explained below.

The Role of Worship in Christian Learning

This last section discusses the active role of worship and its components in teaching Christian education to the church as a community place of learning. In examining the role of worship in Christian learning, Jeff Astley brings attention to the implicit catechesis that takes place within the worship of the church. He explains this further:

> This latter process, deriving as it does from ritual (words) and ceremonial (acts) of worship, is hardly an intentional activity and certainly not a systematic one. However it does result in a change in a person as a consequence of conscious experience. We may say, therefore, that it produces 'learning', even if it is not itself 'education.' . . . What is thus learned in Christian worship is a range of emotions, experiences and attitudes that lie at the heart of Christian spirituality.[65]

Worship is an end in itself, without any ulterior motive or purpose. With this in mind, Astley portrays worship as an activity which "expresses" certain religious attitudes, affections, and experiences and tends to "evoke" them.[66] In their worship, he explains, Christians express Christian attitudes and emotions. Such expressions serve to reinforce those attitudes and emotions in some worshippers and to evoke them in others. In addition, they also supply other people with "secondhand" expressions of what it means to be Christian. Because worship expresses religious experience, other people learn "about" a Christian's religious experience from his or her worship. In so far as worship sustains, deepens, and evokes

65. Astley, "Role of Worship," 244.
66. Astley, "Role of Worship," 245.

religious experience, he suggests that it helps both the worshippers and others to learn from their religious experiences about the nature of religious reality.

Astley continues by affirming that at the heart of worship is a numinous or spiritual sense of the Holy God. The numen or spirit is experienced "outside oneself, over against the worshipper."[67] This type of mystical occurrence can be found within Christian worship. It is here, that God is known in the "journey inwards," in the ultimate union with the worshipper's own deepest being. Regardless of whatever account of objective religious experience is accepted, the point for Astley is that worship may serve to prepare for, allow, and evoke such experiences of God: "It may put people in the place, psychologically and epistemologically, where God can be 'seen' and 'heard.'"[68] Following Dewey's theory on experiential learning, this type of religious understanding and worship is learning through experience with a vengeance.

Astley also draws on the definition of catechesis as defined by John Berntsen. Berntsen proposes that catechesis is the "shaping of religious emotions and affections in the context of teaching doctrine," contending that there cannot be a wedge driven between emotion/experience and belief/doctrine.[69] He argues that all human acts are cognitive-affective and cannot be separated since merely affective or merely cognitive acts do not exist. Astley continues this line of study by emphasizing that even the more explicit educational processes that take place before, during, and after worship go along with these more implicit shapings of religious affections and attitudes. He declares that the explicit educational processes are the verbal, cognitive, often analytical, and critical "left lobe" activities, and the implicit shapings are the intuitive, aesthetic, imaginative, and non-verbal "right lobe" activities. Astley explains this further:

> The good health of Christian education is dependent upon the operation of both lobes of the brain, so that Christian truth is learned both affectively and cognitively. It is when reason and emotion are divorced that religion most rapidly loses its sense and its power for people. Religion is a cognitive-affective activity.[70]

67. Astley, "Role of Worship," 249.
68. Astley, "Role of Worship," 249.
69. Astley, "Role of Worship," 249.
70. Astley, "Role of Worship," 250.

Astley concludes by suggesting that the teaching of Christian doctrine and the formation of Christian attitudes must take place together—neither process can take place authentically without the other. Christian worship is the paradigm situation for the joint activity to take place.[71]

> In the explicit catechesis of liturgy, the Christian story, always the basic format for Christian doctrine, is proclaimed in the context of affective, experiential worship so that it can be felt and experienced. There, salvation is preached and people feel it; God speaks and we hear God for ourselves. And there, too, through the implicit catechesis of liturgy, we come to learn the Christian mode of being in the world as our attitudes, emotions and experiences are formed through the symbolic power of ritual and ceremonial. There it is that we become fully Christian.[72]

Anne Streaty Wimberly and Black Worship as Nurturing Experience

The black worship experience is highlighted by Ann Streaty Wimberly in her work on congregational worship.[73] She focuses on the evocative manner in which worship life in the black church nurtures the faith and hope of the worshipping congregation. Wimberly defines nurture as the basic meaning of the vitality of life and insists that without its nourishment, life would diminish. Therefore, all of those who comprise the black worshipping congregation, the pastor, liturgists, musicians, and worshipers are those who serve as communal nurturing agents who make possible the forming and sustaining of an alive faith and hope.

Evocative nurture "builds on the view that worshipers desire and are ready for nurture and have the wherewithal to receive nurture and discern its meaning for their lives."[74] Wimberly points out that black worshipers come into the worshiping congregation seeking a nourishment that affirms and responds to their capacity to receive it, struggle with it, and to discover, build on, and act on what is enormously important to their lives as Christians. She states, "I am using this term here to denote what we, as black persons, hold within us, as we worship, about the positive and troubling realities of life in general and our own lives

71. Astley, "Role of Worship," 250.
72. Astley, "Role of Worship," 250.
73. See Wimberly, *Faith & Hope.*
74. Wimberly, *Faith & Hope,* xv.

in particular."[75] Wimberly names God as the evocator who reaches out and invites the people of God to reach back and to vow that they will not look backwards but will move forward, "to see what the end will be."[76] In this context, faith and hope become verbs that reflect matters of the head and heart. She describes faith as the belief or trust in the relationship with God and God's relationship with God's people through Jesus Christ and the Holy Spirit. Hope points to the expectation and endeavors to live confidently and courageously in community after the model of Jesus in times of triumph and in the midst of hard trial and tribulations:

> This book is intended to explore in depth how faith and hope are formed in persons in an age of nihilism. Moreover, the exploration of nurture in the black worshiping congregation seeks to capture new awareness that worship is a central context for the educational ministry of the church.[77]

Wimberly's premise that the evocative manner in which worship life in the black church nurtures the faith and hope of the worshipping congregation will be viewed through the lens of three nurturing activities that emerge out of every worship service: the activities of preaching, music, and prayer.

Preaching, Music, and Prayer as Nurturing and Teachable Pathways

Preaching

According to Wimberly, black preaching is one of three essential pathways through which the nurture of faith and hope are carried out in the black worshiping congregation. As a nurturing pathway, the sermon is an evocative trigger that motivates black worshipers to live faith-full and hope-filled lives after the pattern of Jesus Christ. The preacher is compelled to say something that addresses the needs of the people, directing the message to heart and head, and the intended communication on which nurture centers is at once relational, practical, specific, and intended to have evocative power.

75. Wimberly, *Faith & Hope*, xv.
76. Wimberly, *Faith & Hope*, xix.
77. Wimberly, *Faith & Hope*, xxvi.

Wimberly points out that preaching in the black worshiping congregation which nurtures faith and hope incorporates three primary functions; *prophetic*, *priestly*, and *apostolic* functions. Her definition of *prophetic* preaching includes the literal building of a case—especially through story—that can evoke in worshipers a deepening faith in the nearness of God. This function in black preaching includes an aspect of nurture that involves unsettling worshipers in a way that pushes them beyond a position of complacency toward the necessary and intentional struggle for justice in everyday life:

> Here, my focus is on describing the prophetic function of sermons that nurtures worshipers in a way that brings about heightened awareness and an existence that exemplifies an alive faith and hope in church and world. The phrase "a homiletic of protest" is a helpful descriptor of the prophetic function.[78]

Underlying this aspect of the protest sermon, Wimberly shows that the dealing of the oppression or dehumanizing treatment of human beings is as much an inner struggle as it is an outer battle. Therefore, the prophetic sermon reflects the notion that dealing with any form of subjugation, denigration, or cruelty requires one to become uncomfortable and dissatisfied with any evidence of these forms of inequities that one observes, participates in, and too often creates.

Likewise, prophetic evocation prompts the wakefulness of the One who calls humanity to justice, kindness, and a humble relationship with God.[79] Wimberly proposes that the prophetic word is to evoke the congregation's embrace of faith and hope as verbs; actions in response to God, the ultimate evocator, who beckons the congregation to move into the unknown future with the will to be reflections of Jesus Christ in a hurting world. Consequently, evocative nurture means not only arousing a worshipper's awareness of the gospel message in the Bible but also raising and posing hard questions in ways that stimulate reflection, in light of scripture, on the self's attitudes, behaviors, and contemporary life in general.

Wimberly claims that the critique of human behavior in the sermons of black preachers exposes a prophetic function through straightforward descriptions of behaviors that counter the biblical norm or requirement for faith-full and hope-filled Christian life. The intentional insertion of

78. Wimberly, *Faith & Hope*, 133.
79. Wimberly, *Faith & Hope*, 132.

personal pronouns is a tactic that draws the worshipers into a self-critical mode and toward the formation of "internal propheticism." She explains.

> In fact, the formation of an "internal propheticism" requires self-awareness and self-criticism of attitudes and commitments that, on the one hand, paralyze our abilities to address critical issues and that, on the other hand, empower our abilities. In this way, first-person language contributes to nurturing faith and hope through preaching.[80]

This is an example of Dewey's theory of the formulation of community and the mutual education that socially undergirds it so that it might be labeled a functioning community. As stated earlier, what links a people together to form a community is the commonality found within the shared knowledge, aims, belief systems, and growing aspirations of the people themselves. As Dewey asserts, regardless of the context, a community is only formed once all members of the community are cognizant of their shared common end and make an effort, through communication, to regulate specific activity in view of this common end.[81] Dewey's theory is applicable to the prophetic function in black preaching because this view of nurture unsettles worshipers in a way that pushes them beyond a position of complacency toward the necessary and intentional struggle for justice in everyday life. The congregation is pushed together to form a community of care and concern that promotes intentional actions of justice for the good of humanity. The growing aspirations of the congregation to do deeds of justice and to analyze personal inner struggles can empower it to move forward in like mindedness to a positive end.

For Wimberly, the task of the *priestly sermon* in the black worshiping congregation is to raise a surety of who the congregation is, as Christians, and who they belong to, as Christian believers. The priestly sermon:

> is to evoke in us what Olin Moyd describes as "the courage to struggle against the dehumanizing forces and the power to transcend the human-caused trials and tribulations in countless otherwise hopeless situations." Through these sermons, we are to be moved to imagine a worthy future and to move toward and into that future.[82]

---

80. Wimberly, *Faith & Hope*, 137.

81. Dewey, *Democracy and Education*, 5.

82. Wimberly, *Faith & Hope*, 132.

Accordingly, she indicates that the central focus of this function is build-ing faith and hope within worshipers through intentional attention to the worshipers' identity-formation, views of life, and coping strategies amidst life's trauma. Moreover Wimberly points out that through the priestly word, the preacher helps the worshipers to envision a vocation and specific Christian life skills that are critical to living in families and in the world as Christians, even "when their backs are often pressed to the wall" by the challenges of life.

Another aspect of the priestly function in preaching is that it cen-ters on evoking in worshipers self-examination, a deepening, self-under-standing affirmation of the valued identity of Christians that is given by God and lived out in community, and sustenance for the journey ahead. It takes seriously the fact that worshipers come into the worshiping con-gregation with numerous issues and facets of their lives:

> We come with stories great and small, promising and problem-atic about our identities, the places we live, our relationships, the direction of our lives, and the meanings we assign to our lives. Preaching that carries out the priestly function tends to these themes of worshipers' stories and arouses in the commu-nity of faith its individual and communal understanding of the faith as being fully open to life and God's purpose for our being in the world.[83]

It is within this function that the hope and faith of the individual wor-shiper and the community of worshipers is both evoked and nurtured through the application of the biblical word. Such an examination results in the discovery and the exploration of the purposes God has for both the individual and the congregation as a community of faith.

The *apostolic function* of sermons, according to Wimberly, refers to the disclosure of the faithful heart and mind of the preacher, which is able to evoke, in the heart and mind of the worshiper, a response to the gospel. The term "apostolic" refers to the function that centers on the establish-ment of the gospel in a believer which includes the preacher.[84] Wimberly proposes that preaching as evocative nurture relates the symmetry be-tween the life of the preacher and the preaching of the preacher, that is, the pastor's character gets preached through the life of the preacher.

---

83. Wimberly, *Faith & Hope*, 141.
84. Wimberly, *Faith & Hope*, 132.

One of the criticisms of the black church is the hypocrisy and the lack of congruency between what Christians profess and how they live. Wimberly contends that nurture through preaching becomes a wholly believable endeavor only insofar as the preacher is a person of integrity, reflects authentic personhood, and expresses authority that is representative of the sacred. She cites Thomas Swears to support her contention:

> "Authentic preaching," says Swears, "requires of the preacher authentic living, which is best accomplished by the preacher's commitment to live intentionally in the presence of Christ." Authenticity is the evidence that the preacher has a relationship with God through Jesus Christ that shows in the preached word and in the very life the preacher lives, and the truthful, caring relationships the preacher enters with others. Authenticity requires that the preacher is a listening presence with others in order to grasp who they are and the nature of their stories.[85]

Nurturing faith and hope through preaching requires an authentic and compassionate response to the existential conditions of people's lives. It also reflects the preacher's personal witness through appropriate disclosure of his or her story, or disclosure that is relevant to the problems or experiences of the worshipers, or that illuminates meanings of faith and hope with which they can identify. Consequently, apostolic preaching requires of the preacher the very same things the preached word itself requires of those in the congregation who hear it. It requires an attentive response that illuminates the hearers to respond justly and righteously as those who are labeled followers of Christ.

Music

The imaginative nurture of music gives congregants an unparalleled opportunity for imagining meanings of faith. The imaginative function of songs nurtures a critical awareness of the various generations' involvement together in the worshiping congregation. Wimberly states:

> Indeed, this function makes of music a pathway for our imagining, redefining, and affirming our identity as black people and people of faith and hope. . . . Moreover, the externalization of what we and others know or believe draws us all into imagining, wondering, considering, and affirming the meaning of

85. Wimberly, *Faith & Hope*, 142.

that knowing and believing in light of our own stories; and it summons children and others who may be new to the Christian faith into the same process.[86]

Wimberly emphasizes that music in the black worshiping congregation moves the worshiping congregation beyond simply rote of unmindful copied expression. It engages them in evocative experience that summons their thinking, reflecting, and feeling selves on the promise they have as children of God, and creates a foundation for persons' ongoing participation in the worshiping congregation and, indeed, in the church's ministry.[87]

Wimberly explains that the expressive nurture components of music within the black worshiping congregation does not ordinarily happen without bodily responses such as clapping, swaying, tapping the feet, swaying, or dancing. This is witnessed through the variety of musical styles of congregational singing, choir selections, or instrumental music—which are the congregations' direct response to the move of the Holy Spirit. This spiritual relationship with the Holy Spirit is similar to the example of the African slaves, the Invisible Church, and the Ring Shout discussed in chapter 1. This connection arouses in the body of black worshipers kinesthetic meanings of faith in God, the ability to give way to expressive capacities, and what it means to hope or to continue in the unknown future with vitality and diligence as Christians. As described in chapter 1, this expressive nurture through music engages the black worshipers' "kinesthetic intelligence" to move because there is an indescribable intuitive knowing which can only be responded to by movement.

Music is one form of expression that communicates the depths of the inner soul and summons the whole self to respond. Such examples give opportunity for spontaneous movement or liturgical dance choreography to be done as the answer to the call. Such a relationship awakens a kind of black expressive spirituality. On the other hand, Wimberly points out that black worshiping congregations are sometimes challenged to see the importance of stillness and quiet that allows for another level of hearing and responding to the Spirit. She writes:

The challenge is to critically reflect on and assess the extent to which the intensity and profusion of action and sound overwhelms our ability to grasp the importance of stillness,

86. Wimberly, *Faith & Hope*, 149.
87. Wimberly, *Faith & Hope*, 149.

especially active stillness that is anticipative listening and openness to the Spirit.[88]

Regardless of the musical expression and the response of either kinesthetic movement or stillness, music as a nurture bearer has the potential
to renew and even transform the worshiping congregation by arousing
the imagination, emotions, and attitudes that lie at the heart of Christian
spirituality.

Another aspect of the nurturing components of music in the black
worshiping congregation is its inclination to foster a spontaneous and
improvisational style of expression. Wimberly labels this type of activity as "spiritual free play," which is a result of the heart's and the body's
response to the movement of the Holy Spirit, and the mind's connection
with the message or content on which the music centers. In "spiritual
free play," the whole self is released to delight in the personal experience
of seeing and hearing God, and it is through this experience that one
creates and adds new sounds, rhythms, movement accompaniment, and
thoughts that respond to and add further meaning to a truth or belief
disclosed in a song. "'Spiritual free play,' creates a climate of imaginative experience and artistry that builds creative musical capacities from
which life outside the congregation is embellished."[89] Consequently, it
enhances the understanding of faith and hope that guides life outside the
congregation.

Wimberly suggests that there are at least five aspects of imaginative
and expressive functions of nurture which engage the black worshiping
congregation through "spiritual free play."[90] First, she points to improvisation as an act of responding and drawing attention to the mysterious
work of God's Spirit that cannot be comprehended on the printed page.
Through improvisation, black worshipers become open to the qualities of
luminosity and wholly affective religious experience that appends what
is seen, learn, and reproduced from a musical score. The second is the
improvisatory aspect of music making in the black worshiping congregation, which is a pathway for nurturing the surrendering of self to the
musical cord to sing, clap, shout, dance, and pray when the Spirit says
to do so. Improvisation serves as a function to evoke the awareness of
the "push" within the worshiper to "lean" into the future, second by sec-

88. Wimberly, *Faith & Hope*, 150.
89. Wimberly, *Faith & Hope*, 152.
90. Wimberly, *Faith & Hope*, 152–153.

ond, relinquishing a certain degree of momentary control. The third is the power of the improvisatory musical experience to nurture within the black worshiping congregation to reflect and stimulate the awareness that life unfolds according to unexpected twists and turns. The improvisational character of music affirms and reminds the worshiper—consciously or unconsciously—that unexpected life events call one to create, to improvise, and to proceed on the journey faithfully and imaginatively, "to see what the end will be."[91] Fourth is that, by its very nature, improvisation is comprised of unique, nonrepeatable, and nonretrievable moments. Improvisational musical expression calls attention to the affective domain of educational ministry in which appreciation, reverence, and creative participation in every moment of life must be seen as a valid part of living with faith and hope. Finally, the fifth is the evocative nurturing power of improvisatory musical experience to nurture openness to God's speaking to and through the worshiper. The congregation can move forward with resolute faith in the able God who is with them, and with an expectancy of living confidently and courageously in community after the model of Jesus in times of triumph and, in the midst of suffering, narrow escapes, failures, reversals, and hard trials.

However, the aesthetic, nonverbal "right-brain and left-hand" mode of nurture is often seen as antithetical and of lesser value than the more intellectual, analytical, verbal, and cognitive "left-brain and right-hand" mode of religious learning.[92] Wimberly cites Jeff Astley to counter such criticism:

> This modeling in black congregational worship affirms an emerging position in religious educational circles that there should not be a wedge between emotion or experience and what we do to promote a person's grasp of belief or doctrine. To use Astley's words, "emotions have a logic: a grammar, form and determinacy which derive from, and must be understood in conjunction with, the accompanying thoughts, beliefs and objects of the emotion. The point is that the good health of Christian education is dependent on the operation of both lobes of the brain, so that Christian truth is learned both affectively and cognitively." This point is no less true in the nurture of faith and hope.[93]

91. Wimberly, *Faith & Hope*, 153.
92. Wimberly, *Faith & Hope*, 154.
93. Wimberly, *Faith & Hope*, 154–55.

As mentioned earlier, Dewey maintains that when one has an aesthetic experience, it is then that the material experienced runs its course to fulfillment. These experiences are classified by those situations and episodes that are spontaneously referred to as being "real experiences."[94] In an experience, flow is from something to something; as one part leads into another and as one part carries on with what went on before, each gains distinctness in itself.[95] These experiences enhance learning in ways that are both intellectual and emotional. Dewey's explanation of the aesthetic experience is echoed in Wimberly's explanations of the imaginative and expressive functions of nurture that are found in the improvisatory nature of "spiritual free play." Each of the five aspects heightens the learning and expressive nature music has upon the black worshiping congregation, both individually and collectively. Since black worship experience affords the opportunities for such musical explorations to occur, God's nature and God's relationship with God's people are lessons that are at the forefront of such experiences. There is a unity found within the exploration and the comprehension of the aesthetic experience. Therefore, as both Astley and Wimberly agree, healthy Christian truth is learned both affectively and cognitively.

Prayer

According to Wimberly, the nurture occurring through prayer in black worship is an experiential endeavor that affirms the faithful and hope-giving nature of God, and it validates through the language of prayer the faith and hope-centered character of that relationship with God. As she explains, the very entry into the experience of prayer in and of itself communicates the need for it, yet, it is the actual participation in hearing and articulating the language of prayer that lets one know more surely the depth of this need. Nurturing faith and hope through prayer in the black worshiping congregation also happens as black worshipers engage in prayer language that calls attention to the need of human beings for God. She submits that "nurture through prayer evokes in us an awareness of the reciprocal relationship between God and us."[96]

---

94. Dewey, *Art as Experience*, 36.
95. Dewey, *Art as Experience*, 36.
96. Wimberly, *Faith & Hope*, 160.

Prayer as a validating language of the divine-human relationship is described by Wimberly as the opportunity given to worshipers to build a language to express their personal concerns and needs as well as the wider concerns and needs of churches, communities, social structures, and the world for God. She explains that praying is revealed as a divine-human encounter that extends beyond instruction and that cannot be encapsulated in the word nurture. Prayer simply engages and draws the worshiping congregation into relationship with God, the Source of all strength and the Author of faith and hope. Experiences of prayer engage black people in and help them to express heart rendering thoughts and feelings that include prayers of lament, confession, intercession, and commitments to God. For example, she points to the prayers of lament as validating the awareness of a compassionate God, who reaches out to the people of God and welcomes them to reach back:

> Through these prayers, we become willing participants in the divine pedagogy in which the able God . . . is the divine Listener and the divine Evocator who seeks to arouse in us a profound sense of faith in God's presence and healing activity.[97]

Thus, Wimberly reminds us that the nurturing message of the prayers of lament is that God can be trusted with our cries and that a perspective of hope cannot be wholly formed without the full disclosure of the depths of hurt and despair.

The prayers of confession allow the black worshiping congregation to confess sinfulness, appeal for forgiveness, and commit to Christian discipleship which clergy, liturgists, and worshipers disclose. In the worshiping congregations, these prayers heighten the awareness of the human difficulty to acknowledge the imperfections, the inability to manage them, and the tendency to be servants of the mind and will rather than servants of God.

Hope-filled prayer is the act of guiding the believer to trust God's ultimate disclosure. Faith and hope-filled prayer teaches the believer to wait on the Lord who will renew the believer's strength and it nurtures the believer in the exercise of "revolutionary patience"[98]:

> With this kind of faith and patience we recognize that an answer to a prayer may not come in the near or even far-flung future, but it is envisioned and spoken nonetheless in the heart and

97. Wimberly, *Faith & Hope*, 162.
98. Wimberly, *Faith & Hope*, 166.

leaned toward by the verve of the spirit that is lifted and carried by the Spirit of the living God.[99]

Therefore, the times of prayer in the black worshiping congregation are "teachable moments" that nurture the understanding of what it means to be a thinking and feeling community in creative conversation with God. Praying through song provides an added dimension of "teachable moments," in which black worshipers form another expressive way of thinking, feeling, and talking with God.[100] In prayer songs, the worshipers are allowed to repeat ideas, rhyme thoughts, and clap or engage in other bodily movements as so often happens in musical appeals such as the song, "Guide My Feet While I Run this Race."[101] According to Wimberly, what evolves from the experiences of praying through singing is an awareness that, in song, the worshiper is enabled to express thoughts and feelings to God that are found inexpressible in spoken language. Regardless of the form of prayer utilized, within the black worshiping congregation, they generate conscious awareness of a passionate style of praying, and these experiences have the effect of nurturing or evoking a desire for this style in new members and future generations.

Wimberly's notion of nurturing faith and hope through the exploration of the black worshiping congregation as a model for Christian education corresponds with Dewey's principles of continuity and interaction. As mentioned earlier, Dewey provides the measure of the educative significance and value of the experience through the principles of continuity and interaction.[102] What must be at the forefront for learning to transpire are the situations in which educative interactions takes place. In this case, Wimberly's black worshiping congregation provides both continuity and interaction between the preacher, choir, musicians, liturgists, and congregation. Dewey contends that the objective conditions, which include the "what" and the "how," are somewhat regulated by the educator. Wimberly's research brings together the elements of preaching, music, and prayer as the "how" moments of Christian educational learning for the worshiping congregation to focus on becoming more Christlike through these vehicles. As Dewey proposed, such conditions involve the educators' preparations, their "what" and their "how," the equipment

99. Wimberly, *Faith & Hope*, 166.
100. Wimberly, *Faith & Hope*, 167.
101. Carpenter and Williams, *African American Hymnal*, 131.
102. See Dewey, *Experience and Education*.

and materials utilized in engaging the students, and, most importantly, the total social set-up of the situations in which they are engaged.[103] In this case, the social set up is the entire worshiping congregation, and the educator is the Holy Spirit, who facilitates learning through the vehicles of preaching, music, and prayer in order to teach in and through all who make up the collective worshiping body.

Within the black worshiping congregation, these three elements illuminate the endless and creative possibilities by which Christian education can transpire. Dewey's principle of continuity within the educational application takes into account "the future at every stage of the educational process."[104] Wimberly's use of the black worshiping congregation is not only the most conducive environment for the educative interaction to take place but also continually prepares the worshiping congregation for later experiences of a deeper and more expansive quality. And as Dewey contends, this "is the very meaning of growth, continuity, [and] reconstruction of experience."[105]

Conclusion

This chapter set out to bridge a connection between John Dewey's concept of education as attained through experiential learning and the work of religious educators who view religious experience as the centerpiece of their work with learners. The church can be classified as a community of learning and where a plethora of religious teachings can promote diversified learning experiences for the congregation, regardless of age, gender, learning abilities, culture, and economic status. Learning what Christianity is and what it means to be Christian is a lifelong task for both clergy and laity—but such a teaching must be taken seriously if the teaching is to extend beyond the walls of the church.

Dewey's philosophical principles about learning through education and experience provide lifelong learning opportunities that have social and imaginative implications for the religious educator and the religious community. Education and experience must be purposeful for continuity, interaction, and the objective conditions to transform both the teaching and learning moment. The use of the aesthetic within teaching can

103. Dewey, *Experience and Education*, 45.
104. Dewey, *Experience and Education*, 47.
105. Dewey, *Experience and Education*, 47.

help bring this about. Dewey's understanding of the social function of education is foundational to the educational experience of the church as a community place of learning. What is truly essential for Dewey is that learning has to be both transformative and lead to the furthering of more educational experiences. This is dynamic education.

The work of Charles Foster offers a rubric of ideas on how Christian education can be enriched, renewed, and kept purposeful for every member of the congregation. Whether it is viewed as a form that is emancipatory, transformational, or utterly creative, it ultimately must reflect the mystery of God. This is what Foster claims. Not only must it reflect this mystery but it must also reveal how Christians are to embrace that mystery in order to live out faith, not only in present time but to believe in it enough to allow it to take Christians into future time as well.

The work of Norma Cook Everist acknowledges the gifts of the entire congregation as those who can both teach and learn. Everist insists that religious education is not a set of lessons written down simply to be recited, but it is the understanding that the inspired revelation of God and the love of God can touch all humanity through the power of the cross. For Everist, the congregation is made up of differently-abled people who are called to share their many varied gifts with one another for the church to become a community place of sincere and divine learning.

Finally, the work of Anne E. Streaty Wimberly points to the necessity of nurturing faith and hope through the elements of preaching, music, and prayer as witnessed through the black worshiping congregation. The entire worshiping event promotes learning, creativity, and deep reflection for all, both individually and collectively, regardless of position or task. Within black worship Wimberly presents numerous tools for Christian educators to use in order to promote a Christ-likeness for those who call themselves followers of Christ in this time of postmodernity.

Religious education as experientially imaginative, it is argued, can push every Christian to live their lives not for selfish motives, but purely for others who live both inside the walls of the church and on the outside periphery of the church. These are the people who may never have the opportunity to know the still small voice of God that reaches out to their hearts. To the question who will go and share this message, this chapter suggests that it is the congregation, the church, the community of learners who reply, "Send us, we will go and experience God with them, together!"

The next chapter defines and describes liturgical dance as an educative tool within the church by drawing from information supplied by written texts and structured interviews. It identifies its creative, imaginative, and educational attributes through the use of description, interpretation, and evaluation of movement, gesture, and language in the context of specific church teaching and learning events. Liturgical dance is acknowledged as movement that not only teaches within the four walls of the church, but its educative landscape reaches outside to the surrounding community and beyond.

Chapter 4

Praise God with Dancing

An Investigation into the Meaning and Application of Liturgical Dance

Introduction

Curt Sachs writes that "dance is the mother of the arts."[1] Sachs explains that dance breaks down the distinctions of body and soul, of abandoned expression of the emotions and controlled behavior, of social life and the expression of individuality, of play, religion, battle, and drama, which are all the distinctions that a more advanced civilization has established. The need *to* dance is found in the ecstasy *of* dance, which Sachs claims is the conduit by which humanity bridges the chasm between this present domain and the other spiritual domain of demons, spirits, and God. Religious dance—and the commonness found within it—is both widespread and universal within the realms of both time and space. J.G. Davies affirms this with the following observation:

> No matter whether one turns to the records of ancient Egypt, of classical Greece, of imperial Rome, of the European Middles Ages, of India, China, Africa, Australia, or the Americas, they all witness to the practice of dance as a religious activity right down

---

1. Sachs, *History of Dance*, 3.

to the present day. Moreover, dance had (and still continues to have) a part in the ritual of most of the world religions.[2]

Known by many names, religious dance or sacred dance dates back to the pre-historic period, but, according to W. O. E. Oesterley, there is no proof to support any theories of its origins.[3] What is certain is that, since the sacred dance originated during a very primitive stage of culture, it must have been something very naïve and childlike. Oesterley proposes that one of the most ingrained characteristics of human nature is the imitative propensity that is more pronounced in the child than in the adult, and what holds good for the individual applies also to the race. Therefore, the more uncultured humanity is, the more humanity replicates a childlike nature, and the further back one goes in investigating the human race, the more pronounced and childlike will be that imitative propensity. Aristotle maintained that dancing is imitative; in all its forms, it is an artistic imitation of physical movement expressive of emotions or ideas. Thus, Oesterley contends, sacred dance owes it origin to this imitative propensity that exists in all human life.[4]

This chapter investigates the meaning and application of liturgical dance. This is done by first concentrating on the origins of sacred dance within Israelite worship, through examples extracted from the Old Testament of how dance was useful in the learning and the identification of religious belief. As mentioned in the introduction, starting with the Old Testament is important for establishing the connection between the sacred dance and religious belief. For example, Oesterely writes:

> The Old Testament offers, either explicitly or implicitly, as we hope to show, evidence of the existence among the ancient Israelites of most of the typical sacred dances of antiquity. By "typical" we do not mean dances in their outward form, but in the intention and object for which they were performed. In dealing with sacred dances, it is only by considering their intention and purpose that a classification of them can be attempted. The Old Testament gives with the compass of its pages certain *points d'appui* which afford convenient starting-points for the consideration of these different types of the sacred dance.[5]

2. Davies, *Liturgical Dance*, 3.

3. See Oesterley, *Sacred Dance*.

4. Oesterley, *Sacred Dance*, 14.

5. Oesterley, *Sacred Dance*, 8.

These examples explore the general history of symbolic movement in worship as suggested by Margaret Fisk Taylor.[6] Next, an analysis of particular types of religious dances is given. Oesterley contends that after the gathering of data found on the topic of sacred dance within the Old Testament, it is possible to discern certain categories or styles of religious dance that were exhibited. This can be arranged by analyzing the connection and appearance of each sacred dance within the Israelite worship setting: "Although it is not to be supposed that there was, generally speaking, any idea of having particular kinds of dance reserved for different occasions, it is possible to attempt some kind of classification."[7] Four classifications of dance styles found within the Hebrew Scriptures are examined: the *processional dance*, with a focus on the dance of King David (2 Sam 6:5 and 6:12–15); the *ritual dance round a sacred object*, with a focus on Joshua and the circling around the city of Jericho (Josh 6:8–20); the *ecstatic dance*, with a focus on King Saul joining the prophets (1 Sam 10:5–6 and 10:10–13); and the *victory dance*, with a focus on Miriam's dance (Exod 15:20–21).

Vital to the existence of dance within Christian worship is the examination of both the condemnation and the acceptance of dance found amongst the early Christian Church and Church Fathers. Reasons for those who opposed it will include the influence of pagan worship on the sacred dance, which fostered a compromise in Christian lifestyles, and the rising doctrine of asceticism. The Church Fathers who accepted the use of sacred dance patterned their reasons after the communal honoring of God through the circle dance form and the dance of King David, whose dance signified intense joy and the honoring of God.

The second half of the chapter focuses on the working meaning of liturgical dance for Christians in the 21st century. This will include formalizing a working definition of liturgical dance by examining the work of several authors, including J. G. Davies, Carla DeSola, and Arthur Easton. In formulizing a working definition, several themes are explored, including dance as a proper way to respond to God, dance as a worship response and as prayer, the appropriateness of dance in worship, and welcoming dance into the liturgy. These themes highlight the teaching components found within liturgical dance, and the necessity for such an

6. See Taylor, "History of Symbolic Movement."

7. Oesterley, *Sacred Dance*, 35.

expression to be an integral element within the worshiping activities of the church.

To clarify terminology, definitions for worship, liturgy, and liturgical dance are given. Worship, in this context, refers to the faithful human response to the revelation of God's being, character, beneficence, and will.[8] Phenomenologically, worship takes place in cultic acts where such rites are intended as the vehicle of an inward and total devotion; they both form and express the believers who carry them out. John G. Davies explains that Christian worship is Trinitarian in theme and structure, such as in the Eucharistic prayer which is normally offered to the Father through Christ in the Holy Spirit. The term liturgy denotes an act of worship, more specifically the Eucharist. Davies explains the term further:

> Derived from the Greek *leitourgia*, it was used in Hellenistic Greek of an act of public service. In the NT it is employed of an act of service or ministry. In time, it was confined in Christian usage to the idea of service to God, and finally, since worship was regarded as the supreme service to God, it was applied to the Eucharist. Consequently, to study liturgies is to examine the forms which the Eucharistic rite has taken throughout the centuries.[9]

The term liturgical dance, in this context, refers to Christian liturgical dance, which can take the forms of a story or choreo-drama, expressional movement, embodied prayer, or it can accompany psalms, hymns and spiritual songs, spoken word, or silence.[10] Davies states that it is a way of exploring physically the meaning of stories, promoting participation and *shalom*, while allowing worship to be rendered by the totality of a person. Davies concludes that Christian liturgical dance is "an act of worship in itself, being sacramental in character in that it unifies the physical and spiritual aspects of human nature; it encourages creativity; it gives scope for enrichment; it allows greater diversity; it can present a challenge."[11] The use of these terms in this writing will be founded on the bases of the aforementioned definitions.

The voices of those who have incorporated liturgical dance from a variety of positions and perspectives within the church is also included in

8. Davies, *Westminster Dictionary*, 505.

9. Davies, *Westminster Dictionary*, 314.

10. For the definition of choreo-drama, see footnote in chapter 4.

11. Davies, *Westminster Dictionary*, 208.

this writing. These positions include the pastorate, director of music for denominational and ecumenical worship, church parishioners, liturgical dancers, and choreographers and directors of liturgical dance organizations. The chapter concludes with a working definition of liturgical dance that describes it as an educational and instructional tool for religious education. Such a description paves the way for the creation of curriculum formats that supply settings that directly engage the use of liturgical dance with religious education. These formational settings are to be explored in the final chapter.

History of Symbolic Movement[12]

According to Margaret Taylor, symbolic movement was not grafted into Christianity in the twentieth century, but the connection between religious feeling and expressive movement has been coeval with human history.[13] She contends that symbolic movement was probably the first of the arts since it required no material outside of the human body. Religion was a major part of life among the early indigenous cultures, thus religious dances were a natural way to express religious beliefs. Similarly, Taylor uses the term *dance* in its broad sense of moving in rhythm with a pattern of expression. When used among the early indigenous religions this term implied a pattern with gestures in which all the tribe could join and not a special form of exhibition or entertainment by a chosen few.[14]

The various references to the use of dance in the Old Testament may be grouped in two categories. The first is impulsive, unplanned, or spontaneous, which arises out of a need to rejoice with the whole being, and the second is folk, where people joined in for traditional festivals or accepted ways of expressing praise. Taylor shares a number of scriptures from the Old Testament that give evidence to Hebrew dancing.[15] They include: Miriam's dance (Exod 15:20), the singing and dancing after David's

12. The historical titles used to express dances done for religious purposes are numerous. The terms sacred dance, religious dance, and symbolic movement have been utilized in research supplied by Oesterley, Davies, and Taylor respectively. As there is not one universal term that has been used to symbolize religious dance historically, such terms as those previously mentioned—as well as the contemporary term, liturgical dance—will be used intermittently throughout chapters 4 and 5.

13. See Taylor, "History of Symbolic Movement."

14. Taylor, *Time to Dance*, 68.

15. See Taylor, "History of Symbolic Movement."

killing of Goliath (1 Sam 18:6–7 and 29:5), David's dancing before the ark (2 Sam 6:14), the mentioning of dance as praise unto God in (Ps 149:3 and Ps 150:4), and the turning of mourning into dancing (Ps 30:11). She also mentions the Apocryphal book of Judith, where the women sang and danced in Judith's honor:

> All the women of Israel gathered to see her, and blessed her, and some of them performed a dance in her honor. She took ivy-wreathed wands in her hands and distributed them to the women who were with her and she and those who were with her crowned themselves with olive wreaths. She went before all the people in the dance, leading all the women, while all the men of Israel followed, bearing their arms and wearing garlands and singing hymns. (Jdt 15:12–13)

Examples such as these appear to indicate that the use of dance as both celebratory and instructional was found to be embedded within the Hebraic culture. She contends that, growing out of a strong Hebraic tradition, Christianity was cognizant of this natural, spontaneous, and accustomed way of human expression.[16]

In the early writings of the Christian tradition, the word *choros*, as in "choral dancing," was used—although the Greek choir also sang, spoke, and danced with the purpose of intensifying a mood.[17] This term was used continuously in describing the actions of Greek choral dancing. In the classic Greek dramas, choral dances were used to emphasize a particular mood or to reveal a vital meaning. *Choros* (and its plural form, *choroi*) was translated to mean "dance," although choral movement involved folk participation in acts of worship. Taylor explains that Greek choral dancing had a special dignity and beauty because of its harmonious movements. The Greeks believed that dance was the art that most influenced the soul, and provided the expressive way for that overflow of awareness for which there were no words.[18]

---

16. Taylor, "History of Symbolic Movement," 16.
17. Taylor, *Time to Dance*, 69–70.
18. Taylor, "History of Symbolic Movement," 16.

Sacred Dances of Israel

There is evidence in the Old Testament of the most typical sacred dances of antiquity among the ancient Israelites. Oesterley suggests that it is only by considering the intention and purpose of the sacred dance that a classification of them can be created. The emotions and aspirations of the Israelites, like those common to humanity, were expressed in the sacred dances they did.

Oesterley notes the absence of provisions for ritual dancing within the Mosaic law. He states that "without question, the priestly historians and legislators resolutely excluded, as far as possible, everything that could infer any similarity between the worship of Jahwe and that of heathen deities."[19] Oesterley posits that it is doubtful whether the subject of sacred dance would have come into consideration within such a connection, since it was a practice too deeply ingrained in human nature. As a means of expressing religious emotions it was uncertain to suggest that the sacred dance implied assimilation to non-Israelite worship. For both the Israelites and the non-Israelites, the bringing of oblations and the offering of sacrifices were common to not only them but to all races. A reason for such an omission is suggested by Oesterley:

> The Mosaic legislation makes no provision for the posture to be assumed in the presence of the deity, nor does it say anything about singing in worship; but it is difficult to believe that there were not fixed modes in regard to these which had been in vogue from time immemorial; and therefore they needed no mention. The same may be postulated in the case of the sacred dance. A thing which all the evidence shows to have been a world-wide means of expressing religious emotion and of honouring the deity during a long period in the history of religious development, was not likely to have been wanting among the Israelites.[20]

In the passages found in the Old Testament that record sacred dancing, there is no hint of disapproval or prohibition, therefore, Oesterley contends that it must have been looked upon as a usual, repeated, and integral occurrence within Israel's worship environment. The sacred dance continued to be an important element in worship on special occasions among the Jews in post-biblical times and, therefore, he surmises, sacred dance, throughout the entire Israelite tradition, was not an innovation

19 Oesterley, *Sacred Dance*, 33.
20. Oesterley, *Sacred Dance*, 34.

but a continuation—and, in some cases, an elaboration—of a rite familiar to the Jewish people. If there were any stipulations, one appeared to
have been that the religious dances of Israel were basically performed by
the sexes separately. There are four examples that exhibit such an understanding: the *processional dance*, the *round the sacred object dance*, the
ecstatic dance, and the *victory dance*.

The Processional Dance

The sacred processional dance that appears in the Old Testament among
the Israelites was always done in honor of Israel's God. David's processional dance, found in 2 Samuel 6:5 and 6:12–15, is a specific example of
a dance honoring God due to the presence of God above the Ark[21]:

> David and all the house of Israel were dancing before the Lord
> with all their might, with songs and lyres and harps and tam-
> bourines and castanets and cymbals. (2 Sam 6:5)

> It was told King David, "The Lord has blessed the household of
> Obed-edom and all that belongs to him, because of the ark of
> God." So David went and brought up the ark of God from the
> house of Obed-edom to the city of David with rejoicing. and
> when those who bore the ark of the Lord had gone six paces, he
> sacrificed an ox and a fatling. David danced before the Lord with
> all his might; David was girded with a linen ephod. So David
> and all the house of Israel brought up the ark of the Lord with
> shouting, and with the sound of the trumpet. (2 Sam 6:12–15)

Oesterley deconstructs the physical actions of David and highlights the
movements of rotation, whirling, jumping, and skipping within the processional dance. He states:

> The picture is that of an imposing procession, headed by the
> king going in front of the Ark into Jerusalem. The entire body of
> those forming the procession is described as dancing, but spe-
> cial attention is drawn to David, and the words used in reference
> to his mode of dancing are instructive; he not only dances in the
> ordinary sense of the word (*sahaq*), but he "rotates (*k'rar*) with
> all his might," and "jumps" (*p'zaz*), and "whirls round" (*hal*); and
> in the parallel passage (1 Chr 15:29), his dancing is described
> as "skipping" (*raqad*) or the like . . . The self-abandonment of

---

21. David's dance is also recorded in 1 Chronicles 15:15–16 and 15:25–29.

this dancing can be imagined in the light of Michal's jibe that the king had shamelessly uncovered himself. Nevertheless, the religious character of the processional dance is obvious, and is emphasized by the phrase "before Jahwe," and by the fact that David "was girded with a linen ephod," the officiating priest's dress (see 1 Sam 2:18).[22]

Within this particular dance, there is an association of excitement that accompanies the processional movement, exemplified through the whirling motion. Whirling is considered to be movement that turns, rotates, or revolves rapidly around within a circular formation. It is from the dancer's perspective alone that the full understanding of the impact and responsiveness of the whirling act can be explained, particularly from the perspective of both dancer and observer participant.

> From the dancers' perspective, the whirling action presents a feeling of exuberance as the circular formation and rapid spins accelerate in speed. The excitement begins internally then expands to create an external excitement for those who are witnessing the action. The whirling action becomes almost uncontrollable for the one dancing; however the exhilaration becomes contagious as the whirling movement continues. The excitement expressed by the observers can take on many forms including responses that are both audible and physical. It is very rare that such a whirling action seeped in joy and gratitude will warrant stillness, staleness, and absolute silence from those participating in the processional.[23]

R. A. Carlson agrees with Oesterley's assessment that David's dance included whirling actions. He states, "He dances with rotating movement, *mekarker*, interspersed with leaps, *mefazzez*, which may also be interpreted as a whirling dance round the Ark."[24] Marilyn Daniels also agrees:

> The most outstanding example of a principal dancer being followed and probably greatly imitated by the others was King David. In a religious procession organized in honor of Yahweh such as the removal of the Ark, David, dressed in the official

---

22. Oesterley, *Sacred Dance*, 54–55.
23. Turner, "If David had not Danced," 43.
24. Carlson, *David*, 87.

robe of the high priest, danced in ecstasy before the deity. It was
a rotary dance rich in gesture accentuated by violent leaps.[25]

Oesterley discusses the role dancing played within the worship life of
the Israelites and explains that there are eleven Hebrew roots to describe
the different characteristics of dance.[26] There are a few terms, however,
that speak specifically about dancing in relationship to the movement
that David did before the ark which are as follows:

> The "whirling" idea is also contained in the root k^2rar (in its
> intensive *pilpel* form, *kirker*), "to whirl about," or "rotate." It
> occurs, in this sense, only once in the Old Testament, 2 Sam
> 6:14–16, of David dancing before Jahwe; and in this passage we
> have another root which does not occur elsewhere in the sense
> of dancing, viz. p^2zaz (again in the intensive form *pizzez*); this
> expresses the idea of agile leaping as part of the dance, the cog-
> nate Arabic root means "to be exceed." The idea of leaping is also
> contained in another root *raqad* (in its intensive form *riqqed*)
> which in its ordinary sense means "to skip about"; as applied to
> dancing it occurs in the passage last mentioned.
>
> So far, then, we have briefly touched on words used in refer-
> ence to dancing which either express or suggest the ideas of its
> being something enjoyable, of its involving the bending about of
> the body, whirling about, leaping, and skipping.[27]

Another vital activity in the midst of the processional dance was
the use of shouting and instrumentation: "David, wearing a linen ephod,
danced before the Lord with all his might, while he and the entire house
of Israel brought up the ark of the Lord with shouts and the sound of
trumpets" (2 Samuel 6:14–15). What is clear from the text is the accompaniment of not only human voices but also instrumentation that allowed
Israel to join in with shouts and musical notes of praise and exclamation.
Carlson comments on the use of shouting with the human voice, and the
musical instrumentation that accompanied it: "The central role of the
Ark is also marked by the 'shouting' and 'the sound of the horn'—common adjuncts of its function in the context of the annual festival."[28]

As the ark was being processed into Jerusalem, David and all of Israel participated in a variety of ways in the processional moment, whether

25. Daniels, *Dance in Christianity*, 10.

26. Oesterley, *Sacred Dance*, 44.

27. Oesterley, *Sacred Dance*, 44–45.

28. Carlson, *David, The Chosen King*, 89.

by dancing, singing, shouting, the playing of an instrument, or by simply observing. It is clear, however, that a processional is an active, moving, celebratory moment, where performer and observer partake simultaneously in the festivities. Whether or not the complexity of the processional action can be imagined or fully comprehended, it is very clear that there were multiple responses from the people of Israel and, more importantly, from the King himself.

What these verses and explanations help to illustrate is the active full bodied response David had for the "alive" presence of God—not only found above the Ark of the Covenant but especially God's "alive" presence found in the very midst of Israel. This processional, with its fullness of shouts, music, and dance, represented for David and Israel a proclamation that the Lord was in the midst of Israel and would remain as the focal point of Israel's worship. It also validated Israel's identity and the proclamation of David as Israel's King. This processional and its fanfare of accompanied action made a resounding statement to all of the surrounding nations that God was in the midst of both Israel and the kingship of David.

The Ritual Dance [a]round a Sacred Object[29]

The ritual dance [a]round a sacred object encircles either an idol, a sacrificial victim, or an altar. Oesterley contends that the movement form of this type of dance was either a march-like step, a running step, or else the worshippers held hands and danced around. There is really no particular Old Testament scripture, however, that supports the latter example of the holding of hands and dancing round in the circle, yet Oesterley believes it is such an obvious form for a dance to take that one can scarcely doubt its having existed among the Israelites.[30]

One scripture that mentions the encirclement round the altar with a song of thanksgiving is found in the Psalms: "I wash my hands in innocence, and go around your altar, O Lord, singing aloud a song of thanksgiving, and telling all your wondrous deeds" (Ps 26:6–7). This particular

29. The ritual dance [a]round a sacred object is the category in which the previously mentioned Ring Shout of the African slaves and the Shaker labor dances can reside. As mentioned in chapter 1, the Ring Shout and some of the Shaker labor dances are done in a circular formation.

30. Oesterley, *Sacred Dance*, 37.

verse exemplifies the ritual in offering sacrifices by the priests.[31] Oesterley describes the ritual encircling of the altar, and the incidental mention of it without further comment seems to imply that it formed part of the ordinary ritual of the priests. Robertson Smith states that the festal song of praise (*tahlil*) properly goes with the dance round the altar, for, in primitive times, song and dance were inseparable.[32]

Another example involves the ritual of the encirclement of a city, as found in Joshua 6:8–20, where the same root as that for the ritual encompassing of the altar is used (*sabab*).[33] Oesterley explains this further:

> Through the whole account the religious element in the undertaking comes strongly to the fore: the encircling procession is a sacred act: the sounding of the rams' horns by the priests, seven in number, the presence of the ark, the sevenfold encirclement on the seventh day, all emphasize its religious character which receives its highest stamp in the words which proclaim the presence of Jahwe Himself in the procession: "And it was so, that when Joshua had spoken unto the people, the seven priests bearing the seven trumpet of rams' horns before Jahwe passed on, and blew with the trumpets: and the ark of the covenant of Jahwe followed them."[34]

As mentioned in the processional dance, the God of Israel is conceived to be either identified with, or present in, the ark. Oesterley points out that the meaning and object of the encirclement is clear from the words of Joshua 6:17, "The city and all that is in it shall be devoted to the Lord." He states that it can be looked upon as a magic circle, based upon the word, "devoted," in order that nothing shall escape and through the encirclement what is inside the circle becomes consecrated. It is also clear that this example of encirclement is different from that in which the encirclement of the altar consecrates the sacrifice that is placed on top of the altar.

31. Oesterley, *Sacred Dance*, 37.
32. Smith, *Religion of the Semites*, 340.
33. To read the account from Joshua 6:8–20, see Appendix G.
34. Oesterley, *Sacred Dance*, 93–94.

The Ecstatic Dance[35]

The appearance of the ecstatic dance in the Old Testament is identified with the appearance and use of instruments found in 1 Samuel:

> After that, you shall come to Gibeath-elohim, at the place where the Philistine garrison is; there, as you come to the town, you will meet a band of prophets coming down from the shrine with harp, tambourine, flute, and lyre playing in front of them; they will be in a prophetic frenzy. Then the spirit of the Lord will possess you, and you will be in a prophetic frenzy along with them and be turned into a different person. (1 Samuel 10:5–6)

Oesteley submits that although there is no direct mention of the sacred dance made in this passage, it can be assumed that a ritual dance is taking place since there is the enumeration of musical instruments, which usually accompanies dancing. He contends that a religious exercise of some kind is made clear by the fact that they had come down from the high place (*bamah*), i.e., a sanctuary. The technical name for such a band of prophets, *hebel*, which is translated to mean "rope" or "string," shows that the procession was in a single file. Oesterley cites Smith as he elaborates on the history of the prophetical bands:

> In speaking of the exercises of the early prophetical bands, Robertson Smith says that "they were sometimes gone through in sacred processions, sometimes at a fixed place, as at the Naioth at Bamah, which ought probably to be rendered 'dwellings'—a sort of coenobium. They were accompanied by music of a somewhat noisy character, in which the hand-drum and the pipe played a part, as was otherwise the case in festal processions to the sanctuary (2 Sam 6:5 and Isa 30:29). Thus the religious exercises of the prophets seem to be a development in a peculiar direction of the ordinary forms of Hebrew worship at the time, and the fact that the 'prophesying' was contagious establishes its analogy to other contagious forms of religious excitement."[36]

For Oesterley, the practice of this type of dance found among other peoples throws light on its mode of performance among the Israelite

---

35. The Ring Shout and the Shaker labor dances as explained in chapter 1 can be associated with the ecstatic dance since both dances had an improvisational and highly charged ecstatic feel when executed during worship.

36. Oesterley, *Sacred Dance*, 108–109.

prophets (1 Sam 10). For him, it is the category of curious phenomenon which appears at a certain stage of religious development all over the world:

> When the means used for producing such results are given in greater detail in many cases, we are justified in believing them to have been similar in a case in which, for some reason or other, the details are only partially described. But if the details of the means used to produce the result are somewhat lacking in the Old Testament account, the result itself is stated clearly enough. The object of all that took place was to be "possessed"—in this case by the spirit of Jahwe; for it was this "possession," this indwelling of the deity, which enforced the "prophesying." In the passage before us the centre of interest, in the eyes of the writer, is Saul. Of him it is said that, as a result of his contact with the "rope" of prophets prophesying, "the spirit of Jahwe" would come "mightily" upon him, and that he, too, would prophesy with them, and "be turned into another man"; the context shows that his contact with the prophets meant joining in their ecstatic dance, the effect of which is graphically described in verses eleven and twelve.[37]

The point Oesterley is reaching for is the "means employed" to get oneself into the ecstatic state required in order to become "possessed." Although there were a variety of ways to reach such a state, one of the most prevalent during this period was the sacred dance accompanied by music. In the passage just referred to, there is no hint of it being anything unusual; the only thing unusual was Saul's "possession": "When all who knew him before saw how he prophesied with the prophets, the people said to one another. 'What has come over the son of Kish? Is Saul also among the prophets?'" (1 Sam 10:11). Referencing to the ecstatic dance amongst the Israelites, Oesterley concludes: "From what we gather as to the existence of the ecstatic dance among other peoples, the fact of its existence among the Israelites does not strike one as other than what one would expect."[38]

The Victory Dance

In early religious cultures, victory dances were normal activities performed to express joy when battles were won. This is one of the reasons

37. Oesterley, *Sacred Dance*, 109–110.
38. Oesterley, *Sacred Dance*, 111.

there were victory dances within Israelite worship. Such dances expressed joy and were celebrations that were performed by women to honor the victorious warriors. Oesterley contends that further investigation is needed in deciphering other reasons for the existence, execution, and necessity for the victory dance:

> In other words, the possibility must be reckoned with that the custom as recorded in the Old Testament was in reality the survival of something which was believed to have a decisive effect in bringing about victory. The dance of the Israelite women on these occasions had a three-fold purpose; it was a means of expressing joy; it was also the way in which the victorious warriors were honoured; and, most important, it was an act of praise and thanksgiving to Jahwe; so that this type of dance was emphatically a religious one. If, as we hope to offer some grounds for believing, this type of dance was, in its origin, a means of effecting victory by magic, it will be an interesting illustration of magic being, as Marett says, "part and parcel of the 'god-stuff' out of which religion fashions itself."[39]

Although there was a solemn preparation for war, war dances are not found within the Old Testament although there was a religious element connected with the act of warfare.[40] The Israelites entered battle knowing that God's protection was upon them if they remained obedient to the religious constraints connected to the wars they fought. The rules of Israel's engagement in war are explained in Deuteronomy, with particular emphasis placed upon the presence and protection of God:

> When you go out to war against your enemies, and see horses and chariots, an army larger than your own, you shall not be afraid of them; for the Lord your God is with you, who brought you up from the land of Egypt. Before you engage in battle, the priests shall come forward and speak to the troops, and shall say to them: "Hear, O Israel! Today you are drawing near to do battle against your enemies. Do not lose heart, or be afraid, or panic, or being in dread of them; for it is the Lord your God who goes with you, to fight for you against your enemies, to give you victory. (Deut 20:1–4)

39. Oesterley, *Sacred Dance*, 160.
40. Oesterley, *Sacred Dance*, 161.

Since the religious element was so strongly emphasized during the times of war, the inclusion of victory dances is certainly warranted and understood. One example of a victory dance is found in Exodus:

> When the horses of Pharaoh with his chariots and his chariot drivers went into the sea, the Lord brought back the waters of the sea upon them; but the Israelites walked through the sea on dry ground. Then the prophet Miriam, Aaron's sister, took a tambourine in her hand; and all the women went out after her with tambourines and with dancing. And Miriam sang to them: "Sing to the Lord, for he has triumphed gloriously; horse and rider he has thrown into the sea." (Exod 15:19–21)

Miriam, whose name means "wish" and "love," sings her triumphant hymn of celebration that is augmented by a series of joyful and praiseful dance movements. Apostolos-Cappadona describes Miriam's image as one that is pious and faithful, who dutifully obeys and worships the Lord following the custom of her people. She states:

> It was an Israelite custom for women to welcome the men with timbrels and dancing when they returned from the battlefield and at other celebrations. She is not described to us in physical terms, but rather in terms of her spiritual status, she is a prophetess, and a singer and dancer of God's praises. This is exactly how she is depicted in the visual tradition.[41]

Apostolos-Cappadona describes Miriam's celebration attire as characteristic of typical Israeli women of that time. She is dressed in a long flowing garment that covers her body and, although the dancing is done by women, there is never any description concerning the sexuality of the women or the physicality of the movements that comprise the victory dance. What is discussed is the instrumentation, which, in this case, is the timbrel. For Apostolos-Cappadona, the timbrel indicates particular movement types that are upward or transcendent due to the use of the timbrel in hand. She concludes that "as a form of worship and celebration, dance has an appropriate role when presented within the rubrics delineated by Miriam."[42]

Dance is also linked to a forgetting of and a freeing from the troubling past, as it was found in the late Beshallach midrash. Although it does not prove that the early Israelites had such a sophisticated understanding

---

41. Apostolos-Cappadona, "Women who Danced," 97.
42. Apostolos-Cappadona, "Women who Danced," 98.

of the effects of dance, Adams contends that the dance from Exodus is an appropriate watershed between slavery and freedom, the past and the future.[43] It is clear that the dancing and singing in this biblical account have the single purpose of thanking God for the victory that is ascribed solely to his intervention and orchestration. Oesterley points out that the Exodus passage presents the highest development of purpose for which this type of dance was performed.

The Condemnation and the Acceptance of Dance among the Early Church Fathers

The Condemnation

Dance in any form was rejected by the early Church Fathers. Several directly spoke out against dancing of any kind amongst those who called themselves Christians. For example, Arnobius, a Christian apologist of the third and fourth century, published a treatise entitled, *Against the Nations.* He attacked the dance done amongst the pagans and questioned if the believers really believed that God sent souls into the world to dance.[44] Arnobius's criticism of the dance amongst the pagans displays his discontent:

> So that human beings should swell out their cheeks in blowing the flute, that they should take the lead in singing impure songs, and raising the loud din of the castanets, by which another crowd should be led in their wantonness to abandon themselves to clumsy motions to dance and sing, form rings of dancers, and finally, raising their haunches and hips, float along with a tremulous motion of the loins.[45]

Another critic of dance was Saint Basil the "Great" of Caesarea (330 to 379) who lived a monastic life and settled as a hermit by the river Iris near Neocaesarea, where he preached missions with Saint Gregory of Nazianzus.[46] Basil gave a homily in which he condemned women who danced on Sundays. He argued that women should spend that day in quiet contemplation because he believed that they were endangering their

43. Adams, "Communal Dance Forms," 40.

44. Davies, *Liturgical Dance,* 20.

45. Davies, *Liturgical Dance,* 20.

46. Livingstone, *Oxford Dictionary,* 167.

own salvation and that of any onlookers whose lustful natures would be aroused by such activity.[47] In the same homily, he also condemned women who danced at the Easter celebrations.

So, too, John Chrysostom, Bishop of Constantinople (347 to 407), condemned dancing. He was known as the "Doctor of the Church," because of his preaching, oratory skills, and numerous sermons on the Books of the Bible. These gained him the title of the greatest of Christian expositors.[48] John Chrysostom denounced dancing and associated the devil with influencing the dancing act. Using examples such as the dancing performance of Herodias's daughter—in requesting the head of John the Baptist—and the dancing at weddings, Chrysostom said:

> Christians do not now deliver up half a kingdom nor another man's head but their own souls to inevitable destruction, if they indulge in such an activity. Cease your attendance at weddings, at dancings, at Satanical performances. . . . It is quite indecent and disgraceful to introduce into one's home lewd fellows and dancers, and all that Satanic pomp. . . . Everything should be full of chasteness, of gravity, of orderliness; but I see the reverse, people frisking like camels and mules. . . . If then, someone may say, neither virgins dance nor married people, who is to dance? No one, for what need is there of dancing? . . . Let no one from the dancing-floor be present, for such expense is superfluous and unbecoming.[49]

Christianity was hostile to dance for a number of reasons, although there was nothing in the New Testament that summoned such a rejection—and the Old Testament supplied numerous examples to encourage it. One reason for its rejection was that dance was connected with pagan worship, pagan purification, and celebration rites. Christians were prompted to ignore dances because so many represented the legends of god and to witness them would have been tantamount to idolatry. As Davies explains:

> Indeed, the compendium of mythological subjects thought suitable to be included in a dancer's repertory covers very thoroughly the activities of the Greek and Roman deities. . . . The

47. Davies, *Liturgical Dance*, 20.
48. Livingstone, *Oxford Dictionary*, 345.
49. Davies, *Liturgical Dance*, 20–21.

castration of Uranus, the begetting of Aphrodite, the battle of the Titans, [and] the birth of Zeus.[50]

Dancing was a concern for the early Church because it was associated with dinner parties. Thus, because of the Lord's Supper and the activities that surrounded it, such as practices of heavy wine consumption, leading to high intoxication and promiscuous dancing, dancing was frowned upon.

At the same time, the Church was experiencing the rising development of the ascetic life-style. Asceticism was associated with moral training, often with the connotation of voluntary abstention from certain pleasures. The term denotes the practices employed to combat vices and develop virtues, the renunciation of various facets of customary social life and comfort, or the adoption of painful conditions for religious reasons.[51] Davies explains:

> Hence an asceticism emerged which, as E. Lampert has so well expressed it, "has often been understood not as a struggle *for* the body and the acquiring of strength for it but as a struggle against the body as the fetters of the spirit." The body then has to be subdued, regulated, punished even, and so there is no possibility for spontaneous movement, for the freedom that comes through dancing. Indeed it is impossible to conceive of Christianity in the period under review endorsing dance when it had such a conception of spiritual progress, such a "bodiless spirituality," and when contemporary dance had so evil a reputation and was closely linked to pagan worship.[52]

There were other religious groups within the empire who did dance, for example, the Jews and certain other heretical movements, but the church was in conflict with them. Hence, this was another reason for the disfavor with which the orthodox regarded the art.

The Acceptance

The New Testament supplies reasons for dance to be looked upon as a tool to express rejoicing. Taylor points out that the words dance and rejoicing are the same word in Aramaic. So when the words "rejoicing

50. Davies, *Liturgical Dance*, 23.

51. Livingstone, *Oxford Dictionary*, 114.

52. Davies, *Liturgical Dance*, 25.

in the spirit" are read, dance is another word that can be translated and substituted for such a passage.[53] Examples of this can be found in several New Testament passages. One is found in Luke, where it is written "Rejoice in that day and leap for joy, for surely your reward is great in heaven for that is what their ancestors did to the prophets" (Luke 6:23). Another scripture is the parable of the prodigal son where the use of the words, dancing, and rejoicing are used as well: "Now his elder son was in the field, and when he came and approached the house, he heard music and dancing. . . . But we had to celebrate and rejoice, because this brother of yours was dead and has come to life; he was lost and has been found." (Luke 15:25 and 15:32). Another example is the Apostle Paul, reminding the early Christians at Corinth that their "bodies are temples of the Holy Spirit" and that they should glorify God in their bodies as well as in their spirits (1 Cor 8:19–20).

Another example of acceptance of dance is the use of the ring dance or circle dance in the early Christian church. There is the hymn-dance supposedly done by the disciples around Jesus during the ceremony of the last supper, as recorded in the Acts of John under the heading of the "Hymn of Jesus."[54] According to Matthew, the institution of the Lord's Supper was done between Jesus and the disciples: "When they had sung a hymn, they went out to the Mount of Olives," (Matt 26:30). The Acts of John implies dance in the following text:

> Now, before he was arrested by the lawless Jews, who received their law from a lawless serpent, he gathered us all together and said, "Before I am delivered up to them, let us sing a hymn to the Father, and go forth to what lies before us." So he commanded us to make a circle, holding one another's hands, and he himself stood in the middle. He said, "Respond Amen to me." He then began to sing a hymn. (Acts John 94:1–6)[55]

After this set of instructions, the composition of the hymn follows a particular format which includes a doxology (Acts John 94:7–13); a series of antithetical affirmations (Acts John 95:1–9); a series of references, including NT scriptural verses and universal inclusions within the dance (Acts John 95:10–16); another series of antithetical affirmations (Acts John 95:17–22); a short series of affirmations (Acts John 95:23–26); a series

---

53. Taylor, "History of Symbolic Movement," 16.
54. To read the "Hymn of Jesus" from the Acts of John, see Appendix H.
55. Elliot, *Aprocryphal*, 318.

of instructions concerning suffering and wisdom (Acts John 96:1–13); a short doxology (Acts John 96:14–15); and closing statements with a final "Amen" (Acts John 96:16–20). After the hymn, chapter 97 picks up the narrative of Jesus's suffering before and after going to the cross while describing the dazed state of the disciples.

Oesterley's description of the circle dance involves worshipers holding hands and dancing in a round.[56] He claims that, "The circle dance was a symbolic representation of the movement of the heavenly bodies."[57] This analysis makes sense as it alludes to the verse Jesus speaks in chapter 95 of the Acts of John:

> "An Ogdoad is singing with us."
> "Amen."
> "The Twelfth number is dancing above."
> "Amen."
> "The whole universe takes part in the dancing."
> "Amen." (Acts John 95:10–16)

Since this dance appeared to have occurred outdoors, this statement gives a sense that the disciples and Jesus were not dancing solely by themselves but were joined by the angels and the heavenly hosts.

The movements found within the circle dance are further explained by Daniels:

> The steps to this particular dance have been lost, but we do have recorded a similar ancient dance of the Andamanese. It too is an imageless circle dance. The magical goal of the imageless exhilaration dance is the attainment of a state of ecstasy in which the dancer transcends the human and physical and, released from his self, wins the power of interfering with the events of the world. . . . The circle later takes on a spiritual significance. This is not the result of a development of understanding but rather of the connection between an idea and its motor reflex: to encircle an object is to take it into possession . . . or it may have as its center a person, as in the "Hymn of Jesus," whose power is supposed radiate to those in the circle.[58]

56. The Ring Shout of the African slaves can also be associated with the circle dance recorded in the Hymn of Jesus since both dances had a call and response song text and were done in a circle formation.

57. Oesterley, *Sacred Dance*, 37.

58. Daniels, *Dance in Christianity*, 15.

Daniels suggests that this type of dance, though not included in the traditional Christian literature, was significant since it illustrates that this type of dance was a part of the religious expression of the early Church.

The acceptance of the ring dance form was displayed in the writings of Gregory of Nazianzus (329 to 389) who was an eminent scholar of theology, the Bishop of Nazianzus, and later the Bishop of Constantinople.[59] Gregory of Nazianzus was given the name, "The Theologian," because of his accuracy in the Trinitarian doctrine. He authored a total of 45 orations, a series of poems, and a collection of 244 letters.[60] About the ring dance, Saint Gregory stated, "May we flee from all the chains of the devil, in performing triumphant ring dances."[61] In another address, Gregory urged the people to attend ceremonies using dances at the graves of martyrs "for the manifest casting out of devils, the prevention of sickness, and the knowledge of things to come."[62]

It appears that the singing of a hymn and dancing was associated with the casting out of devils affiliated with sickness and disease. Adams records that during the twelfth century, on Easter, a hymn and a dance was done to cast out devils and to prevent further sickness. He claims there was a long association between dance and healing in early Christianity and out that during the medieval period there were dances that utilized the trampling of the feet in order to shake off the devil and to heal disease.[63] He states:

> Another medieval hymn sings of dancing and 'trampling vices under foot.' Although only fragments, these records reveal the common use of the dance within the early church to shake off the devil, disease, and all else that enslaves people and holds them down.[64]

59. Backman, *Religious Dances*, 30.

60. Strayer, *Middle Ages*, 666.

61. Adams, "Communal Dance Forms," 40.

62. Adams, "Communal Dance Forms," 40.

63. It is acknowledged that there are dances affiliated with Catholicism during the medieval period and with Protestantism during the reformation period, however, this writing does not investigate the dances of these specific time periods.

64. Adams, "Communal Dance Forms," 40.

The Influence of David's Dance

Many church fathers made reference to Miriam's dance and the dance of David as examples of the acceptable type of dance that should be done inside the church:

> The Patriarchs refer expressly on the one hand to the Jewish sacral dances and on the other hand to certain words of the evangel as a motive for the dance inside the church. David's dance before the Ark, especially, is referred to again and again; the same may be said of Miriam's dance after the Jewish people, with God's help had passed unscathed through the Red Sea.[65]

Two patriarchs who specifically referred to David's dance were Saint Gregory of Nyssa and Saint Ambrose.

Saint Gregory of Nyssa (335 to 394) became the main spokesperson of the Neo-Nicene Orthodoxy and a close theological adviser of the imperial court after his brother, Saint Basil, died in 379 and Saint Gregory of Nazianzus had retired from active ministry life in 381.[66] His theological writings include a twelve-book discourse, *Against Eunomius*, several treatises and orations, and several spiritual interpretations on biblical texts—in which his fifteen set of homilies on the Song of Songs is also included. Gregory's reference to the dance of David and his seeming justification for sacred dancing can be found in these homilies: "David's dance signified 'intense joy,'" he writes, and "by the rhythmic motions of his body, [David] thus showed in public his inner state of soul."[67]

Saint Ambrose (340 to 397) is known for his writings and activities as bishop in defense of the Catholic faith against the Arians and his vindication of Christian moral principles and the independence of the Church against the power of the Roman emperor.[68] He influenced the lives of Saint Augustine, Saint Gregory the Great, and Saint Jerome. This leadership labeled him one of the four "Doctors of the Church."[69] Ambrose refers to David's dancing before the ark in his writing entitled, "Concerning Repentance":

65. Backman, *Religious Dances*, 14.

66. Strayer, *Middle Ages*, 666.

67. Taylor, *Time to Dance*, 75.

68. Strayer, *Middle Ages*, 230.

69. Strayer, *Middle Ages*, 230.

> But the dancing is commended which David practiced before
> the ark of God. For everything is seemly which is done for reli-
> gion, so that we need be ashamed of no service which tends to
> the worship and honoring of Christ.[70]

During the first five centuries of the Christian era, dance was recognized by the church as a natural way of expressing joy, a way of salvation,
and a way of adoration.[71] The faith of the early Christians was not just an
intellectual acceptance of certain beliefs but also an experience of abundant life and spiritual joy. David's dance illustrated the human feelings
of love and devotion and how such feelings could be displayed toward
God. The use of David's dance, in particular, serves as an entry point to
the way one approaches God in spirit and in truth while it also represents
the intense joy and love one can display toward God. Such movement
is a pattern that worships and honors the Godhead. Even for this present time, each historical writing continues to reveal the stipulation upon
which dance is acceptable within the walls of the church. The writings of
Saint Gregory of Nyssa and Saint Ambrose unanimously conclude that
the only type of dance allowed within the church is the type of sacred
movement that speaks to God, that seeks to find God, and that honors
God. Hence, David's dance serves as a biblical point of departure by
which liturgical dance movement can be created, utilized, and function
as a worship and teaching tool within the corporate worship experience.

The Meaning of Liturgical Dance
for Christians in the 21st Century

A Working Description of Liturgical Dance

To explore and arrive at some tentative definitions of liturgical dance for
Christians, Davies proposes that there are three important questions that
have to be addressed:

> First, to what extent is dance an activity suitable to find a place
> in Christian worship? Second, how is dance to be integrated
> with worship and in particular with the [Eucharist], since this
> latter is recognized by the majority of Christians as the principal

---

70. Schaff & Wace, "Repentance," 351.

71. Taylor, "History of Symbolic Movement," 19.

service? Third, how is dance to be interpreted within the context of the liturgy?[72]

Combined with these questions I would also inquire about the instructional and creative characteristics of liturgical dance in order to warrant it as a necessary tool for the church as a community place of learning. To regard the church as a community place of learning means to include its worship services, educational programs, evangelism and outreach endeavors, and any other activities the 21st century church embarks upon. Therefore the driving question still remains: *what are the characteristics embedded in liturgical dance which identify it as religious education within the church as a community place of learning?* Questions such as this one calls for the formulation of a working definition of liturgical dance that addresses not only its usefulness within church worship, but its educational and instructional capacities for the church's learning and instructional life.

Carla DeSola's insight is helpful for this task. She suggests that as a communal form of worship, liturgical dance offers a renewed awareness of who the people in the congregation are as a community. This is evident when the bodies of the congregation sway in unison and their arms lift up in prayer. The people become conscious, in an experiential way, that they are a living, breathing family of God.[73] The Reverend Dr. Floyd H. Flake, Senior Pastor of The Greater Allen African Methodist Episcopal Church of New York, describes his understanding of why there is a special reason for having dance in the house of God:

> There are some people who will be blessed by virtue of the word that goes forth in sermon; there are some people who will be blessed by what is sung; there are some people who will be blessed by the dance. . . . They will be blessed by the energy as they look within themselves and they see what is lacking, and they look out and begin to participate in their own way in the move of the rhythm that somehow takes them out of the condition in which they find themselves, and bring them to a place where they are responding and reacting and emoting in ways that they never could have imagined. . . . when they begin to think of the goodness of God in having given them life, they realize that life is about movement, life is not about stagnation.[74]

72. Davies, *Liturgical Dance*, 126.
73. DeSola, "Word Became Dance," 153.
74. Flake, Floyd H. in an interview with the author, December 2011. Reverend

When practiced by liturgical artists, DeSola points out that dance serves and functions as a conduit from the inner workings of the spirit to the outer expression of today's worship. This definition can mean a variety of understandings, depending upon the liturgical dancer or the one who appreciates what liturgical dance does. For example, Doreen Holland, a sixteen-year member of the Allen Liturgical Dance Ministry, states that, "It allows me to express *everything* that I feel for the Lord and what I want others to know about the Lord through movement. So it is using the entire body, . . . your entire self—body, mind, soul, and spirit."[75] Robert Evans, Founding Director of the Dance Ministry Institute in Westchester, New York, talks about the communicative attributes of liturgical dance and the awesomeness of God to use dance as a tool:

> Dance is such a visual, creative art form, it has the ability to reach people in a somewhat private nonthreatening way. They can sit and wrestle with it and they can mask the wrestle but they cannot deny what God is doing to them on the inside. . . . There is something in the dance that causes people to be convicted to change, or it lifts a burden someone is carrying. It ushers others to worship and to abandon oneself to praise and worship God. I think it is such an awesome thing for GOD to use something like dance as a tool.[76]

Mary Jones is an international liturgical dancer, teacher, and cho-reographer based in Sydney, Australia. Jones notes the broad meaning of liturgical dance as a movement expression of the Christian faith. She explains that "liturgical dance is dance used in the liturgy of churches that have a set liturgy for their services such as Catholic, Lutheran, Episcopal/Anglican. . . . In this case, the dance is usually choreographed rather than spontaneous."[77] As parishioners and parents of children who do liturgical dance, Jay Dekie describes liturgical dance as "praise and worship expressed in dance," while his wife Lori believes, liturgical dance

---

Flake was one of the first AME pastors to allow liturgical dance to take place at Allen through the creation of the Allen Liturgical Dance Ministry in 1978.

75. Holland, Doreen in an interview with the author, November, 2011.

76. Evans, Robert in an interview with the author, January 2012.

77. Jones, Mary in an interview with the author, January 2012. Jones was also the founder of the Christian Dance Fellowship of Australia in 1978 and the International Christian Dance Fellowship in 1988.

"is worship before God and God's people, with not only our mind but our physical being."[78]

Davies submits that just as worship is classified as a "'response to God,' so too could dance be labeled a response to God."[79] He clarifies that the "*how* we worship, the ways in which we express our relation to God, *determines the kind of experience we have of God*."[80] Dancing, for Davies, must be regarded as an entirely proper way of responding to and acknowledging the divine presence, and to refuse to dance would be to identify God with immutable stability.

Yvonne Peters is an international liturgical dancer, teacher, and choreographer located in Lutz, Florida. She was also director of the International Celebration of the Feasts of Tabernacles in Jerusalem for the past twenty-two years. Peters explains that liturgical dance fulfills the biblical command to "halal," the Lord.

> From the very definition, [it] denotes that which pertains to public prayer and worship and that is what liturgical means. The "how" is the form of full body movement. It is the demonstration of full expression of praise to the God of all creation using our bodies as our voice. . . . through a spectrum ranging from crafted praise or choreography to clamorous spontaneity.[81]

Psalm 150 details a way dance gives praise and honor to God. Walter Bruggermann explains the six verses of Psalm 150 as summonses.[82] The hymn structure of Old Testament praise characteristically includes a *summons* to praise, and the *reasons* or *motivations* for the act.[83] Brueggemann explains, however, that the verse text found in Psalm 150 is remarkable because it contains no reason or motivations to praise God at all:

> Psalm 150 is situated literally at the end of the process of praise. It is also located theologically at the end of the process of praise and obedience, after all of Israel's motivations have been expressed and no more reasons need to be given. By Psalm 150, Israel fully knows the reasons for praise, perhaps learned through the course of the book of Psalms. At the end of the book, Israel

---

78. Dekie, Jay, and Lori Dekie in an interview with the author, December, 2011.

79. Davies, *Liturgical Dance*, 132.

80. Davies, *Liturgical Dance*, 132–133.

81. Peters, Yvonne in an interview with the author, January, 2012.

82. To read Psalm 150, see Appendix I.

83. Bruggermann, *Psalms*, 192.

will not restate them. Instead, this psalm is a determined, en-
thusiastic, uninterrupted, relentless, and unrelieved summons
that will not be content until all creatures-all of life-are 'ready
and willing' to participate in an unending song of praise that
is sung without reserve or qualification. The psalm expresses
a lyrical self-abandonment, an utter yielding of self, without
vested interest, calculation, desire, or hidden agenda. This praise
is nothing other than a glad offer of self in lyrical surrender to
the God appropriately addressed in praise. The Psalter, in correspondence to Israel's life with God when lived faithfully, ends
in glad, unconditional praise: completely, and without embar-
rassment or distraction, focused on God. No characterization of
God is given; it is enough that the one to be praised is fully and
utterly God and therefore must be praised.[84]

Bruggermann explains that such an exuberant yielding and self-abandonment can only take place when one comes to terms emotionally,
psychologically, dramatically, and theologically with the demanding,
sovereign reality of God. It is the affirmation of this God that becomes
the reason, motivation, warrant, ground, and substance of this type of
praise. Brueggemann concludes that "Psalm 150, at the end of the Psalter, celebrates Yahweh, who keeps the world as safe and reliable as Psalm
1 anticipates."[85] So when the psalmist says, "Praise [God] with dance,"
Davies believes that the psalmist could have been describing what was
being done, commanding that it be done, or may have been issuing a
performative utterance; in all of these cases the dance *is* the praise.[86] If
the physical activity of speaking can be praise, Davies contends, so the
physical activity of dancing can likewise be praise. What is essential is
that the dance movement executed must be suitable to the subject of the
praise, which, in this case, is God and the verbs to thank, rejoice, repent,
or worship are the words employed in movement. The liturgical dancer
hears a call and responds with a dance from the heart and the desire to
communicate what has occurred inwardly within the dancer arises and
takes shape through liturgical movement, as DeSola proposes.[87]

In explaining liturgical dance as a useful tool for the church, Bishop
Charles Ellis identifies the need for the church to look at liturgical dance

---

84. Bruggermann, *Psalms*, 192–193.

85. Bruggermann, *Psalms*, 194.

86. Davies, *Liturgical Dance*, 151.

87. See DeSola, "Word Became Dance."

as a tool and a gift to be rendered unto God.[88] He addresses the need for the twenty-first-century church to fully gather what it has to offer in the categories of worship and education when it comes to liturgical dance:

> [Liturgical Dance] has come after music and once it comes for the first time in our lives, it has to be scrutinized, it has to be investigated and looked at with a fine tooth comb for its usefulness, its purpose, and to see how it lines up with our practice of religion and our worship to God. Culture many times gets in our way of being all of what we can be in terms of utilizing our gifts and talents to God. Case in point: dance and song have *always* been a part of Israel's life; Israel, the first church; it was not either or. Liturgical dance, if you read the bible, will always be a part of our gifts to God. We read about David dancing out of his cloths, and people say, "That was then and not now."[89]

Adams also warns of the importance to avoid the development of an irreconcilable stress between responding to God and living in community. Like Bishop Ellis, he emphasizes that worship does attempt to create a tension between the present conditions of community and the gifts and demands of God so as to stimulate the church's actions. Adams states: "Nevertheless, worship must be corporate so that the resolution of this tension is sought in corporate action and improvement rather than through individual withdrawal."[90]

Without dance and other corporate expressions in worship, one could see the relationship with God as opposed to the demands of the community, and therefore withdraw from the community. Unlike meditation and prayer, dance includes body movement, which, in normal life activity, does not disturb but rather allows life to continue. Like Bishop Ellis, Adams can see the secular in the sacred, all caught up together:

> These dynamics are clarified by Gerardus van der Leeuw's suggestion that the separation that leads one to distinguish sacred from profane arises only as the dance diminishes. The

88. Ellis, Charles in an interview with the author, October 2011. Bishop Charles Ellis is Senior Pastor of The Greater Grace Temple Church of the Apostolic Faith in Detroit, Michigan and the presiding bishop of the Apostolic Faith, a division of the Pentecostal Denomination. Bishop Ellis is one of the forerunners of the "illustrated sermon," a sermon that is illustrated through drama, music, dance, set design, props, and stage lighting with the preacher as the conduit that links the entire dramatic ministry together.

89. Ellis, interview.

90. Adams, "Communal Dance Forms," 38–39.

re-emergence of the dance, he continued, is likely to sweep away separations that the critically minded person created by sitting and not dancing. Communal dance is preferable to individual so that one comes to look upon the constraints of living in community as a part of the response to God: a condition one should accept and not an evil one should try to escape.[91]

As a proper worship tool, it is an activity of the whole person. Dance expresses the physical and spiritual unity found within the human person in movement. As Davies proposes, worship can become not just a matter of the sense of hearing, as if only those parts of human life that make noise are fitted to praise God, nor solely of sight nor, where the Eucharist is concerned, of taste, nor if incense is used, of smell, but of touch also.[92]

The Role of the Dancer as Minister

The role of the dancer can be viewed as one who ministers. According to Webster's New College Dictionary, a person who ministers is one who attends to the needs and to the wants of others.[93] DeSola suggests that the dancer is a mirror that reflects and magnifies what is hidden or not accessible to the human eye alone. She explains that, "By grounding these perceptions in the body, a dancer then becomes as a mirror of the 'within' of things."[94] By paying attention to both physical and human realities and their spiritual dimensions, while simultaneously interpreting Scripture, the dancer is able to give new life and meaning to the passion of human emotions. In addition, the dancer/choreographer is perceived as both a teacher and a prophet. In the prophetic sense, DeSola references the pioneering and usage of dance in the church, when it is still unclear in some Christian denominations about the role of movement and dance in the liturgy. Reverend Flake remembers the change of culture that took place within Allen, when dance was introduced in worship:

When I think of its beginning in the church, and dance not belonging in the church, the whole transformational phase in getting some of the older members to understand that dance like singing is an art. Its impact on Allen has probably been the most

91. Adams, "Communal Dance Forms," 39.
92. Davies, *Liturgical Dance*, 137.
93. Pickett, ed., *Webster's Dictionary*.
94. DeSola, "Word Became Dance," 155.

secure, because its connection is not limited to the dancers, but
its integration with music, and gospel word, when it becomes a
complete strength and focus, and ministry becomes known to
be not one dimensional. You feel this down in your very soul,
and the measure of it is not the internal evaluation of it, but the
external evaluation. I don't think you can grow churches without energy, and liturgical dance with music gives forth an energy that energizes everyone to live for God and to do for God.[95]

Doreen Holland speaks of the difference in roles she has experienced as a member of the Allen Liturgical Dance Ministry:

I came from a church that did not allow dance at all. . . . Because
I wanted to please God, I gave it up. But when I came to Allen and saw that they were able to use the dance in worship, I
was ecstatic. You mean to tell me I can dance for God? When I
first joined it was basically just technical, wanting to fulfill the
movement properly, but when I got more into it, it became more
of a study, more of an understanding of why I am doing what
I am doing. So it caused my intimacy with God to grow and
to become deeper. It's not any longer for religion sake but for
ministry purposes. I see it and approach it differently than I did
sixteen years ago. . . . What is the scriptural base behind what I
am doing, and how am I portraying the steps to those who are
watching?[96]

Mary Jones also remembers how dancing was not allowed in her
church, but she soon found out about liturgical dance and its connection
to faith growth and faith expression:

I started to dance as an adult in my early 30's having been
brought up in an evangelical Anglican minister's family where
it was accepted that Christians didn't dance. For me dance was
a calling from God when I was searching for ministry direction.
My immediate discovery was that it involved body, mind, emotions, spirit, and artistic creativity and what a joy that was to be
able to respond to God and express my faith with everything
that I was. This happened at the same time as I became involved
in the charismatic renewal and was experiencing a deeper experience of the Holy Spirit. The Holy Spirit worked through the

95. Flake, interview.
96. Holland, interview.

dance to bring my personality into a more balanced expression with more freedom and less emphasis on the mind.[97]

As a parishioner, Jay Dekie acknowledges the liberating feeling liturgical dance gives him:

> It is something that may have been uncomfortable at the beginning, but when you hear about David dancing and how he was overjoyed and overwhelmed in the experience . . . he expressed it in movement with freedom in the body. Personally, it has truly been liberating, now there is no hesitation your hands are waving, you're pulling down strongholds, it is so free.[98]

Lori Dekie speaks from the vantage point of both a parishioner and a parent whose daughters are involved in liturgical dance.

> When I see it I see strongholds released, I can go out of my box to do the liturgical. . . . When I see my children doing liturgical dance there is such a comfort in knowing that seeds are being planted. . . . Only a mother could appreciate beyond what we are trying to do day to day and year to year, to see my child lift up her arms to the Lord in communication that was taught to her in a particular way and she is using it; it is just phenomenal.[99]

In leading communal circle and processional dances, DeSola explains that the dancer serves as a "gatherer," welding the community together with dance and interpretations of songs or chants. What DeSola means when she describes the dancer as a gatherer is "the role of the dancer who calls forth movements of dances from the people, and tests them out for use or further development."[100] The movements that are not appropriate will simply disappear while those that do will continue to serve as language that feeds the soul. Yvonne Peters recalls participating in the international celebration of the Feast of Tabernacles, an annual event that takes place in Israel with international dancers[101]:

97. Jones, interview.

98. Dekie and Dekie, interview.

99. Dekie and Dekie, interview.

100. DeSola, "Word Became Dance," 158.

101. "The Feast of Tabernacles (Lev 23:33–43) is elsewhere called the Festival of Ingathering (Exod 23:16). At the end of a rainless summer, from May to September, processing of the year's harvest was completed, the products gathered for protection and storage, and the ending of the agricultural year celebrated. Deuteronomy presents the days of the festival as a family affair filled with rejoicing (Deut 16:14)" (Harrelson, *New Interpreter's Study Bible*, 180).

The international celebration of the Feast of Tabernacles in Israel began during the early 1980s, I found myself in and among the nations from all over the world expressing their worship in the same way despite language, facial features, skin color, raising their hands, and dancing. They were led by a few international dancers from all over the world, but we were all on one accord using dance. I realized that this was something that God was depositing in my own ear from a small space in Florida, but it included all the nations and that dance was a valid expression of worship unto the Lord.

From the year 1984 to several years ago, I made my pilgrimage back to Jerusalem for five to six weeks out of the year to dance, choreograph, and direct this international celebration of the Feast of Tabernacles. Those who traveled back to their lands began to share these very movements within their congregations.[102]

DeSola explains that, in this respect the dancer serves as a living "icon" of good news and enables people through movement to rejoice, wonder, and open their hearts to their innermost feelings. Doreen Holland shares how influential liturgical dance has been to the congregants who view it:

As a dancer and an observer, one who has sat in the pews and watched, the church has been influenced by the beauty and the awe of the liturgical dance, especially with our dance ministry and it being so large, we surround the people, it is not just frontal but we envelop the entire congregation with the worship and the awe of God.[103] So it invites them in and makes them feel a part of what is going on. As an observer, they are not just sitting here, it uses all of the senses, it is not just hearing, it's not just seeing, all of the senses, witnessing the waving of the flag, feeling the people rushing through the aisles. Everyone is involved and you don't feel like you are just sitting there, but it becomes a bridge and when they allow themselves to enter in deeper they are invited in to see heaven, they see worship and it becomes more than just a nice dance.[104]

102. Peters, interview.

103. The Allen Liturgical Dance Ministry, which was founded by the author in 1978, is a ministry that involves male and female children, teens, and adults. It has been known to have an active enrollment of up to 300 dancers at a time.

104. Holland, interview.

The dancer reminds the community that they are people with feeling; they can rejoice, weep, move, be freedom-loving, physical, and capable of "resurrection."[105] As a witness, the dancer brings into heightened awareness what is already present in the community. The contributions of dance range from demonstration of the ways a congregation becomes more open and spontaneous with movement and gesture to being an integral part of an entire liturgy. The Reverend Eyesha K. Marable explains the connection liturgical dance has with the congregation and with liturgy:

> Dance is seen and not heard, and so people need to ask the dancer what are you saying through your body? What message are you conveying without the use of the spoken word? What are your actions saying that is louder than any words can say? Their questions are asked so the congregation can get their healing, get their deliverance, and get their restoration.

> [Liturgical dance] allows one to prepare not only the whole person physically, but emotionally, spiritually, psychologically, physiologically, for a worship encounter. The difference between the sacred and the praise is that liturgy is required in liturgical dance. And that requires that we study the word of God, to show ourselves approved. The liturgy is required. The Catholic Church follows a liturgy; our Jewish family follows a liturgy in reading the Torah in a three-year period. Liturgy is order. Dance ministry requires that we follow a liturgy.[106]

Dr. Patrick Evans, a sacred musician, once described liturgical dance in relationship to music, although this viewpoint has changed since participating in body prayers during chapel services held at the Marquand Chapel at Yale Divinity School:

> I think liturgical dance is interpreting a song and hymn but I have been stretched to see liturgical dance without music. Some of the most moving experiences in seeing liturgical dance that I have experienced as a musician have been in people doing Body Prayers in silence. When seeing someone lead the congregation, and explaining what is being done and explaining the meaning

105. DeSola, "Word Became Dance," 158.

106. Marable, Eyesha K. in an interview with the author, January 2012. The Reverend Eyesha Katurah Marable is an itinerant elder in the AME church as well as the founding director of the National Liturgical Dance Network, an international liturgical dance organization.

of the gestures and then repeat them three times in silence. Also in use of the proclamation of a spoken text, a poem, or scripture, sometimes with some drumming, not necessarily while people are singing, and not to a recorded piece of music, or to an organ improvisation. Fifteen years ago I would have thought liturgical dance is choreography to a piece of music. It's more than that.[107]

Davies believes that to dance is to abandon oneself wholly to the activity and this is a form of self-oblation that is of the essence of Eucharistic worship. To give oneself is to empty oneself and worship is giving oneself to God, and dancing, with the accompanying expenditure of psychic and physical energy, is another such means.[108] According to Davies, too many times worship is understood and regarded as a way not to give, but only to receive, but this is the wrong attitude to take, since so many leave worship empty handed. To empty oneself in liturgical dance, however, is to be open to the possibility of being filled with divine grace.[109]

It is essential for liturgical dancers to understand their role as gathers, initiators, and those who help carry a word of encouragement throughout the worship experience. They must be clear and open to the move of God that moves them to dance, but also speaks to them while they dance. The understanding of the role of the liturgical dancer as minister is essential. Bishop Ellis speaks about understanding the gift:

I do not mind dancers, but do they understand their purpose in God? They have to understand their gift. Regardless of singer, dancer, usher, reader of scripture, my question is do they understand their gift. . . . I believe it belongs in ministry but it must be taught and people must understand what it is and what they are doing with that gift.[110]

At the same token individualism and pride has no place within the heart of the liturgical dancer. Reverend Flake explains this so to alert the dancer of the boundaries that should be set when dancing within the worship setting:

107. Evans, Patrick in an interview with the author, January 2012. Dr. Patrick Evans is a former Associate Professor of the Practice of Sacred Music at the Institute of Sacred Music at Yale Divinity School (YDS) and was the former director of music for the Marquand Chapel, which supplied daily ecumenical worship at YDS.

108. Davies, *Liturgical Dance*, 153.

109. Davies, *Liturgical Dance*, 153.

110. Ellis, interview.

I'm going to give you two rules . . . Because I want you to understand that there must be a clear distinction between your dance
in secular society and your dance in the liturgical context. The
two rules that you must follow: Rule #1: Never for self. Understand that you never dance for self, but you dance for the edification of God. If you're dancing for self, you'll mess up the step,
you'll cause things to be out of order; [but] to be in order you
dance to the glory of God. . . . For the edification of God. Rule
#2: Not for show but for worship. If this becomes your show,
God will close the curtain. It's not for self and it's not a show
and if you understand that, you have the basic ingredients for
successful ministry in dance.[111]

Robert Evans also agrees that the promotion of pride is not to be found
within the operation of the liturgical dancer. He gives instruction that the
ultimate attention is directed toward God and God only:

[Dance] has a tendency to bring in this prideful nature and we
have to make sure we do not become prideful . . . The ultimate
attention goes to God and we have to make sure that we do not
take that attention or the glory away from God and place it on
our artistic expressions. . . . Everyone has an offering to give with
their gifts, talents, skills, and abilities unto the Lord to be used
for his glory. These gifts, talents, and skills are sometimes on
stage, sometimes behind stage, sometimes administrative, and
sometimes they are organizational. Let us find a place where we
can come together collectively as a community of worshiping
artists; whether I dance, sing, sew, sculpt we bring our gifts together for a glorifying end.[112]

The *theory* of liturgical dance considers the role of the dancer in
the liturgical community; the role of dance in the liturgical structure,
including the varieties of religious themes which may be danced; and the
communal nature or dimension of dance and worship.[113] The *practice* of
liturgical dance DeSola describes may be divided into the preparation of
the dancer and community, and the shared experience of the liturgical
dancer and the community during the liturgy.

---

111. Flake, interview.
112. Evans, Robert, interview.
113. DeSola, "Word Became Dance," 155.

The preparation of the liturgical dancer is divided into several components which include the spiritual, technical, and analytical.[114] DeSola delineates the spiritual training of the liturgical dancer to include embodied ways of prayer as well as aspects of traditional religious education such as ongoing worship involvement, studies, and instruction in prayer; and meditation such as personal and centering prayer, group prayers, and the reading of Scripture. She defines liturgical dance in relationship to prayer as follows:

> If prayer is the central core of life, then dance becomes prayer when we are expressing our relationship to God, to others, and to all the world of matter and spirit, through movement originating from our deepest selves-this same central point of worship. The movements of dance-prayer start from our deep center, flow outward like rivulets into the stream of life, and impart life everywhere. So dance can be a part of prayer, just as stillness can be a part of movement and silence can be a part of music. There is one root; all the rest, movement or stillness, silence or sound, is its expression. The closer to the source, the purer the song.[115]

Reverend Marable speaks about embodied prayer in the context of both a teaching method and choreographic structure by which liturgical dances are created:

> Embodied prayer is really "in the beginning was the Word and the Word was God" and "the Word was made flesh" (John 1:1). Embodied prayer is reading the psalm and becoming that psalm. Reading it and meditating on it and asking God how can we experience that word in our fingers, toes, eyes, etc.? So when we embody our prayers, when we embody our praise to God, we tell God I need you, I need healing, but I will dance it out, there is a physical release, there is a physical exchange. I am going to give you my praise and leave our best gifts in the sanctuary; it is then that we feel a relief and release, that healing will come in the circumstance. It may not come immediately but we are changed, our outlooks are changed in the midst of our dancing. So we are not dancing for dance sake but we are dancing the word of God.[116]

114. DeSola, "Word Became Dance," 161.

115. DeSola, *Spirit Moves*, 10.

116. Marable, interview.

DeSola explains that the technical training involves the dancer's preparatory warm-up prior to the liturgy, such as loosening-up exercises to activate the body through stretching and other techniques. These activities are just an abbreviated extension of the dancer's overall training which can include the learning of a variety of dance techniques (ballet, modern/contemporary, folk, and an array of cultural dances that give identification and meaning to Christians who live within the international community).[117] This training can also include improvisational and choreographic techniques in movement discovery to support spontaneous movement language in prayer, praise, and worship.[118]

The analytical training or the development of subject matter, consists of studies in Scripture, liturgy, and ritual, together with study of psychological and spiritual components of the personality, as DeSola points out. Attention to the themes and subject matter of dances and development of a point of view about the material are based on personal experience that has political, sociological, and economic dimensions.[119] In the context of the analytical training, dance can be considered within the realm of religious studies which is an educational approach to the understanding of liturgical dance. This type of approach underlines the presupposition that one learns by and through dancing. The elements of the spiritual, technical, and analytical are essential in the preparation and educational training of the liturgical dancer and choreographer. While these practices are valuable for religious studies, they can be done independently of any liturgical consideration.

Liturgical Dance as a Worship Response

If dance is to become an acceptable feature within a church service, then it must be integrated with and not just added to the celebration of the liturgy. When dance is an act of praise or adoration, then it cannot become just a filler, bringing the course of the liturgy to a halt. Davies warns that an improper relationship between dance and worship would have been fostered if members of a congregation think that once dance is brought into the corporate worship experience, everything stops in order to display this artistic presentation; and then afterwards, worship continues.

117. Turner, "If David had not Danced," 49–52.
118. Turner, "If David had not Danced," 51.
119. DeSola, "Word Became Dance," 161–62.

This type of irrational presupposition will not bring the collective and supportive harmonies that are found between liturgical dance and worship. Therefore, it must be understood that whoever is asked to bring dancing inside the worship space of the church must be aware that they are being invited to contribute to an event in which God is the focus, and God is encountered. They are not executing a program that warrants theatrical applause at the end. Davies contends that the inside of the church is hallowed and holy ground, and a place where God can be met. Therefore dancing must aid such a meeting between the creator and the created, and in such a doing its integration with worship has been achieved. Davis cautions:

> The reference here is of course to dance which in itself is an act of devotion, but this statement has to be freed from ambiguity by defining precisely what kind of dance is in mind, since there are many varieties not all of which could be identified in this way with worship.[120]

When dance is integrated in worship, there is a gain in three aspects according to Davis. The three aspects are *diversity*, which is increased, *creativity*, which is encouraged, and *participation*, which is intensified.[121] The Apostle Paul's suggestive account of the *diversity* to be found in the Corinthian church is recorded in 1 Corinthians, which states:

> What should be done then, my friends? When you come together, each one has a hymn, a lesson, a revelation, a tongue, or an interpretation. Let all things be done for building up. (1 Cor 14:26)

Davies posits it was the Holy Spirit who determined what parts were revealed in the worship gathering, whether they were the gift of teaching, prophecy, etc. and when these gifts are suppressed or not expressed there is a quenching of the Spirit (1 Thess 5:19). So the question becomes what then of those whose gift it is to dance? Are they to be left out of the liturgical celebration? Davies believes that if music, singing, sculpture, painting, and all of the arts have a place in the Christian culture or setting, then why not dance? He supports this question with a quote from the North American Roman Catholic bishops who stated, "All words and

120. Davies, *Liturgical Dance*, 138.
121. Davies, *Liturgical Dance*, 143.

art forms can be used to praise God in the liturgical assembly."[122] This statement is applicable to those individual artists who can and wish to worship God by dancing. As a musician, Patrick Evans speaks about the denominational and personal barriers that promote the use of the mind over the use of the body:

> Especially in mainline congregations—especially as a Presbyterian, we are so in our *heads* and so *not* in our bodies, which is so bad for music. And the psalms say worship God with timbrel and dance; they do not say worship God with your thoughts, worship God with your mind, worship God with the text you are reading on theology. But in most educational whether it is church school, worship, whether that is seminary education, we are so privileging the life of the mind and we either ignore or shame the life of the body, and I think it is awful. Liturgical Dance is so important for people to claim their bodies and get to some deep spiritual place that you cannot get to through intellect alone.[123]

Liturgical dance is not simply a prayer, or a dance of praise and worship, but it is that and so much more. *Creativity* is needed and barriers should be removed within the realm of liturgical dance. Davies warns that liturgical dance can become sentimental, superficial, and anything but a fitting rendering of glory to God. But once a seasoned and experienced liturgical dancer is allowed into the church, the result is likely to be disturbing. Dances about suffering and hardship can arise, and choreodramas,[124] which are sermons in dance, can be delivered so the word of God is witnessed and experienced in revolutionary and creative modalities.[125] Davies submits that creativity does not fashion a safe haven, but it challenges the congregation to experience the word of God and faith development in radical ways: "This can upset members of a congregation, many of whom will be conservative and, even if prepared

122. Davies, *Liturgical Dance*, 143.

123. Evans, Patrick, interview.

124. Choreo-drama is a term that was first introduced to the author by choreographer and director Dianne McIntyre, whose dance company, Sounds In Motion, and the choreographic and theatrical (including Off Broadway) projects the author had the opportunity to participate in as both performer and assistant to the choreographer. The term has come to represent sermons performed in dance with the use of multi-dimensional sound collages, including music, spoken word, and sound effects as well as visual imagery, props, and choreography.

125. Turner, "If David had not Danced," 49–50.

to tolerate dance, will want it to be inoffensive. This could be to impose shackles on creativity."[126]

If shackles are not placed on the creative spectrum of liturgical dance, however, then its educative value is endless. Jay Dekie speaks about his time as a member of the Allen Liturgical Dance Ministry and as a member of the Marriage Enrichment Ministry of the Greater Allen Cathedral who used liturgical and ballroom dancing as a way to teach Christian concepts applicable to the institution of marriage. He explains how dance was so meaningful to him in both instances:

> There were a couple of pieces that affected me. But "Conquerors"[127]; there was a special meaning and when you are a part of liturgical and you are struggling with something, you are able to internalize it, the darts, everything coming at you and yet you are able to fend it, you are able to show it warring with it, and showing that God is with you. It's something when you *do* it, watching it you get something, but doing it. It's like singing in the choir versus listening to the choir; there's a different release when you *sing*.

> But to *do* liturgical, to be a part of it. When we did the marriage dance,[128] to be a part of the wonderful display of the dance, to know what each movement meant. What the dance meant you can't express it with words. There is nothing like it.[129]

Lori Dekie recalls her reaction when she participated in the marriage dance.

> The effect is huge. Doing the marriage dance, rehearsing in our little tiny space I was reminded about his security and his love. I was reminded why I choose him and it was intimacy by default. Dancing and praying before God there is nothing like it. The effect was huge. The "ah-hah" moment was so great, the

---

126. Davies, *Liturgical Dance*, 144.

127. "Conquerors," was a choreodrama (a sermon in dance) choreographed by the author for Royal Priesthood—the adult male members of the Allen Liturgical Dance Ministry—in the Fall of 1997.

128. "From the Upper Room to the Ballroom," was a dance choreographed for the members of the Marriage Enrichment Ministry of the Greater Allen AME Cathedral of New York by the author and her husband in June 2011.

129. Dekie and Dekie, interview.

ceremonial dance that we did affected us for months after the dance was done.[130]

Dance can be integrated with worship as a vital factor to increase *participation* and it can further this in several ways. It can first reduce shyness and promote corporateness; second it draws people out of isolation since the movements are visible, the emotions and rhythm are common, and the enjoyment of God becomes the shared activity of a fellowship; and third, dance enables each one to become part of a totality that is greater than the individual self.[131] This is reflected in the comments of Patrick Evans, who highlights the importance of being imitators of Christ when the congregation is asked to imitate a song or movement in the worship gathering:

> If singing a new song to the Lord is a faithful act of worship, then preparing to sing a new song to the Lord is also a faithful act of worship. The learning itself is an act of worship, the teaching itself is an act of worship, not an interruption of worship. If we are to be imitators of Christ's imitation, you give a gesture and we imitate it; it embodies what we claim as Christians that we are to imitate Christ. Every time we enact teaching and learning in worship we are naming theologically the metaphor for what we proclaim to be as Christians.[132]

Evans acknowledges that the teaching act within worship is one such method in establishing the diversity, creativity, and increased participation of the entire congregation. If this is understood by the worship leader and the congregation, then both the observation and imitation can produce learning results. He explains this further:

> If they are being invited to do a body prayer or singing a certain way, you do not have to do it. Because learning also takes place by watching, until one is comfortable enough to join in.
>
> Whatever excellence we want to offer to God in worship, we need to make plenty of room to be human and that we are truly able to bring our whole selves which includes our brokenness, our inability, which includes our sorrow, not just our rejoicing, and not just our brilliance, and not just what we are best at. Anytime worship leaders are inviting worship, we must always

130. Dekie and Dekie, interview.

131. Davies, *Liturgical Dance*, 145.

132. Evans, Patrick, interview.

be sure the invitation to try something and not be immediate experts at it is clear to everyone gathered.[133]

These are all ways that the understanding of liturgical dance can be administered to the congregation. DeSola points out that this can also be accomplished through the religious education of the people by workshops or preliminary instructions with the congregation. The dual objective is to prepare the community to participate in the dances and to create collaborative work with the celebrant and/or liturgical team.[134] She recommends that the congregation and leaders of churches need to become more aware of the potential for dance and dancers to express the richness and complexity of the Christian faith. The inclusion of dance in a sacred context is not peripheral, ornamental, or a diversion from the service, but on the contrary the dancer embodies unrealized hopes and dreams of the people.[135] She proposes that a trained and spirit-filled body of the dancer teaches through dance as does an icon or a religious painting or a fine piece of music.

Liturgical Dance within the Worship Service and Beyond

Albert Rouet describes liturgy as that which gathers the community of believers together and presents them as distant persons of the cross who hunger for their faithful journey to continue. The liturgical event and the quality of the event is not the factor that determines the success of the event, but what is imperative and what must be revealed is the depth of the conversion from which each one celebrates from.[136] Successful liturgy moves a congregation more toward conversion, more toward hearts being transformed because of the continual conversion experience. For Rouet, the arts can be helpful in fostering this continued conversion experience. Rouet comments on the state of the celebrant, including the liturgical dancer during the worship gathering:

> Worshipping people are beggars. Because they know their poverty, their liturgy becomes the praise of that One who gives them everything. Liturgy succeeds when those who celebrate realize

133. Evans, Patrick, interview.

134. DeSola, "Word Became Dance," 162.

135. DeSola, "Word Became Dance," 160.

136. Rouet, *Liturgy and Arts*, 19.

that they have been pushed beyond themselves, whatever their natural abilities or their skills.[137]

Therefore, Rouet contends, faith asks dance to translate into art those spaces where words cannot reach, but where the human spirit moves forward and where Christ himself ventured ahead of the church. Reverend Marable explains the necessity for instructional gatherings that teach the importance of liturgy and the components that make up church liturgy in the liturgical colors, objects, songs, etc. She describes one such conference gathering "from the first dance ministry conference," in which,

> Dancers came from across the nation to learn how to study, and follow the liturgy of the Christian church, to understand the word, the colors that are rendered during certain seasons, the ceremonies that surround the Christian church.[138] How to build altars of praise, and liturgy requires that if we read the word, we will understand what God did in the past, present, and what we are to become in the future. "Praise dance" does not require that, everything can praise the Lord. There are no rules, everyone can praise the Lord, high praise, there is no set standard in which to follow in order to understand what to render to God during particular seasons of the Christian calendar. The bible is our instructional tool that tells us as Christians how to live, how to praise, how to worship. It tells us what God did in the past and what is he doing now and what prophetic word God is going to speak.[139]

DeSola quotes the work of Thomas A. Kane, who presents a helpful analysis of the role of dance within the liturgical structure. Kane suggests that instead of describing all the possible places and ways dance can support liturgy, he directs people to consider dance according to its function in the liturgy. Liturgical dance can fall into five different categories: processional, prayer (including acclamation and invocation), proclamation, meditation, and celebration.[140] Religious themes are interwoven within this structure and the variety becomes endless. He states "the dancer can express the multiple and sacred dimensions of life—joys, fears, dreams,

137. Rouet, *Liturgy and Arts*, 10.

138. The Allen Liturgical Dance Ministry presented their first national liturgical dance ministry conference under the direction of the author in 1998 entitled, "Dancing Before God's Throne." This is the conference that Reverend Marable is referring to.

139. Marable, interview.

140. DeSola, "Word Became Dance, 159.

questions, disappointments, themes of peace and justice, faith, action and the sacredness of everyday life."[141] Jay Dekie shares an experience of liturgical dance during a worship service at Allen:

> From the congregational perspective I watch the congregation. We find that a lot of the married couples are now free to lift up their hands, arms, during worship. When you see the pageantry, the worship and the flags, sounds, movement, you can only imagine what heaven would be like. [During the service] . . . there was a song that the children were dancing and with the words of the song . . . the congregation was overwhelmed by the song and the choreography. It was so amazing and the song had such power that the spirit overwhelmed the congregation, the congregation was overtaken that the sermon couldn't be preached.[142]

Lori Dekie continues:

> There was such a collaboration between the music, movement and theme, and the choreography was so important that when all came together there was such a synergy that took place![143]

The Dekies continue sharing another memory of the use of liturgical dance for the first time by their daughters during a worship service at a neighboring church and how the experience changed the dynamic of the parishioners:

> We had an experience with a church that we visit near our home in Long Island where our daughters brought liturgical dance to them. This congregation never witnessed it before and at the end they were all crying. At the end of the service, the pastor and people came to us and thanked us for allowing our daughters to dance, because they never witnessed it before, and they were grateful for such a new experience, especially since the church is made up of seniors. They were so grateful.[144]

Under the heading of prayer within the worship service, Reverend Robert VerEecke, SJ, describes liturgical dance prayer as all those movements, gestures, and rhythmic expressions of the body that are not merely functional but rather have an intention of prayer and communal

---

141. DeSola, "Word Became Dance, 159.

142. Dekie and Dekie, interview.

143. Dekie and Dekie, interview.

144. Dekie and Dekie, interview.

celebration. He points out that there are the moments in liturgy which use the symbolic language of the non-verbal to cry out on behalf of the whole community, to express a depth of human experience that cannot be spoken in words:

> Movements of sorrow, anguish, of faith-filled joy and ecstasy that are given life and liveliness through the body are the "stuff" of liturgical danced prayer. From the simple lifting up of the arms at the beginning of the Eucharistic prayer to a more festive dance at the closing of the celebration, liturgical danced prayer can capture and express the hearts of the faithful if it is allowed to speak and are seen for what it is, a valid form of prayer.[145]

Liturgical dance can be found in many countries. For example, Yvonne Peters highlights the use of liturgical dance as prayer and intercession in Israel. She states, "Intercession and dance within Israel brings to light the promises of God for Israel and so they dance, intercede, and worship God with these thoughts in mind."[146] She points to the use of prayer and dance among Brazilian Christians, and notes the wide number of Brazilian males who dance and intercede on behalf of their country:

> Brazil is an exuberate nation and in the worship setting, they have great intercession for not only themselves but for their nation. They bring national flags within their worship and present their nation before the Lord for the Lord to lead and to transform them and this is done through the word, music, and the dance. The plethora of males, men from 18 and up who do liturgical dance, they have almost as many male dancers as they do female dancers. Because they do not come from the western mindset that dance is effeminate, for them dance is an expression of strength, so they are so many excellent male dancers emerging out of Brazil.[147]

Within the worship gathering, the use of liturgical dance as storytelling is explained by Davies through the term, narrative dance.[148] Davies suggests that one of the major uses of dance within Christianity

145. Gagne et al., *Dance in Christian Worship*, 138.

146. Peters, interview.

147. Peters, interview.

148 There are many terms utilized within the choreographic categories of liturgical dance. There are also numerous terms used to describe the use of dance in narration or the storytelling capacities of liturgical dance, such as "choreo-drama" (see footnote above).

is to function as the re-enactment mechanism in translating the sacred history, which is foundational to the Christian faith. This can be done through narrative dance that accompanies, illustrates, and accompanies biblical readings and stories. This can replace the sermon, not simply of the didactic but also of the kerygmatic type, where the proclamation of the gospel takes place. He states, "One should not only preach one's religion but dance it; one should not just pay verbal testimony to one's faith but incarnate it."[149] He also explains that within the narrative dance the meaning of the stories can be explored physically through understanding and learning that takes place both cognitively and creatively as explained in chapter 2 and through experiential learning as explained in chapter 3. Dance can be prophetic as it calls things into question, whether they are actions, policies, behavior, preconceived ideas, etc. Davies states:

> Dance too can assist us to find the ultimate in the immediate by transcending the present and opening it up to eschatological possibilities. Prophetic dance does not simply mirror the present nor depict solely the historical context of an original story; it points beyond that which is to what may be. It can awaken responsibility and lead to an appreciation of values rooted in actual living.[150]

One example of dramatic narration of a biblical story is the illustrated sermon.[151] Bishop Charles Ellis, one of the pioneers in its use explains why he uses this creative methodology at least four times a year at his church: New Year's Eve (an original illustrative sermon), Good Friday, "The Whip, Hammer, and Cross," Easter Sunday (an original illustrative

149. Davies, *Liturgical Dance*, 139.

150. Davies, *Liturgical Dance*, 139.

151. In the interview with Bishop Charles Ellis, he explained that it was Tommy Barnett, pastor of the First Phoenix Assembly of God in Phoenix, Arizona, who was the first one to introduce him to "illustrative sermons." Illustrative sermons are the integration of both sermon and drama. They are productions where the sermon is fully illustrated by way of drama, dance, music, stage props, and stage sets—set design, and graphic designs with production makeup, costume etc. The illustrative sermon is connected by way of the preacher, Bishop Ellis, who connects the biblical account, the action/dance/song with sermonic proclamations, prophetic utterances, and introspective questions to the congregation. The illustrative sermons are done in the sanctuary where the entire sanctuary through set design is transformed into the scene where the illustrative sermon takes place.

sermon), and the Friday before Halloween, "From Hell and Back."[152] He states:

> I think we are very careful because our productions (and I guess I have to use the word "production" because, if I just use the word "sermon," then people will just think that someone just opened up the bible and talking about stuff, that [they] don't know) . . . I do use the word "production" because I want people to feel a sense of a "professional presentation," whether it is lighting, staging, or special effects, costuming, or makeup, I want them to feel this is going to be professional. . . . You're not going to have to imagine it. . . . You are going to see it. That is why I use that word production, but they see ministry. That is why we use illustrated sermon, with the makeup, costuming . . . People question, "Is it a sermon or is it a play?" and it gets them out. Then people say, "Now I know what an illustrated sermon is." . . . Barnett was the first to cut the lights on for me to help me have an appreciation for an integration of the two, you have the spoken word and the dramatization.[153]

The work of Robert Evans, such as *The Nativity*, is an example of a full ministry story performed through liturgical dance and presented outside the church building. He explains how the production of *The Nativity* came about:

> God instructed me to do *The Nativity* and to flip the script. Instead of presenting a musical singing version with many singers with one to two dancers, do the entire production through dance and use live singing to enhance the dance. I told the Lord that there was no model for me to follow and he reminded me of my viewing Dance Theatre of Harlem and their ability to tell a story solely through movement, but when I saw their production of *Medea*, and though I was unfamiliar with the text, I could follow the storyline completely, because they were so thorough in the storytelling on stage through movement. And that became the model. How do we develop character; how do we move from one conversation to another; what dance movement language does this character need? Those things became the framework that I can then put walls onto.[154]

152. The author saw the live production of "From Hell and Back," and will make reference to it and "Whip, Hammer, and Cross," in chapter 5.

153. Ellis, interview.

154. Evans, Robert, interview.

Evans recalls the instructional capacities of liturgical dance as experienced by one of his neighbors who saw a production of *The Nativity*:

> My neighbor saw the production in 2005 and her comment was, 'Robert I get it . . . I get the whole birth thing now, I have heard sermons about it before, but I finally get it.' Instructional . . . yeah, it reminds us what this Christmas season is about . . . this season of Santa Claus and reindeer and all of this other stuff . . . the authentic message of Christmas is this little baby that became the ultimate gift for us.[155]

For the dancer and the student of religion, the story becomes personalized, and a connection develops from which new points of view emerge. "When a biblical story is danced, it becomes 'part of one's bones.'"[156] This type of liturgical dance becomes an integrated, living memory, and it has the potential to affect one's life in far-reaching ways. As DeSola puts it: "Through our bodies, we have entered into an integral relationship with the gospel. Reading the Scriptures and prayers with and through the body is a new kind of hermeneutics."[157] She also describes the communal dimensions of dance and worship and its effectiveness in the learning process. When the congregation is dancing together they feel the combined energy of all the people moving. "They are led to comprehend, in a lived, felt way, what their community is about."[158] Such an understanding may give rise of what is implied in the phrases "the body of Christ," "the prayers of the faithful," and "the celebration of the banquet." Thus, the sacred, communal dance of today has the same potential of involving people in a learning and living experience of their religious beliefs.[159]

Conclusion

While liturgical dance is any dance in the context of worship, it is most closely defined when it is itself seen as liturgy.[160] The movement and choreographic language of liturgical dance has been enhanced by modern/contemporary dances:

155. Evans, Robert, interview.
156. DeSola, "Word Became Dance," 165.
157. DeSola, "Word Became Dance," 165.
158. DeSola, "Word Became Dance," 161.
159. DeSola, "Word Became Dance," 101.
160. Davies, *Liturgical Dance*, 155.

> The possibility of this category of dance, which is in itself wor-
> ship and prayer, has been immensely increased by the emergence
> of modern dance; indeed it is difficult to conceive of liturgical
> dance in this sense, as distinct from narrative dance, as existing
> without it. No longer is a knowledge of the five positions of clas-
> sical ballet essential nor has attention to be fixed on the exact
> placements of the arms and legs. Free creative movement that is
> an activity of the entire physical/spiritual being is now possible
> to express and embody one's worship.[161]

Therefore, liturgical dance does not seem to consist of following pre-
established exterior norms, like those found in ballet choreography. It
emanates from the interior drive of the dancers as they give honor to
God, and it is appropriate to the divine mystery, which should suppress
from time to time the vocal in favor of a voiceless but bodily communion.
A spiritual goal of dance is to open new channels for prayer and worship,
as DeSola asserts: "Ultimately, the liturgical dance serves to transform
and become a common praise and 'work of the people.'"[162]

This chapter explained the history of dance within religious custom
as that which was found within the culture of early human life. From
there a historical journey of the use of dance in religion, whether known
as symbolic movement, sacred dance, or religious dance, paved the way
to examine how it was demonstrated in the Old Testament. The four types
of dances most commonly utilized by the Israelites helped to promote
dance in worshiping and developing faith in God. The early Christian
Church struggled with why dance should be allowed inside Christian
worship, and it appears that the 21st century church is still struggling
with these same issues.

To help clarify what liturgical dance is for the 21st century church
this chapter sought to widen its definition to include characteristics that
identify it as a tool for the teaching of religious education within the
church as a community place of learning. Thus, it is proposed that in
formulating a working definition of liturgical dance, the characteristics
gathered from chapters 1, 2 and 3 must be included. These characteristics
include liturgical dance as creative expression, imaginative exploration,
experiential, educative and instructional, introspective, narrative and
prayerful, inspired by love and thanksgiving, healing and reconciling,
while fostering religious identity within the church community through

161. Davies, *Liturgical Dance*, 155.
162. DeSola, "Word Became Dance," 165.

bodily movement that investigates space, time, and design. Flowing from this is a newly crafted working definition of liturgical dance for Christians that has been created by the writer. Thus liturgical dance "is expressive and imaginative movement that is used both inside and outside of worship that creatively educates and instructs Christians to comprehend the Bible and their faith in the Trinity through the elements of space, time, and design. Liturgical dance has a relationship with music, spoken word, and silence. For both the individual dancer and congregant, the church is identified as community through individual and mutual movement, and dance explorations that cultivate love, prayer, healing, and reconciliation, while fostering Christian identity throughout the liturgical calendar. Because of its experiential properties non-Christians can be exposed to liturgical dance and be influenced by it."

This newly form working definition of liturgical dance gives foundation to the last chapter, "And We Shall Learn through the Dance." This chapter presents formats that reveal the diversified partnership found between liturgical dance and religious education and how such a partnership can function inside and outside of the church. These formats help to design activities in the areas of worship, bible study, missions, conversational gatherings, prayer, and ministry outreach.

Chapter 5

And We Shall Learn through the Dance

Exploring the Instructional Relationship between
Liturgical Dance and Religious Education

Introduction

This chapter analyzes the relationship liturgical dance has with religious education in the life of the church as a community place of learning. This affiliation is viewed through the imaginative imagery of two partners dancing together in a choreographed dance. In dance as in the circus arts, partnering can happen between two people or within a group of dancers. In some dance styles, the two people can be of the same gender, as in a duet, where they represent two voices dancing different choreography simultaneously, or dancing the same movement in unison. However, there are other dance styles where they are to support each other's weight in a variety of wonderful and imaginative lifts. In addition, each partner compliments and highlights the other partner as in a ballet's *pas de deux* or they dance as one, as in ballroom dances like the waltz.[1] In both of

1. "The *pas de deux* originated in ballet choreography and appears throughout the ballet, but it is also known to end the ballet, with a spectacular *pas de deux*. It is comprised of the ballerina and her partner. This *pas de deux* usually developed according to a strict form: first came a stately section (the adagio) for both performers, emphasizing lyrical and sustained movements. Then came two solos (called 'variations'), the first for the man and the second for the ballerina. Finally, in the coda, the stars appeared together again, the choreography emphasizing quick, flashy steps. If the *pas*

these cases the partners are made up of one male dancer and one female dancer. Whether the correlation between the partners is seen through unison choreographed movement, improvisational movement, solo moments when each partner is featured separate from the other, or during the acrobatics of real partnering where one partner lifts the other, all of these images place the two partners in the position of being collaborators who are dancing toward a finished end. So, too with liturgical dance and religious education. The aim of this chapter is to suggest that liturgical dance has a valid role in the instructional life of the church, and this role is witnessed through its ongoing relationship with religious education.

In identifying the variety of partnering formations that can take place within a choreographed dance, this chapter identifies four partnering positions that represent four instructional formats which place liturgical dance and religious education together as teaching partners operating in activities both inside and outside the walls of the church. These four arrangements are derived and crafted from the accumulated research found in chapters 2, 3 and 4. First, these four designs reflect the meaning and purpose of liturgical dance as defined in the conclusion of chapter 4. Second, they will reflect the research gleaned from Maxine Greene, John Dewey, Jennifer Zakkai, Charles Foster, Norma Cook Everist, Anne Streaty Wimberly, and Carla DeSola. As in chapter 4, the use of the ten samples from the conducted interviews completes the information needed to support the four instructional strategies. One principle that undergirds each of the four teaching strategies is the principle of listening and why listening is imperative for the teaching success of Christian education in congregational life. The work of Margaret Crain on the sensitivity of listening sets the foundation for this final chapter.

The Importance of Listening

Margaret Crain makes a strong case in describing what the Christian educator needs to address the educational needs of the members of the congregation. What Crain stresses is the need for the Christian educator to know how to listen in order to ask the pertinent questions in matters pertaining to religious education for the life of the congregation. Such an act requires that religious educators learn and practice patience,

---

de deux form could degenerate into a formula, it nonetheless permitted adroit displays of male and female movement" (Anderson, *Dance*, 66).

quietness, and endurance when waiting for the questions to materialize. Crain contends that such questions "emerge out of the life events and communal identity of the congregation."[2] She affirms that the theological questions that arise out of the lives of the congregation tend to be unique, and they are shaped by specific personalities, diversity and culture, and detailed experiences of the lives of those who make up the congregation. Hence, such an action requires careful and vigilant listening.

The ability to hear the deep seeded questions will always be limited by the religious educator's own experiences and needs. Since it is impossible to fully understand the needs or questions of another, Crain poses the following question: "How do educators look for these glimpses of God's transformative power within a congregation?"[3] Her answer is simple; she explains that it is looked upon with eyes of love:

> I believe that eyes of love are eyes that do not begin with judgment, but instead seek to see lives and groups as whole and complex, living within a web of forces. . . . Educators must begin by taking seriously the whole of those lives. The issues of that reality should be a foundation of the curriculum for religious education.[4]

According to Crain, the Christian educator cannot see the glimpses of the reign of God that are already present in a congregation until he or she sees the people who are a part of the congregation in the complexity of the lives they lead, recognizing that each one seeks to be faithful, and that each one is a child of God touched by grace. Judgment is not the place to begin but listening is. This means that the Christian educator must listen to every facet of the educational life that comprises the church, whether it is the Sunday school class, the weekly bible study class, the assembled members of the choir, or the Sunday school staff. A Christian educator is to listen with the assumption that the people are speaking from their own lives, which are touched by grace. Crain contends that each one has spiritual needs, shaped by all the experiences of his or her life, and the questions that each one is asking are slightly different because of those unique experiences.

Crain submits that the skills of an ethnographer, specifically speaking the skill to look, to listen, and to reflect on moments where God's

---

2. Crain, "Listening to Churches," 101.

3. Crain, "Listening to Churches," 101.

4. Crain, "Listening to Churches," 101.

grace is present, are the tools the religious educator should use in seeking the answers to the question: "How do I guide the congregation into focusing on one or another of the approaches to Christian education?"[5] It is here that the ethnographic methods will help an educator identify what approaches are already present and are a part of the life of the congregation. Once these approaches are identified and honored, the educator can build and strengthen them. If they are not identified, the educator is too often working at cross-purposes to the presuppositions and comforts of the congregation. However, if the educator honors, utilizes, and encourages those identified practices of the congregation that are already present, they can build and expand the repertoire of learning opportunities in an easier and more successful fashion.

Crain also addresses how an educator can begin to understand the complex webs of interaction and meaning that are part of his or her congregation. Questions asked by the educational ethnographer would be specific to the congregational setting with which they are interacting. The questions should focus on three primary issues, namely, the people and their lives, the dynamics of the congregation, and the environment of the community in which the people reside. In terms of the people, the questioning goal is to discern the issues that command the attention of the people, how their faith affects the ways they engage with these issues, and how the church either assists or inhibits their addressing these issues.[6] In terms of the congregation she suggests that the educator seeks to discern the places where the congregation honestly engages the issues of the people's lives, where the congregation is particularly effective in helping people integrate faith and life, and how truth-telling and honest reflection can be enhanced. Regarding the community, Crain suggests that the Christian educator needs to reflect on the forces that are affecting the lives of the people; how culture, class, and values focus people's attention, and how the congregation can impact the forces that affect, and even define, the meanings with which people live.

Crain proposes three qualities that are essential, effective, and mutual for Christian education. They are:

> (1) The educator must see herself or himself as an interpreter among interpreters; (2) the contexts for learning must create

---

5. Crain, "Listening to Churches," 102.
6. Crain, "Listening to Churches," 105.

hospitable and just space; and (3) the congregation must practice the presence of God.[7]

For the first, she explains that in a congregation of interpreters, the Christian educator seeks to bring possibilities and resources to any question,
but does not seek to control the outcome. This can happen if the teacher
takes on the role of a co-learner, one who must listen carefully to the
questions and answers of all participants, helping each to offer "answers"
in an atmosphere of shared vulnerability and mutual search for truth.[8]
She suggests that when the interpreters who are evaluating and planning
for education discover contexts within the life of the congregation where
mutuality is not occurring, interventions may be necessary.

In addressing the contexts for which learning can create both a hospitable and just space, Crain suggests that listening and shared vulnerability is the starting point:

> A hospitable context is one in which the individual feels the se-
> curity of "home." One feels welcomed. . . . It is dependent upon
> both seeking relationships and honoring differences. To hold
> ourselves in relationship and yet to honor difference is difficult
> at times, yet it promotes growth.[9]

An aid in creating a hospitable and just space, Crain cites the work of
Brother Lawrence and his notion that the route to faithfulness is to
practice the presence God.[10] This notion has caught the imagination of
many Christians because it is so simple and yet so profound. Practicing
the presence of God is the final criterion for evaluating the contexts for
learning in a congregation. Lawrence explains, "When we practice God's
presence, we seek to live in 'an habitual, silent, and secret conversation of
the soul with God.'"[11] Crain explains that as we enter into relationship
with one another we risk knowing that we are also in relationship with
God, and we are to pay attention to one another as we pay attention to
God. Practicing presence also raises one's awareness of how God's grace-
ful presence undergirds one's learning.[12] Another dimension in practicing the presence of God is honoring the whole of the Christian tradition.

7. Crain, "Listening to Churches," 105–6.

8. Crain, "Listening to Churches," 106.

9. Crain, "Listening to Churches," 107.

10. For more on Brother Lawrence of the Resurrection, see Delaney, *Practice*.

11. Crain, "Listening to Churches," 107.

12. Crain, "Listening to Churches," 107.

Such awareness brings to the educator the rich and diverse fund of images, stories, songs, movement gestures, and concepts from the Christian tradition that can prompt questions of faith while supplying guide lines that can be followed. Crain explains this further:

> This means that the interpreter must be steeped in her or his faith tradition. But it also means that the educator must attempt to provide opportunities for everyone in the congregation to acquire a rich fund from the religious tradition. . . . In practicing the presence of God we ask, "What is God's call to us in this situation?" We seek answers in the Bible, in the Christian tradition, in our own experiences and in those of our fellow interpreters, and through the gift of reason. Through it all, we listen for God's answers. God empowers us with moments when we live justly and lovingly. Those moments provide hope and possibilities. We seek to join with God in working toward the reign of God.[13]

Crain provides a landscape of suggestions in aiding the listening ear and heart of the Christian educator when it comes to matters of faith learning and development. These recommendations are particularly useful for the implementation of the four formats that merge liturgical dance and religious education as working and supportive partners in a dance that highlights faith development and Christian love. In proposing these four formats, Crain provides a foundation for how such suggestions can be visualized and implemented.

Format One: Dancing In Unison

Format One displays liturgical dance and religious education as partners dancing in simultaneous unison, while being spatially arranged side by side. This setting presents both partners as equals, and when viewed side by side, each dancer presents not only themselves but they present the uniqueness of the relationship they share with the other. Such a partnership presents the strength and the creative capabilities found within each one, while both dance simultaneously together.

The format setting for this side by side partnership is situated at the beginning of congregational worship, where praise and worship music are utilized to gather the congregation together.[14] By way of song and simple

---

13. Crain, "Listening to Churches," 108.

14. "A Praise-and-Worship approach to corporate liturgy sequences the order of

liturgical dance movement, this gathering identifies the congregation as Christian and confirms the relationship they have with the Godhead.[15] Within this praise and worship setting, liturgical dance and the praise and worship music work hand in hand to support the educational message that Christians come together in time and space to learn more about the Trinity through praise, worship, prayer, and communing with God. Dance is a bridge from the world of intellect to the world of the imagination, according to DeSola and Easton, and through dance, one can grasp in deeper ways the meaning of religious concepts.[16] In this partnership both liturgical dance and religious education are supporting one another in united movement by helping to identify the essence, meaning, and the scriptural text that undergirds each praise and worship song.

------

worship, using contemporary Christian music to lead participants through a series of affective states. . . . The name itself, 'Praise-and-Worship,' parallels the logic of this typology. Proponents make a distinction between praise—usually defined as extolling God by remembering or proclaiming God's character and activity—and worship—usually defined in more relational terms of direct communion with God. The basic movement from praise to worship is achieved by adjusting certain characteristics of the music. At least three are standard. The first is a move in the types of personal pronouns used for God, from third person to second person. As participants progress into worship, they begin to address God with the more intimate 'you.' The second common adjustment is in the tempo, tone, and key of the music. Frequently, Praise-and-Worship services begin upbeat, utilizing songs in major keys to proclaim the goodness of God's character and activity. Somewhere in the progression, the tempo slows and repetition is more frequent and extended. The volume is diminished as worshippers enjoy communion with the living God. The third shift is in the songs' content. Frequently, the Praise-and-Worship progression moves from more objective remembrance of God to songs reflecting upon God's person and our relationship with God" (Bradshaw, *Westminster Dictionary*, 379–380). Within certain Protestant denominations, Praise and Worship songs are led by a praise and worship leader, and a praise and worship team help supply singing support. During the opening of The Greater Allen Cathedral's worship service, a prayer is spoken and then the praise and worship singing begins with the praise leader, praise team, and the congregation.

15. Numerous Christian churches have liturgical dancers active during the praise and worship segment of the worship service. The dancers demonstrate simple movement that the congregation can follow, if they choose to do so. In most cases there is a moving atmosphere found within this portion of the service where the congregation is given the opportunity to either follow fully or in part the liturgical dance movement gestures that are presented by the liturgical dancers. These movement gestures accompany the words of the praise and worship songs that are sung. Both song and dance should work together to support and translate the scriptural meanings that undergird the songs.

16. See DeSola and Easton, "Right Lobe through Dance."

Both partners contribute to the instructional setting of the moment, where the religious themes are uplifted in the words that are sung and in the movement gestures that are danced. Both partners give visualization and comprehension to the meaning of the words. An example of a praise and worship song that is accompanied by liturgical dance movement is the song "Welcome into this Place" that was used as a teaching example on the subject of grace for the entire congregation found in chapter 3.[17] As explained, this example focused on the entire congregation with the assistance of the Praise and Worship leader, the singing worship team, and liturgical dancers. The primary goal of such a partnership is the internalization of the song's meaning and the congregation's critical reflection upon that meaning for themselves and for the "grace" actions that they are encouraged to display toward others in Jesus' name. This type of learning integration exemplifies the portion of the definition of liturgical dance found in chapter 4, which emphasized that it be expressive and imaginative movement used inside the worship experience which creatively educates and instructs in the matters of the Bible and faith in the Trinity through the elements of space, time, and design, and that it has a relationship with music.

Wimberly introduced one aspect of the nurturing components of music within black worship through the spontaneous and improvisational style of expression known as "spiritual free play." In "spiritual free play," its essence is centered in the response of the heart and the body to the movement of the Holy Spirit, and the mind's connection with the message or content of the music. In "spiritual free play," the whole self is released to delight in the personal experience of seeing and hearing God, and it is through this experience that one creates, and adds new sounds, rhythms, movement accompaniment, and thoughts that respond to and add further meaning to a truth or belief disclosed in a song. Wimberly declares that "'spiritual free play,' creates a climate of imaginative experience and artistry that builds creative musical capacities from which life outside the congregation is embellished."[18]

This creative response to the movement of the Holy Spirit is what takes place during praise and worship, where the understanding of God's love for every congregational member is witnessed through the songs

17. See chapter 3 of this book, "Teach Me and Give Me Understanding: Experiential Learning and the Church Community," for the song, movement, and educational underpinnings of the teaching on grace.

18. Wimberly, *Faith and Hope*, 152.

that are sung and the movements that accompany the words. The movements are usually choreographed, however there can also be moments where spontaneous movement occurs. The dancer's creativity is nurtured through the work of improvisation, which is the creation of unplanned movement on the spot. Dance improvisation aids the dancer in finding new ways to move, develop technical skills, and provides another means to develop as an artist.[19] "Spiritual free play," creates enriching moments where new movement gestures through improvisation enriches the educational underpinnings of the spur-of-the-moment change of praise and worship music that is in response to the movement of the Holy Spirit.

During such times, the entire congregation is welcomed to join in, and, as explained earlier, all who gather are termed differently abled according to Norma Cook Everist. As previously described, differently abled is a term that allows people to see how they view one another regardless of their physical, mental, and/or emotional wellbeing. Everist explains that each person in some way is able and each is disabled, regardless if the disability is hidden as in heart disease or lupus, or the disability is revealed as in cerebral palsy or deafness. The goal is not to change, or even to "cure" certain "disabilities," but to care in a way which gives attention to each person individually.[20] It is during times of praise and worship that all differently abled members of the congregation can freely join in and sing and dance the songs of praise and worship and genuinely feel the love of the Lord inside the sanctuary space. Doreen Holland shares a memory of seeing the love of God through the dancing of her differently abled son during a time of praise and worship:

> My middle son is eighteen years old and was diagnosed with autism since he was sixteen months old and he has been with us in the church setting. He feels the beat of the music and he marches, he claps his hands and marches to the beat of the music. If I am in the congregation and I am doing my personal praise and worship as an observer, he mirrors me, if I wave my hands, he is waving his hands, if I am clapping my hands, he is clapping his hands. I would have my oldest son clap his hands and the eighteen-year-old will clap his hands also. He doesn't do this at home, but he knows that this is what we do at church and he does it solely at church. People have gotten use to him doing this.

19. Penrod and Plastino, *Dancer Prepares*, 81.
20. Everist, *Church*, 36.

There was a period where he wasn't doing this, there were a few challenges that he was facing and caused him not to dance in his seat for a few months. There were those in the congregation who asked what was wrong because he wasn't dancing and they had missed him moving. Now that he is up and doing it again, then those in the congregation were excited that he was back and he was dancing to the church music. Again the movement of liturgical dance whether small or great, is a bridge for those who watch it. In this case liturgical dance was the bridge for my middle son and for the congregational members who were use to seeing him move near his seat.[21]

Yvonne Peters shares the importance of the use of liturgical dance as a facilitating tool that can lead others to worship God through the dance:

David selected those musicians who were skilled and excellent in their craft to minister before the Lord and to instruct others. They were literally to prophecy on their instruments and release the expression of their intimate communion with God through the sound of their instruments. Liturgical dancers seek the same. With excellence comes skill, with skill responsibility to impart and teach others. We are called to lift up others into a higher level of worship. Liturgical dancers cannot be just demonstrators in front of congregations but we are to be facilitators, we do not just craft but we instruct and lead others to worship through the dance with their entire selves.[22]

This praise and worship setting reveals just how stable a partner both liturgical dance and religious education are as they function equally through the vehicle of praise and worship music. Both partners are unified in their responsibilities to teach what it means to be Christian in a congregational setting that fosters such instruction through creative and spontaneous expression. The ability to listen deeply to the needs of God's people who assemble in the sanctuary space can bring about the revelation that all of God's people can respond to God in ways that are expressive yet undergirded with opportunities to learn just how good God is. One partner does not upstage the other, but they dance together side by side revealing the educational value that undergirds such a partnership.

21. Holland, interview.
22. Peters, interview.

Format Two: The Dance of Balance and Harmony

Format Two highlights the balancing capabilities of liturgical dance and religious education in a movement relationship that supports each other's total weight equally and harmoniously. This type of movement allows one partner to hold onto the other by the pulling of the hands and arms, or the pushing toward one another through bodily contact of the back, or sides of the body. In each scenario the body weight of one is totally supported by the body weight of the other. To explain this position using the hands, each partner's body is pulled away from the other, and the tension felt between the two through the connection of both hands and arms allows for both to be in total balance with the other. This type of partnership requires a total and complete trust on behalf of each partner, and, if achieved, such interaction produces complete harmony and complete balance. However, if one partner stops supporting the weight of the other, one partner if not both partners lose balance and can possibly fall. This dancing relationship signifies that the contributions of one partner are totally supported by the contributions of the other partner and vice versa. Therefore, in this dancing partnership liturgical dance and religious education are not seen as equals in their individual contributions, but they are equals *because* of the contributions of the other.

Penrod and Plastino present two improvisational exercises that deal with partner awareness through the use of body weight. One exercise has each partner face the other, standing with the feet comfortably balanced and three feet apart, with the arms forward and slightly bent and with the palms of one partner resting against the palms of the other. Each partner is to take turns leaning passively forward into the palms of the other allowing one to support the weight of the other. The overall aim of this exercise is the development of trust.[23] The second exercise highlights the exact positioning liturgical dance and religious education occupy in *format two*. This exercise is explained as follows:

> With feet comfortably together and knees bent, hold hands at the wrist and lean back away from each other. Experiment with sensitively using each other's weight to oppositionally shift the weight forward, backward, and sideward, eventually cooperatively moving downward with control, to sit on the floor.[24]

23. Penrod and Plastino, *Dancer Prepares*, 88.
24. Penrod and Plastino, *Dancer Prepares*, 89.

These are typical partnering exercises that are explored in improvisational classes when the themes of trust and partnership are highlighted.

For Christian education, the setting of this balancing partnership is during worship where the actual teaching of a song or movement to a song takes place. There are many types of worship services within Christian traditions where teaching is a welcomed way to learn and develop faith. This type of setting exists during the various chapel services held on college, seminarian, and even on military campuses as well as in churches that are moderate in size.

Charles Foster explores how the church can participate in the "formative and transformative events of Christian tradition and witness."[25] His work mirrors Dewey's understanding of community as communication, where the participation of people within the learning process is assured because of a common understanding. Foster sets forth suggestions on how to nurture meaning making within a church that considers itself to be a disciple community. One suggestion is to implement disciplined reflection which promotes a better comprehension of an event and the implications of an event upon the lives of the congregation. The ability to honestly reflect on the struggles and the new understandings requires theological and educative perspective. Dewey presses this point in his understanding of experiential learning.[26] Learning does not take place when a routine action is done in which the action is automatic. Learning is only achieved because after the act is performed, there are results which were not noted previously.

Patrick Evans is a proponent of the actual teaching and learning act within the worship service, and how it highlights the notion of Christians being imitators of Christ. However he does have two principles as to how the teaching and learning act should transpire. He explains this further:

> Two principles: (1) knowing that people will be invited to do something that they are not use to doing, (2) creating a place where it is safe to do that and it is okay to make a mistake. To try it and "fail" because you don't ever risk anything if you never do. It is such a different experience in seminary from the classroom where there is such pressure to *never* fail, to get the prefect grade point average, to get Latin honors; so the concept of doing something and learning from the not immediate brilliance success of it is really important. Those principles over a

25. Foster, *Educating Congregations*, 8.
26. Dewey, *Democracy and Education*, 102–3.

long period of time create a situation or help foster a situation in which people are willing to risk. In which even though this is not the way I worship, and I feel uncomfortable doing it, I know that this is important to you and you have found God *in it*, that makes me willing to risk, feeling foolish, or doing something that may not be perfect, because I am an expert and I only want to do things in public that I am expert at.[27]

Deconstructing personal opinions of failure or vulnerability while building up love and transparency can promote an individual's healing and faith nurturing within a worship service. It is here that Crain's earlier question and answer is situated, "how do educators look for these glimpses of God's transformative power within a congregation?"[28] Once again her answer is simple; the glimpses of God's transformative power are looked upon with eyes of love. It is here where the mutual trust in the partnering and balancing dance between liturgical dance and religious education can be witnessed.

To bring the concepts of meaning making, experiential learning, active and alive teaching in worship, and the viewing of God's transformative power within the congregation through the eyes of love in context, the following example of a chapel service shows the mutual trust, balance, and harmony found between liturgical dance and religious education.[29] The chapel service would take place on the campus grounds of a boarding school, college, seminary, or military base, where there is a collective body of people who attend daily or weekly chapel service. The religious nature of this particular faith community is ecumenical, where the knowledge of Christ is upheld, although religious backgrounds can stem from Catholicism to a wide variety of Protestant denominations. This chapel service will be entitled, "You Have Turned My Mourning Into…" based on a passage from the book of Jeremiah:

> Then shall the young women rejoice in the dance, and the young men and the old shall be merry. I will turn their mourning into joy. I will comfort them, and give them gladness for sorrow. (Jer 31:13)

27. Evans, Patrick, interview.

28. Crain, "Listening to Churches," 101.

29. "You Have Turned My Mourning Into . . ." was the title of a chapel service held on the grounds of Yale Divinity School on 21 April, 2008. The author attended Yale Divinity School from 2005–2009.

During the opening welcome it will be explained that this service will be interactive in nature. This means that there will be an element of teaching throughout the thirty-minute service including in the singing of song, the dancing of liturgical movement, and the moving throughout the space to prayer stations. The opening welcome serves as an official invitation for those attending the chapel service to feel free to participate in order to experience the many ways God has turned ones' mourning into song, praise, peace, prayer, hope, and dancing.

This type of service highlights the aesthetic as the driving force behind the learning experiences that will be attained. As explained earlier, Dewey claims that "the [a]esthetic is no intruder in experience from without, whether by way of idle luxury or transcendent ideality, but that it is the clarified and intensified development of traits that belong to every normally complete experience."[30] Artistic expression unites the same relation of doing and undergoing, outgoing, and incoming energy that makes an experience to be an experience. Artistic expression can be seen in an instructional tool as in this present example, or the creation of a work of art to be observed. Whichever the case, the attitude of the perceiver is embodied within the work being created. This incorporation allows the art to be an aesthetic work. For Dewey, the perceiver must create one's own experience. In the partnership suggested here, the artistic expressions of music, word, and dance lend themselves to formulate both artistic and educational experiences for those who created and for those who attend the chapel service.

The opening song, "You've Turned My Mourning into Dancing," is the theme song and serves as the opening and closing song of the service.[31] This song is also the first teaching moment that transpires in the chapel service. It exemplifies those verses from Psalm 30:

> You have turned my mourning into dancing; you have taken
> off my sackcloth and clothed me with joy, so that my soul may

30. Dewey, *Art as Experience*, 46.

31. "You've Turned My Mourning into Dancing," was written and composed by John Tirro, a 2009 MDiv graduate from Yale Divinity School (YDS) and was attending YDS during the same time as the author. During the 2007 to 2009 academic years, both individuals had the opportunity to work on numerous chapel services together that featured both music and liturgical dance as worship and teaching tools for the YDS community. "You Have Turned My Mourning into..." was one such collaboration that was featured in Marquand Chapel. For the words and song format, see Appendix J.

praise you and not be silent. O Lord my God, I will give thanks to you forever. (Psalm 30:11–12)

The song by John Tirro has only two lines which repeat. The first line is repeated four times before moving on to the chorus which is repeated twice before repeating the entire song again. The first line is, "You've turned my mourning, my mourning, my mourning into dancing." The second line is, "You've turned my sorrow into song, you've turned my singing into praise, you've turned my praise to peace, my peace to joy, and dancing!" Once the song is taught, everyone will be asked to stand and then sing the song a few times, in order to begin comprehending the deeper meaning of the song text in relation to the scripture. Once this has been done, then the accompanying movement will be taught to complete this portion of the interactive cycle.

In applying liturgical movement as a teaching tool, it will be explained that the gestures help to bring light to the fullness of both the Psalm 30 text and the song text that was inspired by the scripture, and a demonstration of the mourning movement will be done. The members of the congregation will be encouraged to join in and follow the movements of the leader. The initial movement of the body is a rocking motion from side to side since the musical accompaniment is upbeat and in common time. The mourning position will be explained by having the arms slowly cross each other, while they are being folded inward toward the chest with the head slightly lowered in the forward direction. The movement to accompany the words, "into dancing" will have the arms release slowly from the chest as they are raised gradually upward above the head, one arm at a time (right, left, right, left) in the four count rhythm. The releasing of the arms and their motioning upward resembles the joyous motions of happiness and emancipation, especially the feeling one has once a weight has been lifted off of one's shoulders. This gesture is repeated four times as the song verse is repeated four times.

The second line, which begins with the words, "You've turned my sorrow into song," will continue with the rocking motion of the body since this is the constant full body motion that accompanies the entire song. The arms will fold into the chest, resembling sorrow, but will open and release upward in almost a V shape, once "song" is sung and then the hands will clap five times as the body is rocking side to side, resembling the change of temperament, which is captured in the words, "singing, praise, peace, and joy." The arms push upward two times on the last word of the song, "dancing" while the body continues to rock from side to side. This movement gesture signifies the desire to be in a state of joy, merriment, praise, comfort, and divine peace. This combined song and movement opening will be repeated at least twice so that everyone can get familiar with the accompaniment and they can begin internalizing the educational meanings of both scripture and song text through the use of movement.

Patrick Evans gives dutiful caution when using liturgical dance as a teaching tool within congregational worship. He states,

> There are cautions in doing liturgical dance in congregational settings. You are inviting people to do things with their bodies and they have issues with their bodies. Age and bodies have changed, been physically abused, or sexually abused, and they may not realize until they are touched by someone else that there are deep wounds and deep scars there, but liturgical dance can be healing in these situations. We just have to be mindful when we use it and teach it in congregational worship.[32]

Throughout the service when the congregation sings, hears readings, watch others do liturgical dance,[33] and pray the members of the community are given the space to reflect upon themselves and where they are and how they are responding to what they are doing, seeing, and praying. It is during these moments that the Holy Spirit is welcomed into the service to relieve the congregation of its sorrows, hurts, and concerns through the modalities of song, movement, and prayer. When the opening song is sung at the conclusion of the service, it is anticipated that those who attended the service will be changed in some way and will be moving from a state of mourning to a state of wondrous dancing in Jesus' name. *Format Two* supports the portion of the liturgical dance definition that identifies the church as community though individual and mutual movements and dance explorations that cultivate love, prayer, healing, and reconciliation, while deepening Christian identity. The balance and

32. Evans, Patrick, interview.

33. During this particular service and services like these, one or two dances can be presented by individuals or groups of liturgical dancers that reflect the theme of the service, along with scriptural readings, and reflective songs. The times of prayer are moments that will afford individuals the opportunity to pray at their seats or travel to designated prayer stations to write down their mourning prayers for themselves or to intercede in prayer for others. The entire service is a teaching service utilizing the interactions of the congregation to gather together in order to lift each other up from a state of mourning to a state of joyful dancing.

harmony found between liturgical dance and religious education in this supportive and trusting partnership is one that points to the continual theme of God's desire to transform the state of God's children from that of mourning to a state of peace, song, praise, joy, and dancing.

Format Three: To Be Lifted Up

In the first two examples liturgical dance was utilized in a setting that addressed predominately non-dancers. Both settings took place inside the sanctuary during worship, where the congregation is made up of an assortment of people, ranging in age, gender, and capabilities. However *format three* will look at liturgical dance as the primary subject to be taught while religious education is the secondary underlining subject that gives credence and stability to it. This example also addresses the teaching audience composed of liturgical dancers or those who are interested in learning more about the subject. Here the dancing partnership between liturgical dance and religious education favors that of a *pas de deux* where the male and female dancers are doing a meaningful adagio, which encompasses slow, continuous, and sustained movement with an incorporation of wonderful and effortless lifts with the male dancer lifting up the female dancer. Thus this format will show liturgical dance is the subject being taught and religious education is the subject that give it its foundation.

Wimberly explained in chapter 3 that evocative nurture "builds on the view that worshipers desire and are ready for nurture and have the wherewithal to receive nurture and discern its meaning for their lives."[34] She pointed out that black worshipers come into the worshiping congregation seeking nourishment that affirms and responds to their capacity to receive it, struggle with it, and to discover, build on, and act on what is enormously important to their lives as Christians. God is the evocator who reaches out and invites the people of God to reach back and to vow that they will not look backwards but will move forward "to see what the end will be."[35]

Evocative nurture is the type of teaching the liturgical dancer needs. This type of nurture is what DeSola and Easton describes as "the corresponding spirituality for the dancer as a total union of body, spirit, music,

---

34. Wimberly, *Faith and Hope*, xv.

35. Wimberly, *Faith and Hope*, xix.

and space forgetting the self in actualizing the dance."[36] For her liturgical dance is assumed to be the result of a personal, meditative experience of God; the movement's sources come from the heart's response, in an overflowing of gratitude or speech to God. As explained earlier, Christ is the partner in an ever-new dance which is inspired by the Holy Spirit and is offered to God. However, there should be a teaching approach that guides the liturgical dancer to comprehend exactly what liturgical dance is and how it affects both those who watch it, and the dancers of faith who participate in it.

Marable shares some of the problems the liturgical dancer could face if proper and meaningful instruction is not created, established, or implemented. She states:

> There are those who are studying the Word of God and there are those who are not studying and speaking from Word, but they are dancing in God's name. The real precaution are those who are studying on line and getting these online degrees and giving themselves titles of reverend, apostle, and prophet and they are going into churches and sabotaging God's pure praise. When pastors experience them and there is a profane spirit moving though the worship and arts movement, the pastor and congregation say that we do not want this. We have to be mindful that the body speaks such strong languages and the enemy (Satan) is angry. So we have dancers who dance with exposed bodies, and that either offends members of the congregation or it entices pedophiles who may be present, or the rate of teenage pregnancies escalate because of the lack of teaching and learning concerning liturgical dance and the worship and the arts. A profanity can enter into the church and we have to make sure to study and study correctly.[37]

From another perspective, DeSola and Easton warns against the overwhelming attention given towards the dancer's technique which can be based on imitation or copying the style of present or former teachers. Since much of a dancer's life is spent doing repetitive exercises that train the body to perform actions with as little strain as possible, the dancer is seldom guided through those maturing steps from technique to performance level of interpretation and, ultimately, to spiritual understanding and freedom. DeSola and Easton explains this further:

36. DeSola and Easton, "Right Lobe through Dance," 73.

37. Marable, interview.

We are not saying that technique is wrong, but the emphasis
is misplaced when the goal of the dancer becomes glamorized,
when the only objective is to dazzle and to prove one's worth as
a performer.

The church can offer opportunities to both dancers and
non-dancers by helping them to share selflessly in services and
festive events; such participation lifts individuals from personality preoccupation to holistic experience.[38]

Crain's principle of listening can assist in the area of instructing liturgical dancers particularly addressing the concerns of both Marable and
DeSola and Easton. The questions asked by the educational ethnographer
are appropriate for this instructional setting to gain a deeper awareness
of the individuals who call themselves liturgical dancers or who are interested in learning more about the subject. The three issues Crain suggests
specifically target the dancers and their lives, the dynamics of the congregations they serve, and the environment of the community in which
the people reside. In terms of the liturgical dancer, the questioning goal
is to discern these issues, and how the church either assists or inhibits the
way they address these issues. With this type of questioning, DeSola and
Easton's suggestion of the church giving opportunities for the liturgical
dancer to selflessly give to the church and its liturgical and festive events
would help in this area. Regarding the liturgical dance ministry of the
church, Crain's suggestion that the educator seeks to discern the places
where the dancers honestly engages the issues of both their lives and the
lives of the congregation, is essential for helping the dancers integrate
faith and life. Concerning the community, she suggests that the Christian
educator reflect on the forces that are affecting the lives of the dancers;
how culture, class, and values focus people's attention, and how the liturgical dancers can impact the forces that affect, and even define, the
meanings with which they and those in the congregation live.

Marable, DeSola, Easton, and Crain's observations highlight the
need for liturgical dancers to gain strength by learning a variety of subjects that are related to the field whether the subject is dance technique
that can span a variety of disciplines, or that of biblical studies, or the
use of liturgical dance in liturgy. In addition to these areas there is a discernment process that the liturgical dancer must engage in as it relates to
faith building, and the use of movement in liturgical choreography. Discernment sustains a knowing about movement, movement choices, and

38. DeSola and Easton, "Right Lobe through Dance," 75.

the movements that are or are not appropriate to use under the rubrics of liturgical dance. As Marable and DeSola and Easton have indicated, movements that place a heavier emphasis on the personal self and on the physicality of the body are primarily movements that highlight the dancer and not the Trinity. The use of such movements cause confusion and division among the dancers and the congregations they serve. As a parent of daughters who do liturgical dance, Lori Dekie emphasizes how important it is to teach liturgical dance in such a way that its intent is clearly Godly. She states:

> It could be an instructional tool, it needs to be taught and un-derstood in such a way so that the movement and its intent is clearly Godly. We have to watch out for the secular influence of movement not to have a place within liturgical dance. It must be taught in such a way that the biblical understanding and asso-ciation of the word of God coincides with the movement. There should not be a certain musical language and movements, like gyrations inside liturgical dance. There is a difference between understanding how it is done and the manifestation of the ac-tual movement being done. There is a difference in teaching older people what to do and the teaching of teens. There is such a difference and the teacher must be aware enough so to correct if the movement interpretation is more worldly than it is sup-posed to be. The meaning of the movements and the meaning of the dance must be explained and taught. Secular dance has an emphasis on the self and liturgical dance highlights God and our worship of God. If the congregation is not taught correctly about liturgical dance, then their understanding will be off.[39]

Therefore, the type of teaching and evocative nurturing the liturgical dancer needs should be developed from a foundation that is undergirded by religious education. Such a foundation promotes a curriculum of learning, investigation, deep inquiry, and exploration, while promoting a need to seek God through tools, instruments, and available subject mate-rial. Some of the subjects that could be included in such a curriculum are as follows:

- Bible study—exegetical investigations that bring comprehension and light to the biblical text;
- History—learning the history of liturgical dance starting with the earliest of cultures, to the Old Testament, to the early church, to

39. Dekie and Dekie, interview.

present day Christian faith traditions, and organizations that have implemented dance and worship.

- Prayer—both verbal and embodied that develops the inner soul and spirit of the dancer to learn how to pray both verbally and physically through movement.

- Movement technique—including strengthening and stretching;

- Composition—learning the craft of choreography and movement development through improvisation and compositional forms, using biblical themes.

- Attire and Accessories—comprehending, designing, and apprehending the appropriate liturgical attire to wear while dancing, and accessing what pageantry accessories are available to use in creating liturgical dance choreography.

- Liturgy—Understanding what liturgy is, what it does, and how formational it is when it includes the use of dance and the arts within the worship setting.

- Collaboration—how to work successfully and creatively with other ministries within the church under the guidance of religious education and liturgical studies.

- Evangelism—exploring ways to take the ministry of dance outside the walls of the church and out to the streets.

In addressing the implementation of liturgical dance within the church, suggestions surfaced during the interviews that addressed this issue. Yvonne Peters makes several suggestions to the religious educator and the liturgist on how to utilize liturgical dance within the worship setting that will help educate the liturgical dancer, the pastoral leadership, and the congregation:

> (1) Keep the roots of dance as an active expression to God not as a spectacle before Him; (2) Worship is active not passive. One enters into worship to the degree one is willing to invest themselves in the worship experience. To lead worship, to teach worship, one must remain and be an active worshipper. Unlike other disciplines, there is no end to exploring the realms of worship. In this respect, student and teacher are ever pursuing; and

(3) Liturgical dance must be fitted into the entire context of the liturgy. There is grave danger of adding it on a as a new flavor or spice to the liturgical service. To do this may cause the dance expression to become entertainment instead of a tool of facilitating corporate worship.[40]

Marable explains one technique she uses in teaching liturgical dancers how to approach choreographing liturgical dance based on a particular scripture:

The preacher is required to exegete the biblical text in bringing forth the Word of God in the sermon, by studying the Greek and the Hebrew significance of the word, read commentaries and read other authors, and challenge the ideas and interpretations of other authors. So should the dancer. Choreographically I challenge the physical language of others, what does this text mean to you? In choreographing, "My Help," I used the Psalm, "I will lift up mine eyes unto the hills, from whence cometh my help" (Ps 121:1). I am bringing in their language in the study of the text. I am then going to find out what God meant by "help" and how help was used in other parts of the bible. Was it a help where we prostrate before him, or the type of help where we have to reach toward him? I am exegeting the text in a theological perspective and in a social context, what does that help look like socially. Who needs help in our community? We may need to bring in characters in the dance who are homeless, hungry, pregnant, or that they are bearing a cross because they need that type of help. It is a very instructional tool, because it is trying to preach a sermon through movement.[41]

Setting up such a curriculum is not necessarily new, however, there were past efforts to do such a work and these efforts took on a variety of forms and shapes. For example, Mary Jones and fifteen other people met and formed the Christian Dance Fellowship of Austria in 1978. Jones explains the aims of the organization:

The aim of the new organization was to join over the huge distances those scattered people who were already involved in trying to use dance in worship and provide training, encouragement, and resources for them. The Fellowship would also aim to increase people's understanding and experience of sacred dance through literature, workshops, and demonstrations,

40. Peters, interview.
41. Marable, interview.

encouraging it as prayer, worship, teaching, and evangelism, coming from a personal faith commitment.[42]

As the fellowship developed, Jones expanded the aims to also include the following:

- Stimulate interest in and exchange information about using movement to celebrate and explore our life and worship together in Christian community;

- Increase people's understanding of the history and theology of dance in the church;

- Reach those outside the church with the message of the Gospel presented through dance, mime, and drama;

- Encourage and train both individuals and groups in dance ministry;

- Encourage the formation of branches of the Fellowship around Australia;

- Promote performances, conferences, and other functions in furtherance of these objectives.[43]

Marable describes the beginnings of the National Liturgical Dance Network, as follows:

> During the final morning worship of the first conference (1998), one of the directors asked how do we stay in touch? God gave me the mandate to create a national liturgical dance network to keep us all together so that when we come together in another eleven months instruction would have been given to these churches on how to maintain and feed your liturgical dance ministry. Dance not only out of their flesh and out of their feelings but to learn how to dance the Word of God. We created a curriculum, a pedagogy that worked at Allen and is being replicated around the world on how to feed, teach, and maintain dance ministries. Ministries throughout the world are sitting down to be feed spiritually, educationally, and scripturally to learn how to dance the word.[44]

42. Jones, *Dance Movement*, 35.

43. Jones, *Dance Movement*, 40.

44. Marable, interview. The National Liturgical Dance Network was created after the first Liturgical Dance Conference in 1998, sponsored by The Allen Liturgical Dance Ministry of the Greater Allen AME Cathedral of New York: "The Network was developed to provide organizational development and leadership training to

Recently accredited college and graduate programs that are offering dance and theology, or liturgical dance as regular courses in the curriculum. Mary Jones cites the International Institute for Creative Ministries, an accredited theological college, which is an interdenominational college associated with Christian Life Centre in Sydney, offering courses in dance, drama, music, art, and theology.[45] The creation of the college was the result of a joint vision of director David Johnston, a native of California, and Frank Houston, the New Zealand-born pastor of Christian Life Centre. Jones explains that the college has a uniquely conceived curriculum that ensures that each student has general experience in all areas of theology and the arts offered by the college, while specializing in one or two specific areas.

Also Marable describes the newly established graduate program at Drew seminary where there is a concentration in liturgical dance:

> At Drew Seminary, it is fascinating to mix the pedagogy of worship and the arts there. There are believers and nonbelievers, agnostics, Mennonites, Methodists, confused people, and pastors. It is amazing that at that instructional place they do not just hear the word, study different theologians but they have a space to dance it out. At Drew, they created the first ATS accredited curriculum on liturgical dance, where people can get a Masters of Arts in Liturgical Dance, where people are studying all the dynamics of theology, but we are given space to embody

Christians who participate in, lead, or have a vision to begin liturgical dance ministries at their respective churches. It is designed: (1) To help dance ministries best witness to the unsaved through dance, and to edify God's kingdom by enhancing the praise and worship experience for the church universal; (2) To promote the development of an intimate relationship with God through praise and worship; (3) To share, encourage, edify, lift up dance ministers functioning in the body of Christ; (4) To provide ongoing training, support, and resources for dance ministers that will help them continually mature as leaders over their respective ministries; and (5) To transform people into leaders that can submit, support, and complement the authority of their church; direct a group with authority, compassion, confidence, and commitment" (National Liturgical Dance Network, "Statement and Purpose").

45. Mary Jones points out that the International Institute for Creative Ministries became Wesley Institute when it changed ownership from an AOG church to Wesley Mission (Methodist/Uniting). David Johnston continues currently as principal. The course of study at Wesley once was for Christians and included Dance Ministry as well as all the regular dance courses, but now there is a majority of non-Christians in the courses and the person in charge of the department has a different vision for it. Plus there is always the economic factor. However they'll have to take biblical studies and theology (Jones, interview).

our theology. What does it look like to believe God, to preach the word? This semester I am teaching a class on Preaching the Word through the Body, Performing Arts, and Preaching. We are teaching people how to preach from the pulpit but how to use their bodies, how to use other people's bodies from the congregation. To actualize and to visualize what the word looks like. Using the story of Lazarus being raised from the dead, you can have someone wrapped in toilet tissue and then they are released. They do not have to dance, but dance is a visual in the learning.[46]

The partnership of liturgical dance allows it to be considered as a course of study not only for the liturgical dancer, as in the example displayed in *Format Three*, but also as a course of study for clergy, congregations, religious educators, and liturgists. Such a partnership reveals its validity as both a topic of study for collegiate and seminarian study, and as a viable method of study by which other religious topics can be investigated. In either example, both the instructor and learner can fulfill and reflect the Psalm which states, "Let everything that breathes praise the Lord! Praise the Lord!" (Ps 150:6).

Format Four: The Partnership of One

Format Four is the final format, and it will make use of the imagination to such a degree as to visualize the extreme uniqueness found in the partnership between liturgical dance and religious education. In this duet, the many relational opportunities found between both partners are viewed though the different choreographic movements and lifts displayed. From collaborative and unison movements, to postures that solely rely on the element of trust, to distinctive and extraordinary lifts that display both liturgical dance and religious education, this last format will include evangelism and outreach found both outside and inside the walls of the church. What evangelism looks like is immeasurable to imagine, however when it is creatively devised it can help surface components of restoration and healing that are underscored by the agape love of Christ. In this last format, both liturgical dance and religious education are joint partners whose choreographic and performing endeavors seek to uplift and share the name of Christ to a world that at times appears to be unlovable and immensely broken.

46. Marable, interview.

Evangelism in the Christian context can help form and create community. Evangelism in this regard typifies the Marcan scripture which speaks of the great commission. In Mark 16:15 Jesus told the disciples to "Go into all the world and proclaim the good news to the whole creation." The imagination is helpful in establishing a setting where the good news of evangelism can formulate community. For example, Maxine Greene's notion of the imagination is important for forming community. In describing community, Greene emphasizes process words such as making, creating, weaving, saying, and the like. Community is achieved by persons who offer the space to discover what they recognize together and to appreciate in common with one another; they have to find ways to make intersubjective sense: "It ought to be a space infused by the kind of imaginative awareness that enables those involved to imagine alternative possibilities for their own becoming and their group's becoming."[47] For Greene, community is not the encountering social contracts that are the most reasonable to enter, but it is the question of what might contribute to the pursuit of shared goods: what ways of being together, of attaining mutuality, of reaching toward some common world.[48] Community, such as the one described by Greene, can be easily established within a church and within an evangelistic event where the sharing of the good news can be experienced by all especially if it is shared with the use of the imagination through the partnership of liturgical dance and religious education.

One example of an evangelistic outreach is described by Lori Dekie concerning her youngest daughter who was fulfilling her Girl Scout "Silver Award" requirements and used liturgical dance to do so:

> Our youngest daughter is a Girl Scout and there is a second to last step, the Silver Award and her project had her bring liturgical dance to the girls in all of the Girl Scout troops across Suffolk County and she taught them liturgical dance and they performed it in nursing homes which was part of her project. The community has been influenced by liturgical dance, something that she has learned and taken out of the church and into the surrounding community.[49]

Such an example not only influenced Lori's daughter, but she found it appealing to build a community through the use of religious education and

47. Greene, *Releasing the Imagination*, 39.
48. Greene, *Releasing the Imagination*, 39.
49. Dekie and Dekie, interview.

liturgical dance with the members of her Girl Scout troop. They learned the movements, they learned what the movements signified, they learned the various meanings that undergirded the movements—meanings such as hearing the good news of Jesus Christ, living life more abundantly, living with hope, and living to love and to be loved. However the building of community did not stop at that evangelistic setting between the Girl Scout members themselves, but it expanded to the nursing homes where the scouts shared through liturgical dance the love of God, the love of neighbor, and the sharing of the good news to those residing in nursing homes. Such a partnership allows one's imagination to be energized and to expand so to create numerous ways of sharing the gospel that are inspirational, inventive, and educational.

Robert Evans described how important it was to imagine both cognitively and artistically how the structure of *The Nativity* was going to transpire.[50] He asked God:

> How do we develop character; how do we move from one conversation to another; what dance movement language does this character need? Those things became the framework that I can then put walls onto. What songs help describe the characters within *The Nativity*? The question was not which Christmas songs should I use.[51]

Evans understood that in order to clearly craft *The Nativity* so it tells the story accurately, an artistic and a religious educational approach had to be intertwined within the choreographic process.

Evans's use of outreach and community formation initially took place within the casting of *The Nativity*. He believes that dance ministry is not solely for children, as in an activity to keep their attention, or solely for women, because of its gracefulness. But it is also for males from the youngest to the oldest. He explains:

> Dance ministry is ministry and anybody who has ever been ministered to know that it is irregardless of gender, age, ethnic group. In some circles when you talk about males in dance ministry, typically the only dance form that is acceptable is African or manly stuff with fists and stomping. And yes, God is all of that, but sometimes what we are really dealing with is people's

---

50. *The Nativity* is the liturgical dance presentation choreographed and directed by Robert Evans and referred to in chapter 4 during his interview.

51. Evans, Robert, interview.

image of what manhood is or their image of what a man is. God is a God of love and of strength and if you can convey that to your children, to be a father of both strength and love then why can we not be both strong and soothing in and through dance?

I used to have these conversations with God, you give me this stuff that has more male leads than female leads and in *The Nativity*, there are only two female leads, so what is this, a joke? And I am not desperate enough to strap females down to make them shepherds. So the males have to come from some place. And it is a walk by faith. . . . We did not have our shepherds until three weeks to tech, and the shepherd's scene, those guys should have been rehearsed long before that. But we kept plowing through, plowing through, plowing through. But we then began to get phone calls, and I said "yes, tell them to get over here, right now!" One of the things that bring me a great deal of joy is that one of my students from this classroom was a shepherd. He heard me talking about it on the phone and I was going through some of the photos and he said, "What is that?" And I began to tap out some stuff and he began to repeat it and so he would take the trip up to Westchester, Metro North, every Saturday for rehearsal. . . . We had a lot of men in the production and not all were dancers, but they wanted to be apart. My son is also in it and he grew up in DMI starting off as a sheep and assumed lead roles this 2011 production and also choreographed for *The Nativity* as well.[52]

As with *The Nativity*, when doing liturgical dance for evangelistic purposes, during the initial stages the teaching must always begin with the cast and those who are directly related to the production. This gives space for those who are involved to learn the deeper biblical lessons and principles that give foundation to the production. From this educational perspective, those involved in the production can perform and minister the movement and characters with clarity, understanding, and honest conviction so the message transcends outward to the audience. The movements speak but they also teach, give witness, and transform the community.

Another example of creating community through evangelism was during the initial years after the 9/11 tragedy. The September 11, 2001 attacks were the most deadly international terrorist attack in history and the largest attack on United States territory since the Japanese attack on Pearl Harbor on December 7, 1941. Lerner captures the untiring

52. Evans, Robert, interview.

rescuing efforts of those lost in the remains of the collapsed World Twin Tower buildings by the fire-fighters, rescue workers, police officers, and countless others. He states:

> Rescue efforts started immediately as surviving police, firefighters, engineers, construction workers, and other arriving emergency personnel began a determined search for colleagues and civilian survivors. Although intense rescue efforts continued for more than a week, the tremendous force of the collapsing buildings spared few of those trapped inside. The tremendous volume of falling material compacted into a tight and dense mass, providing few spaces that held the possibility of finding survivors. Death for thousands had been swift, and beyond a handful of survivors found in the first hours, no one survived the full fury of the collapse. Despite a twenty-four-hour operation throughout the winter by large and dedicated crews, a full excavation of the site and forensic determinations of human remains would take more than half a year.[53]

There were many organizations that provided a variety of services and spiritual counseling programs to help bring healing to the people of the United States and to the world community. In addition, numerous benefit concerts emerged to help raise funding for the victims and families of the 9/11 tragedy. One organization that participated was the New York City inspirational radio station, KISS Inspirations, which presented a benefit gospel concert annually entitled, "A Night of Healing," held at the Theatre at Madison Square Gardens.[54] The Allen Liturgical Dance Ministry was invited to participate as the only dance ministry on the program—which included noted gospel artists.[55] It was accompanied by an inspirational

53. Lerner, "September 11 Terrorist," 4.

54. "The station presented 'A Night of Healing,' a show that changed the parameters of all other shows owing to its exceptional presentation that went straight through the heart. They were emotionally attached with the stage sequence of the show. . . . The talent line of the show includes Donnie McClurkin, Fred Hammond, The Clark Sisters, Andrae Crouch, Richard Smallwood, Kelly Price, Tye Tribbett, J Moss, and other special guests. . . . The others who extended significant roles in making the show a major hit were Kim Burrell, Natalie Wilson, Smokie Norful, Byron Cage, Hezekiah Walker, The Allen Liturgical Dance Ministry, Martha Munizzi, Israel & New Breed, and Donnie McClurkin" ("Night of Healing").

55. The Allen Liturgical Dance Ministry (ALDM) was invited to participate during the 2003 and 2004 productions of, "A Night of Healing." Under the direction of the author, the ALDM ministered a ten-minute segment of liturgical dance for each benefit concert. In 2003, the ALDM presented two liturgical dances, "Receive Our

message given by a notable preacher. The use of dance in this particular venue was a huge shift from inspirational and gospel music alone. With the combination of music, word, and dance the concert provided healing for many. One website source records reactions from the 2003 benefit concert:

> The kind of response the event gathered was rather surprising. People went crazy after watching the show. While some of them felt awesome and blessed, the others felt that the spirituality was healed by the various artists. . . . The audiences could not forget each and every scene from their memory and the scenes progressed in their minds in full sequence even after watching the show a few days back.[56]

The dancer's preparation for this two-year event was standard as it required bible study, prayer, and numerous rehearsals. However, within any evangelism project the love of God permeates not only through the body's movements, but also in the dancer's facial expressions and demeanor as they entered on and off stage. During the 2003 concert, one of the gospel artists, Bryon Cage, who knew of the dance ministry's work, asked if ALDM could accompany one of his songs. Although this was not a planned component of the concert, the reasons behind this spontaneous change revealed the rich partnership between liturgical dance and religious education. Cage indicated that he wanted the words of the song to jump out and reach the people in the audience, and since he knew of ALDM's movement version, it was allowed to take place. For both the dancer and audience member the words and movements to the song, "The Presence of the Lord is Here," rang true.

Lastly, an example of evangelism that is highlighted though the partnership of liturgical dance and religious education is found inside the walls of the church. The illustrated sermons of Bishop Charles Ellis

---

Praise, Oh God," an original score by Stanley Brown and "We Speak to Nations," by Lakewood Church. The first was ministered by the men and teen boys and the second by a fifty-member representation of ALDM (this representation included girls, boys, teenagers, women, and men). For 2004, ALDM (a fifty-member representation) presented three dances in a form of a choreo-drama that was accompanied by the Greater Allen Cathedral Praise and Worship singers and musicians. Two songs were originals, the first by Benjamin Love entitled, "If My People..." and the repeat of Stanley Brown's "Receive Our Praise Oh God," and the traditional song "Holy, Holy, Holy," text by Reginald Heber and tune by John Dykes (See Carpenter and Williams, *African American Heritage Hymnal*, 329–31).

56. "Night of Healing."

are moments in the seasonal work of Greater Grace Temple that invite not only the members of the congregation, but it ultimately invites people from the community including groups from a variety of non-religious agencies as well as church groups who travel from out of state. The first two, "Whip, Hammer, and Cross" and "From Hell and Back" were given to him from Pastor Tommy Burnett, the originator of the illustrated sermon. Ellis explains the creative license he utilizes in presenting these sermons.

> These two, "From Hell and Back" and "Whip, Hammer, and Cross," are Tommy Barnett's illustrations and gave us free reign to use them. Whip, Hammer, and Cross is Jesus from his triumphant entry into Jerusalem to his ascension up from the grave. It is the story of Christ, but Barnett put it in a dramatized form, and he has given us the access and permission to use the title and to take it and adjust it for our audience and local. Phoenix, AZ is a predominant Caucasian, Hispanic, Native American audience and culture. So a lot of his music, dance, and choreography would not work here in Detroit. So you would have to adapt it to your audience. So if you would watch Barnett's "Whip, Hammer, and Cross," and then mine, well the story is the same, nothing in the story changes, but when you look at the dramatization of it and the music you will see a vast difference between Barnett's and Bishop Ellis. If you see "From Hell and Back," you will see a big difference between Barnett's and Bishop Ellis, but the concepts were given from Barnett for those two and those two are staples that we do every year. I went to Barnett's conference in February of 1997 and then Good Friday of that same year I did "Whip, Hammer, and Cross." That New Year's Eve, 97 to 98, we did "From Hell and Back," and we were off and running, we baptized 100 people that Good Friday and baptized 238 people that New Year's Eve. So we were off and running then.[57]

Ellis explains that the illustrated sermon topics come from him and he shares the assignment of getting it into dramatic form with the director, choreographer, set designer, and musical director. From his perspective, the people who come and witness the illustrated sermons are made up of two types of audiences. The first are Christians, whether they are from Greater Grace or from churches located either near or far away. For those who travel from afar, there are designated seats throughout the sanctuary reserved for these groups, so they will have the best viewing, since they

57. Ellis, interview.

have traveled great distances to see the production. However, good seats are also reserved for those groups from social service agencies who make it an outing to come out and view the multi-dimensional productions.

Ellis's use of the illustrated sermon is another form of witness. However it is one that "pushes the pastoral envelope" since the entire sanctuary is transformed for the setting of the production. He explains the yearly format for the use of the illustrated sermon as follows:

> Now I do a minimal of four illustrations per year. I always do "Whip, Hammer, and Cross," Good Friday, and "From Hell and Back," the Friday before Halloween, and they are predetermined illustrated sermons. Then I do one on Easter Sunday and I do one on New Year's Eve. I usually title them after a popular movie title. That title for Easter will always tie into the resurrection. "Ransom," "The Blind Side," "Tomb Raiders," are movie titles that tie in to the resurrection message. On New Year's Eve, those are movie titles but they go along with what is going on at the time, there are movie titles and it will get that person who may not go to church interested in coming to see what these titles are all about.[58]

The description of the opening scene of the "Whip, Hammer, and Cross" reveals the magnitude of the production and how Bishop Ellis employs professionalism and creativity in presenting the educational underpinnings of the gospel account. In the production the dancers play the followers of Jesus as well as the Jews who despise him. At the beginning of the production, the dancers, both adults and children, use the double level of both the pulpit and sanctuary floor, to open the triumphant entry theme with movement and streamers. This is being done while a group of Roman soldiers are lined up on the back of the pulpit stage on a variety of levels. After the dancers are finished dancing on the stage, they exit as one Roman soldier comes in on a horse and rides on the pulpit stage to see who is coming and what the commotion is all about. As the opening song continues, the dancers return coming from the back of the sanctuary, and they dance down three isles of the sanctuary, while Jesus and the disciples are coming down the main isle. The disciples are dancing as well as the entire cast with the exception of Jesus who is on a donkey. Jesus, the donkey, and the disciples are led onto a huge ramp that connects the lower level of the sanctuary floor to the upper level of the pulpit platform.

58. Ellis, interview.

This opening scene tells the entire story of the triumphant entry into Jerusalem as found in the gospel accounts,[59] as it utilizes dance, both animal and pageantry props, dramatic interpretations, and music. Movements are varied as the dancers perform more full bodied movement combinations while the disciples do more movement gestures that signify the celebration of Jesus as the "one who comes in the name of the Lord!" Whether the movement is full bodied or is gestural, the significance of the movement is key for it helps to bring animation to the events of the triumphant entry as well as it gives religious foundation to the educational underpinnings of the biblical event. What such a production does is to bring life to the biblical accounts while affording the audience moments to contemplate and question their actual relationship to the text.

Bishop Ellis' work is both commended as well as questioned by those both inside and outside of his denomination. He shares teachings on the subject of illustrated sermons yearly so present-day pastors understand the importance of the visual in today's 21st century post-modern church. Pastor Tommy Barnett, Bishop Charles Ellis, Reverend Dr. Floyd H. Flake, and other pastors have been at the forefront of progressive ministry especially as it relates to the use of the arts, liturgical dance, and religious education. True innovation has the ability to change and transform life. As a pastor who has welcomed the use of liturgical dance inside the walls of the church for the past forty years, Reverend Flake shares some advice to those pastors venturing into the pastorate, especially on the subject of innovation. He states:

> Rather than spending time talking about the successful churches and what they have, look at them in terms of being models, where innovative ideas were birthed, then speak with them and see how you can produce the innovative ideas that God has placed within you. Pastors have been limited by the definition of what ministry is supposed to do. What is the business of the ministry? It is to meet the needs of the people daily.[60]

59. Jesus' triumphal entry into Jerusalem can be found in Matthew 21:1–11, Mark 11:1–11, and Luke 19:28–40.

60. Flake, interview.

Conclusion

All four formats in this chapter explain the unique partnership between liturgical dance and religious education. As in a dance, whether it is a well-crafted piece of choreography or it is an improvisational exercise of movement exploration, the two partners learn how to exist one with the other, while also learning how to support one another unselfishly. The work of both learning modalities exposes the uniqueness found within each, while revealing just how effective they can be once paired together to relay the messages of hope and restoration. As the four examples illustrate, whether the format is found within the worship service, a teaching chapel service, a liturgical dance curriculum or a curriculum for those in ministry, or within the work of evangelism, each of them display the meaning of corporation and imaginative creativity.

The correlation between the newly formed definition of liturgical dance and the four formats highlight four basic principles. The *first basic principle* captures liturgical dance as expressive and imaginative movement that is used both inside and outside of worship that creatively educates and instructs Christians to comprehend the Bible and their faith in the Trinity through the elements of space, time, and design. Whether the space is inside the walls of the sanctuary, in a nursing home, on a stage, or in a classroom, religious education takes place through time and through innumerable and imaginative choreographic shapes that edify the mind, body, and spirit.

The *second basic principle* describes the creative and educational relationship liturgical dance has with music, whether the music is instrumental, a newly composed inspirational song, a praise and worship song, or a traditional sacred hymn. Its relationship with the spoken word gives vision and depth to the whole text regardless if its extracted from the Bible, a sermon, a poem, or words from a sacred play. Its relationship with silence truly gives space for the movement itself to speak, to teach, and to be reflective on themes of faith and faith development.

The *third basic principle* promotes the formation of community through individual and mutual movement and dance explorations. Community is formed wherever two or three are gathered in the name of Christ and it is formed through the listening eyes of love. Therefore, genuine community is formed out of the need to extend love in Jesus' name. So whether the community is formed by the congregational members waving their arms in a worship service, by the audience that views a liturgical dance or liturgical dance play, or inside the classroom walls where liturgical dancers are being instructed, a teachable witness of this partnership is enough to form community. Regardless of the setting, the themes of love, prayer, healing, and reconciliation are cultivated.

The *fourth basic principle* emphasizes the nature of liturgical dance, and because of this attribute anyone, regardless of religious affiliation, can be exposed to liturgical dance in the Christian context and be influenced by it. From the smallest gesture to the largest of movements, liturgical dance grounded in partnership with religious education can help exemplify a way of knowing that transcends the ordinary in church worship, but more important in life itself. It opens the heart through bodily expression, to learn the meaning of a love that is non-negotiable and never-ending. To this end, this type of love is in partnership with God and with neighbor and it fuels liturgical dance to be a dance that is transforming.

Appendix A

For I Can't Stay Behind #8[1]

Chorus or Response

I can't stay be-hind, my Lord, I can't stay be-hind!

[1]

Dere's room e-nough, Room e-nough, Room e-nough in de Heaven,
  my Lord;
Room e-nough, Room e-nough, I can't stay be-hind.

[2]

I been all around, I been all around, Been all around de Heaven, my Lord.
All around, All around, I can't stay be-hind.

[3]

I've searched every room, I've searched every room, Searched every room,
de Heaven, my Lord;
Every room, Every room, I can't stay be-hind.

[4]

De angels singin't, De angels singin't, De angels singin't all round de trone;
Angels singin't, Angels singin,t, I can't stay be-hind.

[5]

My Fader call, My Fader call, My Fader call and I must go.
Fader call, Fader call, I can't stay be-hind.

1. Allen et al., *Slave Songs*, 6.

205

[6]

Sto-back, member; sto-back, member; sto-back member.[2]
Sto-back, member; sto-back, member; I can't stay be-hind.

2. Sto-back means "Shout backwards."

Appendix B

King David[1]

Just as soon as you cease
Good Lord,
Children, from your sins
Good Lord,
To take you in . . .

Who's that ridin' the chariot?
Well well well.
One mornin'
Before the evening
Sun was going down
Behind them western hills.
Old Number Twelve
Comin' down the track.
See that black smoke.
See that old engineer . . .[2]

1. In Courlander, *Negro Folk Music*, there appears to be two sets of verses that are labeled under the heading of the song, "King David." Appendix B presents both verses as they appear in the text. The first is found in chapter 3, "Anthems and Spirituals as Oral Literature," and the second appears in chapter 11, "The Music." The latter has the actual song as recorded with the original musical score and verse text.

2. Courlander, *Negro Folk Music*, 40.

King David

King David was
>> good Lord
That shepherd boy
>> good Lord
Didn't he kill Goliath
>> good Lord
and he shout for joy
>> good Lord.
Well the tallest tree
>> good Lord
in Paradise
>> good Lord
them Christians called it
>> good Lord
their tree of life
>> good Lord
(Chorus)
Little David play on your harp, hal-le-lu
>> hal-le-lu
little David play on your harp hal-le-lu.
Didn't you promise to play on your harp, hal-le-lu, hal-le-lu,
didn't you promise to play on your harp, hal-le-lu.

Just watch the sun
>> good Lord
how steady she run
>> good Lord
don't mind she catch you
>> good Lord
with your work undone
>> good Lord.
(Chorus)
Little David play on your harp, hal-le-lu
>> hal-le-lu
little David play on your harp hal-le-lu.
Didn't you promise to play on your harp, hal-le-lu, hal-le-lu,
didn't you promise to play on your harp, hal-le-lu.[3]

3. Courlander, *Negro Folk Music*, 236–37.

Appendix C

The Living Vine (verses 3–12)[4]

This beautiful and bearing Vine now flourishing on Zions hill
Is cultur'd by a hand devine whose blessings on it do distill

Like gentle dews from heaven they fall upon the rue and living Vine
Which makes true branches great & small in harmony and beauty shine

This wonderful Almighty hand does prune the Vine from day to day
Adornd with fruit live branches stand but wither'd ones he takes away

The vine does spread far East & West and yet the fruit is all the same
With which the upright Soul is blest while sinners scorn the lowly name.

The living Vine we know is good we judge it by its precious fruit
The true Believers only food that will his weary soul recruit

Regenerating Souls they are that's joind unto the living Vine
Of them the Father does take care And in his love they do combine.

And those indeed who thus combine their faith will ever stedfast prove
In Christ the true and living Vine the Vine of everlasting love

They are most blind who will not see in scenes of sorrow they'll repine
While Souls in Gospel Liberty rejoice in Christ the living Vine.

4. Andrews, *Gift to be Simple*, 159.

The vine does spread & spread it will in vain does satans pow'r withstand
Thus saith the Lord vain man be still my Gospel shall go through the Land

And when the Gospel has gone thro'and geather'd all true branches in
Amazing horror will persue souls thats left out all bound in sin.

Appendix D

Hannah Cohoon. *The Tree of Life*, 1854.[5]

5. Cohoon, *Tree of Life*.

Appendix E

"Never Would Have Made It"[6]
Written by Marvin Sapp

Never would have made it,

Never could have made it without you.

I would have lost it all.

But now I see how you were there, right there for me.

Now I can say

I'm stronger; I'm wiser;

Now I'm better, so much better;

I've made it, I've made it, I've made it, I've made it.

6. Sapp, "Never Would Have Made It."

Appendix F

"Welcome into this Place"[7]
Text and Tune written by Orlando Jaurez
Arranged by Jimmie Abbington.

Welcome into this place.
Welcome into this broken vessel.
You desire to abide in the praises of Your people,
So we lift our hands
and we lift our hearts
As we offer up this praise unto Your Name.

7. Jaurez, "Welcome into this Place."

Appendix G

Joshua 6:8–20

⁸As Joshua had commanded the people, the seven priests carrying the seven trumpets of rams' horns before the Lord went forward, blowing the trumpets, with the ark of the covenant of the Lord following them. ⁹And the armed men went before the priests who blew the trumpets; the rear guard came after the ark, while the trumpets blew continually. ¹⁰To the people Joshua gave this command: "You shall not shout or let your voice be heard, no shall you utter a word, until the day I tell you to shout. Then you shall shout." ¹¹So the art of the Lord went around the city, circling it once; and they came into the camp, and spent the night in the camp. ¹²Then Joshua rose early in the morning, and the priest took up the ark of the Lord. ¹³The seven priests carrying the seven trumpets of rams' horns before the ark of the Lord passed on, blowing the trumpets continually. The armed men went before the, and the rear guard came after he ark of the Lord, while the trumpets blew continually. ¹⁴On the second day they marched around the city once an then returned to the camp. They did this for six days. ¹⁵On the seventh day they rose early, at dawn, and marched around the city in the same manner seven times. It was only on that day that they marched around the city seven times. ¹⁶And at the seventh time, when the priests had blown the trumpets, Joshua said to the people, "Shout! For the Lord has given you the city. ¹⁷The city and all that is in it shall be devoted to the Lord for destruction. Only Rahab the prostitute and all who are with her in her house shall live because she hid the messengers we sent. ¹⁸As for you, keep away from the things devoted to destruction, so as not to covet and take any of the devoted things and make the camp of Israel an object or destruction, bringing trouble upon

it. [19]But all silver and gold, and vessels of bronze and iron, are sacred to the Lord; they shall go into the treasury of the Lord." [20]So the people shouted, and the trumpets were blown. As soon as the people heard the sound of the trumpets, they raised a great shout, and the wall fell down flat; so the people charged straight ahead into the city and captured it.

Appendix H

The Acts of John[8]

The Hymn of Jesus

94. Now, before he was arrested by the lawless Jews, who received their law from a lawless serpent, he gathered us all together and said, "Before I am delivered up to them, let us sing a hymn to the Father, and go forth to what lies before us." So he commanded us to make a circle, holding one another's hands, and he himself stood in the middle. He said, "Respond Amen to me." He then began to sing a hymn, and to say:

"Glory be to you, Father!"
And we circling him said, "Amen".
     "Glory be to you, Word! Glory be to you, Grace!" "Amen."
     "Glory be to you, Spirit! Glory be to you, Holy One! Glory be to the glory!" "Amen."
     "We praise you, O Father. We give thanks to you, light, in whom darkness does not abide." "Amen."

          95. "Now we give thanks, I say:
          I will be saved, and I will save." "Amen."
          "I will be loosed, and I will loose." "Amen."
          "I will be pierced, and I will pierce." "Amen."
          "I will be born, and I will bear." "Amen."
          "I will eat, and I will be eaten." "Amen."
          "I will hear, and I will be heard." "Amen."

8. Elliott, *Apocryphal New Testament*, 318–20.

"I will be understood, being wholly understanding. "Amen."
"I will be washed, and I will wash." "Amen."

Grace is dancing.
"I will pipe, dance all of you!" "Amen."
"I will mourn, lament all of you!" "Amen."
"An Ogdoad is singing with us." "Amen."
"The Twelfth number is dancing above." "Amen."
"The whole universe takes part in the dancing." "Amen."
"He who does not dance, does not know what is being done."
"Amen."
"I will flee and I will stay." "Amen."
"I will adorn, and I will be adorned." "Amen."
"I will be united, and I will unite." "Amen."
"I have no house, and I have houses." "Amen."
"I have no place, and I have places." "Amen."
"I have no temple, and I have temples." "Amen."
"I am a lamp to you who see me." "Amen."
"I am a mirror to you who perceive." "Amen."
"I am a door to you who knock on me." "Amen."
"I am a way to you, wayfarer." "Amen."

96. Now if you respond to my dancing, see yourself in me who speak; and when you have seen what I do, keep silence about my mysteries! You who dance, perceive what I do; for yours is this passion of mankind which I am to suffer! For you could not at all have comprehended what you suffer if I had not been sent to you as the Word by the Father. When you saw what I suffer, you have seen me as one suffering; and seeing that, you have not stood firm but were wholly moved. Moved to become wise, you have me for a support. Rest upon me! Who am I? You shall know when I go away. What I am now seen to be, that I am not. You shall see when you come. If you knew how to suffer, you would have had the power not to suffer. Learn suffering, and you shall have the power not to suffer. That which you do not know, I will teach you. I am your God, not that of the betrayer. I will that there be prepared holy souls for me. Know the word of wisdom! Say again with me:

> Glory be to you, Father; glory be to you, Word;
> Glory be to you, Holy Ghost!

Now concerning me, if you would know what I was: with a word I once deceived all things, and was not put to shame at all. I have leaped; but understand the whole, and having understood it say, "Glory be to you, Father!" "Amen."

97. After this dance, my beloved, the Lord went out; and we were as men gone astray or dazed with sleep, and we fled all ways. Even I, when I saw him suffer, did not abide at his passion but fled to the Mount of Olives, weeping over what had taken place. And when he was hung upon the cross on Friday, at the sixth hour of the day, there came darkness over all the earth. And my Lord stood in the middle of the cave and lit it up, and said, "John, to the multitude down below in Jerusalem I am being crucified, and pierced with lances and reeds, and gall and vinegar is given me to drink. But to you I am speaking, and pay attention to what I say. I put it into your mind to come up to this mountain, so that you might hear matters needful for a disciple to learn from his teacher, and for a man to learn from his God."

Appendix I

Psalm 150

1

Praise the LORD!
Praise God in his sanctuary;
praise him in his mighty firmament!

2

Praise him for his mighty deeds;
praise him according to his surpassing greatness!

3

Praise him with trumpet sound;
praise him with lute and harp!

4

Praise him with tambourine and dance;
praise him with strings and pipe!

5

Praise him with clanging cymbals;
praise him with loud clashing cymbals!

6

Let everything that breathes praise the LORD!
Praise the LORD!

Appendix J

You've Turned My Mourning Into Dancing[9]

Written and Composed by John Tirro

You've turned my mourning, my mourning, my mourning into dancing.
You've turned my mourning, my mourning, my mourning into dancing.
You've turned my mourning, my mourning, my mourning into dancing.

You've turned my mourning, my mourning, my mourning into dancing.

You've turned my mourning, my mourning, my mourning into dancing.

Chorus

You've turned my sorrow into song, you've turned my singing into praise,

you've turned my praise, to peace, my peace to joy and dancing!

You've turned my sorrow into song, you've turned my singing into praise,

you've turned my praise, to peace, my peace to joy and dancing!

---

9. Tirro, "You've Turned My Mourning Into Dancing."

Bibliography

Adams, Doug. "Communal Dance Forms and Consequences in Biblical Worship." In *Dance as Religious Studies*, edited by Doug Adams and Diane Apostolos-Cappadona, 35–47. New York: Crossroad, 1990.

Alho, Olli. *The Religion of the Slaves*. Helsinki: Academia Scientarium Fennica, 1976.

Allen, William Francis, et al., eds. "I Can't Stay Behind" In *Slave Songs of the United States*, 6–7. New York: Peter Smith, 1951.

Anderson, Jack. *Dance*. New York: Newsweek, 1979.

Andrews, Edward Deming. *The Gift to be Simple: Songs, Dances and Rituals of the American Shakers*. New York: Dover, 1940.

Andrews, Edward Deming and Faith Andrews. *Visions of the Heavenly Sphere: A Study in Shaker Religious Art*. Charlottesville, VA: University Press of Virginia, 1969.

Apostolos-Cappadona, Diane. "Scriptural Women Who Danced." In *Dance as Religious Studies*, edited by Doug Adams and Diane Apostolos-Cappadona, 95–108. New York: Crossroad, 1990.

Armstrong, Thomas. *Multiple Intelligences in the Classroom*. Alexandria, VA: Association for Supervision and Curriculum Development, 2000.

Astley, Jeff. "The Role of Worship in Christian Learning." In *Theological Perspectives on Christian Formation*, edited by Jeff Astley, Leslie Francis, and Colin Crowder, 244–51. Grand Rapids: Eerdmans, 1996.

Backman, E. Louis. *Religious Dances in the Christian Church and in Popular Medicine*. London: Allen & Unwin, 1952.

Bradshaw, Paul, ed. *The New Westminster Dictionary of Liturgy & Worship*. Louisville: Westminster John Knox, 2002.

Brueggemann, Walter. *The Psalms and The Life Of Faith*. Minneapolis, MN: Fortress, 1995.

Carlson, R. A. *David, the Chosen King: A Traditio-Historical Approach to the Second Book of Samuel*. Stockholm: Almqvist & Wiksell, 1964.

Carpenter, Delores, and Nolan Williams, Jr., eds. *African American Heritage Hymnal*. Chicago: GIA, 2001.

Costen, Melva Wilson. *African American Christian Worship*. Nashville: Abingdon, 1993.

———. *In Spirit and In Truth*. Louisville: Westminster John Knox, 2004.

Courlander, Harold. *Negro Folk Music USA*. New York: Columbia University Press, 1963. Repr., New York: Dover, 1992.

Crain, Margaret Ann. "Listening to Churches: Christian Education in the Congregational Life." In *Mapping Christian Education: Approaches to Congregational Learning*, edited by Jack L. Seymour, 93–109. Nashville: Abingdon, 1997.

Cohoon, Hannah. *The Tree of Life*. 1854, ink and water color, Hancock Shaker Village, Hancock, Massachusetts. http://www.hsv.lsw.com/accounts/28/images/20070518040028.jpg.

Daniels, Marilyn. *The Dance in Christianity*. New York: Paulist, 1981.

Davies, J. G. *Liturgical Dance: An Historical, Theological and Practical Handbook*. London: SCM, 1984.

———, ed. *The New Westminster Dictionary of Liturgy and Worship*. Philadelphia: Westminster, 1986.

Delaney, John J. *The Practice of the Presence of God*. New York: Doubleday, 1977.

DeSola, Carla. ". . . And the Word Became Dance: A Theory and Practice of Liturgical Dance." In *Dance as Religious Studies*, edited by Doug Adams and Diane Apostolos-Cappadona, 153–66. New York: Crossroad, 1990.

———. *The Spirit Moves: Handbook of Dance and Prayer*. Austin, TX: Sharing, 1977.

DeSola, Carla, and A. Easton. "Awakening the Right Love Through Dance," in *Aesthetic Dimensions of Religious Education*, edited by Gloria Durka and Joanmarie Smith, 69–81. New York: Paulist, 1979.

Dewey, John. *Art as Experience*. New York: Minton, Balch & Company, 1934. Repr., New York: Perigee, 1980.

———. *Democracy and Education*. New York: Free Press, 1944.

———. *Experience and Education*. New York: Kappa Delta Pi, 1938. Repr., New York: Touchstone, 1997.

———. "Psychology, Pedagogy and Religion." *Religious Education* 69 (1974) 6–11.

Durka, Gloria and Joanmarie Smith, eds. *Aesthetic Dimensions of Religious Education*. New York: Paulist, 1979.

Dykstra, Craig R. "The Formative Power of the Congregation." In *Theological Perspectives on Christian Formation*, edited by Jeff Astley, Leslie Francis and Colin Crowder, 252–265. Grand Rapids: Eerdmans, 1996.

Eisner, Elliot. "Aesthetic Modes of Knowing." In *Learning and Teaching the Ways of Knowing*, edited by Elliot Eisner, 23–36. Chicago: University of Chicago Press, 1985.

———. "Artistry in Education." *Scandinavian Journal of Educational Research* 47.3 (2003) 373–84.

———. *The Arts and the Creation of Mind*. New Haven: Yale University Press, 2002.

———. *The Educational Imagination*, 3rd ed. Upper Saddle River, NJ: Merrill Prentice Hall, 2002.

Elias, John L. *A History of Christian Education: Protestant, Catholic, and Orthodox Perspectives*. Malabar, FL: Kreger, 2002.

Elliott, J. K. *The Apocryphal New Testament*. Oxford: Clarendon, 1993.

Everist, Norma Cook. *The Church as Learning Community*. Nashville: Abingdon, 2002.

Foster, Charles R. *Educating Congregations*. Nashville: Abingdon, 1994.

Gagne, Ronald, et al. *Introducing Dance In Christian Worship*. Washington DC: Pastoral, 1984.

Gardner, Howard. *Creating Minds: An Anatomy of Creativity Seen through the Lives of Freud, Einstein, Picasso, Stravinsky, Eliot, Graham, and Gandhi*. New York: Basic Books, 1993.

———. *Frames of Mind*. New York: Basic Books, 1983. Repr., New York: Basic Books, 2004.

———. *Multiple Intelligences, New Horizons*. New York: Basic Books, 2006.

Greene, Maxine. *Releasing the Imagination.* San Francisco: Jossey-Bass, 1995. Repr., San Francisco: Jossey-Bass, 2000.

Harrelson, Walter J., ed. *The New Interpreter's Study Bible: New Revised Standard Version with the Apocrypha.* Nashville: Abingdon, 2003.

Harris, Maria. "Art and Religious Education: A Conversation." *Journal of Religious Education* 83.3 (1988) 453–73.

———. *Fashion Me A People.* Louisville: Westminster John Knox, 1989.

———. "A Model for Aesthetic Education." In *Aesthetic Dimensions of Religious Education,* edited by Gloria Durka and Joanmarie Smith, 141–52. New York: Paulist, 1979.

———. *Teaching and Religious Imagination.* San Francisco: HarperCollins, 1987. Repr., San Francisco: HarperCollins, 1991.

Jaurez, Orlando. "Welcome into this Place." In *African American Heritage Hymnal,* edited by Dr. Delores Carpenter and Rev. Nolan E. Williams, 114. Chicago: GIA, 2001.

Jones, Mary. *Growth of a Dance Movement.* Melbourne: Christian Dance Fellowship, 1987.

Jordan, Kimberly. "My Flesh Shall Live in Hope: Power and the Black Body Moving in Sacred Space." PhD diss., New York University, 2009.

Lerner, K. Lee. "September 11 Terrorist Attacks on the United States." In *Encyclopedia of Espionage, Intelligence, and Security,* vol. 3, edited by K. Lee Lerner and Brenda Wilmoth Lerner, 68–72. Farmington Hills, MI: Gale, 2004.

Livingstone, E. A., ed. *The Oxford Dictionary of the Christian Church.* New York: Oxford University Press, 2005.

Lovell, John Jr. *Black Song: The Forge and the Flame.* New York: Macmillan, 1972.

Merton, Thomas. *Seeking Paradise: The Spirit of the Shakers.* Maryknoll, NY: Obis, 2003.

National Liturgical Dance Network. "Statement and Purpose." http://www.natldancenetwork.com.

Nelson, C. Ellis. *Congregations: Their Power to Form and Transform.* Atlanta: John Knox, 1988.

"A Night of Healing: 98.7 Kiss FM." *OnlineSeats.com.* 11 March 2012. http://www.onlineseats.com-a-night-of-healing-tickets/index.asp.

Oesterley, W. O. E. *Sacred Dance in the Ancient World.* New York: Dover, 2002.

Olson, Susan Lee. "'If Necessary, Use Words': Modern Dance as Contributor to Liturgical Renewal." PhD diss., Graduate Theological Union, 2005.

Opdahl, Robert C., and Viola E. Woodruff Opdahl. *A Shaker Musical Legacy.* Lebanon, NH: University Press of New England, 2004.

Osmer, Richard Robert. "A New Clue for Religious Education?" In *Forging a Better Religious Education in the Third Millennium,* edited by James Michael Lee, 179–202. Birmingham, AL: Religious Education, 2000.

Patterson, Daniel W. *The Shaker Spiritual.* Mineola, NY: Dover, 1980.

Penrod, James, and Janice Plastino. *The Dance Prepares,* 5th ed. New York: McGraw Hill, 2005.

Pickett, Joseph, ed. *Webster's New College Dictionary,* 3rd ed. Boston: Houghton Mifflin, 2008.

Raboteau, Albert J. *Slave Religion: The "Invisible Institution" in the Antebellum South.* New York: Oxford University Press, 1978.

Rouet, Albert. *Liturgy and the Arts.* Collegeville, MN: Liturgical, 1997.

Sachs, Curt. *World History of the Dance.* New York: Norton, 1937.

Sapp, Marvin. "Never Would Have Made It." *Thirty,* Verity, 2007.

Sawicki, Marianne. *The Gospel in History: Portrait of a Teaching Church: The Origins of Christian Education.* New York: Paulist, 1988.

———. "Historical Methods and Religious Education." *Religious Education* 82.3 (1987) 375–89.

Schaff, Philip, and Henry Wace, eds. "Concerning Repentance, Book II." In *Nicene and Post-Nicene Fathers of The Christian Church,* vol. 10. Grand Rapids: Eerdmans, 1978.

Scott, Kieran. "Curriculum and Religious Education." Fordham University. Spring 2010.

Siegel, Marcia B. *The Shapes of Change: Images of American Dance.* Berkeley, CA: University of California Press, 1979.

Smith, Robertson. *The Religion of the Semites.* New York: Schocken, 1972.

Smith, Yolanda Yvette. "Preserving Faith and Culture in the African American Church: A Tri-Collaborative Model for Teaching the Triple-Heritage through the African American Spirituals." PhD diss., Claremont School of Theology, 1998.

———. *Reclaiming the Spirituals.* Cleveland, OH: Pilgrim, 2004.

Strayer, Joseph R., ed. *Dictionary of the Middle Ages,* vol. 5. New York: Scribner's Sons, 1982.

Stuckey, P. Sterling. "Christian Conversion and the Challenge of Dance." In *Dancing Many Drums: Excavations in African American Dance,* edited by Thomas F. DeFrantz, 39–58. Madison, WI: University of Wisconsin Press, 2002.

Taylor, Margaret Fisk. "A History of Symbolic Movement in Worship." In *Dance as Religious Studies,* edited by Doug Adams and Diane Apostolos-Cappadona, 15–32. New York: Crossroad, 1990.

———. *A Time to Dance.* Philadelphia: United Church, 1967. Repr., North Aurora, IL: The Sharing Company, 1976.

Tirro, John. "You've Turned My Mourning Into Dancing." Mondo Zen Music, 2008.

Turner, Kathleen S. "If David had not Danced." STM thesis, Yale Divinity School, 2009.

VerEecke, Robert, SJ. "Shall We Dance?" *America* 25 (2002) 1–4.

Wimberly, Anne E. Streaty. "A Legacy of Hope: African-American Christian Education During the Era of Slavery." *Journal of Interdenominational Theological Center* 23 (1996) 3–23.

———. *Nurturing Faith & Hope.* Cleveland, OH: Pilgrim, 2004.

Zakkai, Jennifer Donohue. *Dance as a Way of Knowing.* Los Angeles: Stenhouse, 1997.

Index

Jesus Christ, 4, 6, 15, 105, 138–39,
    201–2
Johnston, David, 193, 193n45
Jones, Mary, 144, 144n77, 149–50,
    191–92, 193, 193n45
Joshua 6:8–20, 130, 214–15
Judith, 124

Kane, Thomas A., 162–63
"King David" (song), 16, 207–8
KISS Inspirations, 198–99
knowing, 56–57

labored songs, 24, 24n67
laity, 91–92
language, 37
Lawrence, Brother, 174
learning, 54–63, 74, 93
Lee, Ann, 18–19, 21, 24, 28, 32
"A Legacy of Hope" (Wimberly),
    13–15
Lerner, K. Lee, 197–98
linguistic intelligence, 37, 52
listening, 171–75, 188
liturgical dance
    and aesthetic learning, 100–102
    and balance and harmony,
        180–86
    in congregational worship, 142–
        48, 152, 156–67, 167–69,
        184–91, 185n33
    and dancing in unison, 175–79
    defined, 122
    defined for the 21st Century
        Church, 168–69
    and evangelism, 194–202
    and illustrated sermons,
        199–202
    and narrative dance, 164–67
    and partnership, 170–71
    and praise and worship music,
        175–79, 176n15
    and religious education, 100–
        102, 143, 156, 161, 170–71,
        175–202

and role of dancer as minister,
    148–56
and teaching, 167, 186–94
working definition for
    Christians, 169
working description of, 142–48
liturgy, 122, 148, 152, 154, 156,
    161–64
living curriculum, 98
"The Living Vine" (song), 27,
    209–10
logical-mathematical intelligence, 37
Lovell, John Jr., 10

Marable, Eyesha K., 152, 152n106,
    155, 162, 187–89, 191–93
Marcan scripture, 195
Marcuse, Herbert, 43
marriage, 159–60
Massachusetts, 19
McIntyre, Dianne, 158n124
Meacham, Joseph, 19, 21–22, 24–26,
    32
meaning making, 88–93, 181–82
Merton, Thomas, 31–32
metaphors, 65
millennial church, 22
Millennial Praises (hymnal), 22
ministers, 148–56
ministry of re-membering, 95–98
Miriam, 134, 141
"A Model for Aesthetic Education"
    (Harris), 68–72
modern dance, 62
Mosaic law, 125
Mother Ann. See Lee, Ann
mourning movement, 184–86
movement and dance, 54–63
movement gestures, 30–31, 176n15,
    184–85, 202
Multiple Intelligences (Gardner), 36
Multiple Intelligence theory, 36–41,
    51–52, 59–60
music, 37, 109–13, 152–53, 175–79,
    176n15
The Musical Expositor (Haskell), 23
musical intelligence, 37

CPSIA information can be obtained
at www.ICGtesting.com
Printed in the USA
BVHW050817071021
618239BV00003B/10

9 781532 619496